The Divided Mind
of Protestant America,
1880–1930

The Divided Mind of Protestant America, 1880–1930

Ferenc Morton Szasz

THE UNIVERSITY OF ALABAMA PRESS
University, Alabama

Library of Congress Cataloging in Publication Data

Szasz, Ferenc Morton, 1940–
    The divided mind of Protestant America, 1880–1930.

    Bibliography: p.
    Includes index.
    1. Protestant churches—United States—History—
19th century.   2. Protestant churches—United
States—History—20th century.   3. United States—
Church history—19th century.   4. United States—
Church history—20th century.   5. Liberalism (Reli-
gion)—United States—History—19th century.
6. Liberalism (Religion)—United States—History—
20th century.   7. Evangelicalism—United States—
History—19th century.   8. Evangelicalism—United
States—History—20th century.   I. Title.
BR525.S9   280'.4'0973   81-7597
ISBN 0-8173-0080-5   AACR2

To The Three Generations:
Mary and Ferenc P. Szasz
Margi
Eric, Chris, and Maria

Contents

Acknowledgments

This work owes a great deal to a great many people. I would like to thank Ruth Davies, Hastings Eells, David Jennings, Benjamin Spencer, and especially Richard W. Smith, my instructors at Ohio Wesleyan University, who first enticed me into the fascinating worlds of history and literature. Milton Berman, Willson Coates, and Hayden V. White, among others, expanded the process during my graduate school days at the University of Rochester. I have also benefited considerably from sustained conversations with my colleagues and friends: Joel Blatt, Larry B. Davis, William Ellis, Philip D. Jordan, Gary B. Ostrower, and Howard N. Rabinowitz. Special thanks are owed to Penny Katson, who typed the innumerable drafts of this study and whose knowledge of Greek made it impossible for me to slip a spelling error by her. I would also like to acknowledge the editors of *Nebraska History*, the *Tennessee Historical Quarterly*, and *Mid-America* for generously allowing me to reprint material that first appeared, in altered form, in their journals.

Archivists and librarians seldom get the praise they deserve. I would like to give credit to the following: Mrs. Mary Lane, librarian of the Historical Foundation of the Presbyterian and Reformed Churches, Montreat, North Carolina; V. Nelle Bellamy, archivist of the Church Historical Society, Austin, Texas; A. Ronald Tonks of the Historical Commission, Southern Baptist Convention, Nashville, Tennessee; Edward Starr of the American Baptist Convention, Rochester, New York; Marvin Williams of the Disciples of Christ Historical Society, Nashville; the staff of the Methodist Archives at Lake Junaluska, North Carolina; Gerald W. Gillette of the Presbyterian Historical Society of Philadelphia, Pennsylvania; the staff of the Moody Bible Institute in Chicago; the staff of the Bible Institute of Los Angeles; and Dorothy Wonsmos, head of the Interlibrary Loan Division of Zimmerman Library, the University of New Mexico.

My acknowledgments would not be complete without a special word in praise of Sidney E. Mead, now retired in Tucson, Arizona. Mead read this manuscript in a much expanded form and offered numerous suggestions, which, as always, were full of wisdom. Well does he deserve his reputation as the dean of scholars of the history of religion in America.

Finally, I would like to express my appreciation to my family: to Eric, Chris, and Maria who heard about this project over many an evening meal, and to Margi, who critiqued the manuscript almost as many times as I did. Thanks to her I know what Shakespeare had in mind when he wrote: "He hath a daily beauty in his life."

Preface

This book is about the main line Protestant churches and their impact on American life from 1880 to 1930. As such, it deals both with theology and religious history and with social and intellectual history. This fifty-year period has seldom been recognized as a distinct unit. Few people have a clear mental picture of these years, and they carry no rubric, as do the smaller segments within them: "the Gay Nineties," "Fin de Siècle Decadence," "the Progressive Age of Reform," or the "Roaring Twenties." Yet for American religious history, these years do mark a distinct epoch: they form the "Age of Division" for the main line Protestant churches.

During these fifty years, most mainstream Protestant groups witnessed the emergence of two distinct points of view, which I have chosen to call "liberal" and "conservative." In one form or another, they became part of virtually all the major denominations. Thus, the traditional denominational distinctions, which had held considerable meaning since Reformation days, no longer served as guidelines. Within this fifty-year period, they were largely realigned. Even today, the crucial distinctions among the main line American churches are seldom denominational, but, rather, revolve around the question of whether the church is "liberal" or "conservative." Most of the denominations have reconciled themselves to the fact that they contain both positions. As a result, liberals and conservatives sit side by side on Sunday mornings.

The denominations involved in this realignment were among the largest and most powerful organizations in the country. These churches provided the impetus for the Protestant evangelical ethos, and this ethos, in turn, dominated much of American life and thought during the years under consideration. This was more than an intramural Protestant quarrel. It had major social implications for the entire nation. In these fifty years, the nation witnessed "the demise of the Protestant hegemony in America."[1]

The polarization of American Protestantism took many years to assume full form, but it culminated in the Fundamentalist-Modernist controversy of the

1920s. The comic milieu that surrounded this controversy has led historians to misinterpret it, yet its consequences proved surprisingly significant. In the first place, the clash meant that both organized religion and the clergy were subjected to a great deal of ridicule. Then, too, the fight severely disrupted several important denominations: the Northern Baptists, the Northern Presbyterians and (to a somewhat lesser extent) the Disciples of Christ. But no Protestant group escaped completely. In one way or another, the theological issues raised by the Fundamentalist controversy affected virtually every church. The controversy called to the fore and often helped to polarize all the incipient divisions within each gathering. It reawakened, for example, the old quarrels within the Episcopal church, and it called the Southern Baptists, Methodists, and Presbyterians back to their distinctively conservative positions. In so doing, it set the boundaries for the future development of American Protestantism.

When William Jennings Bryan renewed the issue of evolution, the Fundamentalist controversy left the churches and spilled over into national politics. The question of whether the teaching of evolution in the public schools should be prohibited by law affected everyone, regardless of religious background. This issue came to a head in the Scopes trial in Dayton, Tennessee. The furor surrounding the trial ushered into the popular realm a quarrel between science and religion that has not yet been resolved.

In the wake of this clash, perhaps even because of it, the nation moved farther down the roads of secularization and pluralism. As late as 1910, intelligent men of goodwill could refer to the United States as a Christian (they usually meant Protestant) nation. By the late 1920s, this position was a prerogative of the right wing. In 1955, sociologist Will Herberg, in his widely read *Protestant-Catholic-Jew,* pointed out that the country had not one but three major faiths and these faiths all operated primarily within a secular context.[2] Historian Robert T. Handy has expanded Herberg's spectrum to include Protestant-Catholic-Jew-Greek Orthodox-Mormon-Pentecostal-New Thought-Freethinker, but the principle remains the same.[3] The Protestant domination of the nation had come to an end; religious pluralism was here to stay; and it operated largely within an indifferent, secular society.

Several denominations, both large and small, will be mentioned in this study, but I have drawn most of my evidence from the following groups: Congregationalists, Northern Baptists, Southern Baptists, Northern Presbyterians, Southern Presbyterians, Episcopalians, Northern Methodists, Southern Methodists, and the Disciples of Christ. Lutherans were very strong in numbers, but their major concerns were often internal, and I regret that I have to slight them here. Of the smaller denominations, the Unitarians had influence far beyond their membership, especially in the

Social Gospel. Consequently, they will be drawn upon with more frequency than their numbers might seem to warrant. My reason for stressing some groups over others was based solely on limits of time, energy, and resources. For this I will accept responsibility, if not culpability.

The Divided Mind
of Protestant America,
1880–1930

1
Evolution and the Study of Comparative Religion

The main line American Protestant churches faced the years following the Civil War with great confidence. They viewed the rapidly expanding West and the immigrant-filled, urban East as excellent opportunities for growth. Yet beneath this veneer of optimism lay unresolved intellectual dilemmas that were to cause considerable distress in the years to come.

The major issues that plagued the churches of the period were evolution, comparative religion, and higher criticism of the Scriptures. Because all of these ideas originated in the scholar's study, one of the most challenging tasks in the analysis of late nineteenth-century American thought is to chart the process by which they eventually became the property of ordinary people. Unfortunately, this process cannot be dated with precision, but one can point to certain major milestones along the way. The popularizers may be regarded as more important to this process than the original scholars. It was largely through the efforts of popularizers that the specialized ideas of scholars gradually became widely held social attitudes.

The major issue for late nineteenth-century Protestant America was higher criticism of the Scriptures, which will be discussed in chapters 2 and 3. Here I will argue that evolution and the comparative study of religion—which might have been equally disruptive—were absorbed with relative ease and seemed only mildly threatening to most fin de siècle churchgoers.

"It is wise for the Church to understand the problems of labor," counseled Episcopal rector William M. Hughes in 1894; "is it not still more wise for her to understand the problems of thought?"[1] "Thought" for clerics of Reverend Hughes's generation largely meant coming to grips with the theory of evolution.

Virtually all modern-day discussions make a clear distinction between the concept of evolution—an idea that has come to stay—and the specific theory of Charles Darwin regarding "natural selection"—an idea that has remained controversial up to the present. Some Victorian observers also made this distinction, but many others used the terms "Darwinism" and "evolution" interchangeably. The reason, of course, was that Darwin's *Origin of Species* (1859) firmly catapulted the idea of evolution into the public realm.

Origin of Species is one of the works invariably included in any compilation of great writings of the Western world. Although scholars have discovered that most of Darwin's theoretical positions had already been advocated by others, that has not detracted from his genius. In his 1958 study entitled *Darwin's Century*, Loren Eiseley argued that Darwin's chief importance lay in his role as synthesizer, "a kind of lens or gathering point," to focus these ideas into the midst of Victorian society.[2]

The literature on the impact of the theory of evolution is enormous, for seldom has a single idea had so many ramifications. Darwin's influence has been traced in all the sciences, social theory, philosophy, literature, and theology.[3] Few avenues of nineteenth-century thought were unaffected.

The concept of evolution affected post–Civil War religious life in a myriad of ways. The most important of these, perhaps, was that it unsettled the static and comfortable world of the nineteenth century. Most Americans believed the planet on which they lived to be only a few thousand years old. This world, moreover, was fundamentally static. It was bounded by two specific events—Creation and the Last Judgment—and it was one in which each species brought forth only its own kind. The theory of evolution made such notions obsolete. The history of the world was now seen to extend back to the early mists of time; the present seemed to be continually in flux; and the future was a question. Historian Lynn White, Jr., called the widespread acceptance of the theory of evolution the most important shift in popular thought since the days of Constantine.[4]

On another level, the concept of evolution seemed to deny the idea of the Fall of Man. Evolution, at least as interpreted by most Americans, implied a gradual rise in human understanding from the primitive to the more complex. "That is no fall; that is ascent," remarked Unitarian popularizer Minot J. Savage. "This is what evolution teaches."[5] Yet the theory of the Fall lay at the heart of much Christian teaching.

The substitution of rise for fall as the core of the human story proved crucial for Christian thought. It led to a direct reevaluation of the idea of the Incarnation. What role did Jesus the Redeemer, the Son of God Incarnate, play in a world that now seemed to be steadily improving? Without a Fall, what purpose did a Reconciler serve? During the mid-nineteenth century, theologians alone wrestled with this issue. By the 1920s, when the discussion reached the popular level, it emerged as a bitter dispute over the Virgin Birth.[6]

Darwin's theories of natural selection seemed to contradict the prevailing theory that God's design pervaded all of nature. American Christianity had been able to survive the Enlightenment only by incorporating much of natural religion into its theology. By the early nineteenth century this natural religion—seeing the hand of the Creator in the woods, rivers, animals, plants, and mountains—had almost merged with the idea of Revelation.[7] The beaver's teeth, the duck's feet, the bear's fur—all were attributed to the hand of a loving, concerned God. The harmony that wild animals and plants shared with their natural environment could have come about, it was argued, only through the elaborate forethought of the Creator.

Nowhere was the concept of design more eloquently expressed than in the metaphor of William Paley's "Watchmaker God." Nothing ever happened by accident, Paley suggested. If one were walking in the woods and found a watch, one would have to postulate the existence of a watchmaker. So also did the perfect harmony of the universe suggest the hand of an unseen yet beneficent God.

Some romantic thinkers of the early nineteenth century applied the idea of design to the entire universe. For them, God pervaded all of nature. The strictly orthodox thinkers distinguished between God as the universe and God as transcending the universe. The heterodox thinkers of the time, such as the Transcendentalists, moved close to pantheism. Because most of the early nineteenth-century scientists were religious men, the initial probing of Nature was often a way to discover God's design.[8]

Darwin dealt a severe shock to this cosmology. His theories seemed to elevate chance to a new position of authority and to argue that there was no design in nature. Over millions of years, the innumerable variations in the species "just happened" by "natural selection" as the environment gradually weeded out the unfit. In his autobiography, Darwin wrote, "The old argument of design in nature, as given by Paley, which formerly seemed to me so conclusive, fails, now that the law of natural selection has been discovered. There seems to be no more design in the variability of organic beings and in the action of natural selection than in the course which the wind blows. Everything is the result of fixed laws."[9] At other times, Darwin seemed less certain about the element of design; eventually he concluded that the question was simply beyond human comprehension. Some of Darwin's supporters, such as Harvard botanist Asa Gray, defended design, but the materialistic agnosticism of "Darwin's Bulldog," Thomas Huxley, rose to become the "official" position of the Darwinian movement.[10]

Asa Gray's position on theistic evolution failed to convince many in the scientific community, but his ideas won out with the American public. The version of evolution absorbed by most Americans always had God's design safely locked within it. Here credit should be given to the English writer Herbert Spencer. Following the optimistic theories of Lamarck, Spencer emphasized the positive, creative aspects of evolution. In the 1894 Episcopal Church Congress session titled "The Argument of Design as Affected by the

Theory of Evolution," the various speakers cited Spencer far more often than Darwin. Their general conclusion was that design remained an integral part of evolution. Only a small minority accepted evolution without design, as if, scoffed one critic, the letters of the alphabet could be spilled onto the ground to randomly produce the *Iliad*. "The world is a real world," said the rector of St. Peter's Church in Columbia, Tennessee, "but it is, in mystery, the absolute fiat of Jehovah."[11]

The merging of Darwin's term "natural selection" with Spencer's term "survival of the fittest" gave new life to the metaphors of struggle and war. Traditionally, these phrases have been identified with the industrial struggle of the late nineteenth century to imply that "social Darwinism" simply provided a rationale for large industrialists to do what they would anyway. Yet Irvin G. Wyllie has shown that this rhetoric of struggle was not propounded in the literature read by businessmen themselves. Instead, their writings stressed Christian ethics and stewardship and argued that there was enough of society's benefits for everyone, if all put in the necessary effort.[12] The real impetus to the images of war, struggle, and virtuous victor came only with World War I. It took the fight against Germany to breathe new life into an old idea, and the results were clearly seen in the following decade.

Another area of conflict arose with the publication of Darwin's *Descent of Man* in 1871. In this work Darwin addressed the problem of human origins, suggesting that humanity was directly related to the rest of the animal kingdom. This relationship would not have bothered American Indians, who were well aware of the links between all living creatures, but it distressed many middle-class white Americans, especially in the South, where the Bible had been used to bolster the existing social system. The concept of the interrelatedness of all living things had bothersome social ramifications regarding relations between whites and their black neighbors. The heretical theory of polygenism—many creations rather than one Adam and Eve— received a hearing in the South long after it had died out in the North. Southern resistance to the theory of evolution may have stemmed in part from fear of being linked genetically to southern blacks.[13]

Finally, Darwin's apparent support of agnosticism and his widely known loss of faith, raised doubts in the minds of American religious thinkers. Darwin had considered taking orders in the Church of England, but eventually he gave up faith altogether. At the end of his life, he had become a quintessential Victorian scientist.[14]

Before 1914 the conflict of Darwin's ideas and Christian thought was muted. The theistic evolution that eventually gained acceptance was couched in terms that were acceptable to the majority of those who took notice of them. There were several reasons for this relative harmony. First, *Origin of Species* was published at the outbreak of the Civil War. Except for brief magazine interest in the spring and fall of 1860, an acrimonious debate at the Boston Society of Natural History, and another at the American Academy of Arts and Sciences, there was no public recognition of the explosive implications of Darwin's theories. Careful examination of some twenty scientific, religious, and popular magazines from 1861 to 1865 by historian Sidney Ratner yielded only four articles on evolution.[15]

At first, Darwinism affected only the scientific community, and from the start of the controversy America's two foremost scientists found themselves on opposing sides. Geologist Louis Agassiz opposed Darwin's findings, and botanist Asa Gray supported them.[16] Religious thinkers did not become involved in the quarrel until the *Descent of Man* was published, and even then, only theologians and intellectuals gave it much thought.

As the scientific community was split, so, too, was the religious community. The aged, eminent Presbyterian divine Charles Hodge concluded, in *What Is Darwinism?* (1874), that "it is atheism." James McCosh, president of Princeton University, on the other hand, found that Darwinism supported the Christianity of John Calvin, and he articulated this idea in *The Religious Aspects of Evolution* (1888). George F. Wright, professor of the harmony of science and revelation at Oberlin College, was perhaps the most outspoken defender of the notion that Darwin provided "the Calvinistic interpretation of nature."[17] Seldom, however, did such discussions get beyond scholarly fencing. Hodge, McCosh, and Wright were not widely known. Modern historians have restricted their accounts of this period to analyzing the various intellectuals' responses to Darwinism because that is all the response there was.[18] A contributor to *Bibliotheca Sacra* wrote in 1916:

> There has been more said about the disturbing influence of Darwin's book in theology and the unsettling of religious belief than facts will warrant. Some dry bones may have rattled, but they were neither as numerous nor as representative as is sometimes asserted. My bones never rattled. I passed through the time of whatever perturbation there was in thought because of Darwin's work without agitation myself and I did not find myself lonesome. I found company in plenty in both church and schools.[19]

No dramatic incident occurred to polarize the late Victorian generation over the issue of evolution. The debates in Boston caused no popular reaction, nor were there any real crusaders for or against Darwin's ideas. The only incident that came even close to spreading Darwin's views to the people was the fight among the Southern Presbyterians during the 1880s. In 1884, theology professor James Woodrow (an uncle of Woodrow Wilson) gave an address entitled "Evolution" before the alumni association of the Columbia Theological Seminary in South Carolina. His mild speech was printed in pamphlet form, and soon both Woodrow and evolution became newsworthy. The controversy quickly merged with academic politics, for John L. Girardeau, also a professor at Columbia, strongly disliked Woodrow and took the opposite point of view. The seminary was soon split down the middle. On the verge of collapse, it closed for over a year, during which time all but one of the chairs became vacant.[20]

Supporters of the two points of view set forth their opinions in all the Southern Presbyterian periodicals. Many also printed their arguments in pamphlet form. Woodrow thus found himself caught in the denomination's legal proceedings, but the Presbytery of Augusta found him innocent of "teaching and promulgating opinions and doctrines in conflict with the sacred Scriptures . . . opinions which are calculated to unsettle the mind of the church respecting the accuracy and authenticity of the Holy Scriptures as an infallible rule of faith."[21] The Synod of Georgia, however, overturned this ruling, and the church's General Assembly, meeting at Augusta, concurred. Thus the Presbyterians of the South were the first Protestant group to officially condemn evolution.

The arguments put forth on this subject were almost Byzantine in their complexity, involving such hairsplitting distinctions as supernatural versus contranatural and harmony versus noncontradiction. Yet such discussions filled the pages of the *Southern Presbyterian, Presbyterian Quarterly,* and St. Louis *Presbyterian* for several months. Woodrow despaired at the distortion of his views, stating repeatedly that he had never subordinated Scripture to science.[22] He argued only that the Scriptures were silent on the matter of evolution and that where they were silent, speculation was legitimate.[23]

This discussion gave the idea that evolution was "distinctly atheistic" its first sustained national publicity. In the minds of many, materialism and evolution were identical. The "logical outcome" of evolution, noted one Presbyterian critic, "is mechanical atheism, unsettled morals, and denial of immortality or personality to man or God."[24] Presbyterian feelings ran high on this issue. One critic of Woodrow attacked the evolutionary hypothesis for maintaining that "we came from monkeys," that "our forefathers were at one time nothing but brutes," and that Adam "was born the babe of a monkey and developed into a man."[25] "[T]he first marriage, solemnized by God himself, was not a misalliance," remarked Norfolk conservative minister George D. Armstrong. "There was no more ape-blood in Adam's veins than there was in Eve's." As chief spokesman for the General Assembly's majority report in Augusta, Armstrong claimed that Genesis should be read as actual history. He insisted that the Garden of Eden was a real place.[26]

From 1884 to 1887 evolution was much in the southern news. The *New York Times* followed the Woodrow case, but noted that such a fight could happen only in the South—in the North, clergymen could hold Woodrow's views without censure.[27]

The Woodrow case, actually an academic quarrel, did not become a national crusade; it really affected only the Southern Presbyterians. The rest of the nation would have to wait forty years to experience a similar controversy over evolution. Credit for this period of calm belongs to the many reconcilers who, in opposition to those few who argued that evolution and Christian theology were incompatible, assured Americans that there was no danger from evolution. English agnostic Thomas Huxley visited America for a series of addresses on evolution in 1876, but America lacked its own "Darwin's Bulldog." Virtually all the popularizers of evolution in the United States were reconcilers.

Words of caution came from all sides. In his *Lectures on Preaching* (1873 and widely reprinted thereafter), Phillips Brooks warned ministers not to turn from preaching the word of Christ, which they understood, to discussing scientific questions, which they did not.[28] In the spring of 1885, Henry Ward Beecher preached a series of sermons on the relationship between religion and evolution; these were later published in two widely circulated volumes. Not only did Beecher work toward compromise; he suggested that evolution was laying the ground for greater hope and prosperity for the churches.[29]

The clerical position was bolstered by Asa Gray, who consistently defended Darwinism against the charge that it was atheistic. Gray stressed that the Creator worked His will through all time; the order of the universe, itself, presupposed a mind and a design. The death of Agassiz in 1873 eliminated Gray's major rival, leaving the foremost scientist in the country as a widely known defender of design in nature.[30]

In 1874, Reverend George F. Wright asked Gray if he could republish some of his earlier works, and in 1876 Gray's *Darwiniana*, which contained the old defenses, was brought out in book form. The book received favorable reviews and thrust Gray into the position of the foremost reconciler of Darwinism and Christianity. Gray's lectures to the Yale Divinity School in 1879, published the following year as *Natural Science and Religion*, furthered the defense. He kept this role until his death eight years later.[31]

Although less respected among scientists than Gray, popular lecturers John Fiske and Edward L. Youmans followed the same conciliatory path. Originally a skeptic, Fiske turned to religion in the 1880s for its emotional values and later gained wide fame for his popularization of Spencer and Darwin. His *Outlines of Cosmic Philosophy* (1878) went through sixteen editions.[32] Youmans used the lecture platform and the pages of his *Popular Science Monthly* to spread Spencer's ideas of evolution, for which he received credit in Spencer's 1894 autobiography.[33] The victory of Spencer's optimism over Darwin's agnosticism proved to be what America needed. Many of those who discussed evolution could not distinguish between the two. As an anonymous author said in 1895, "Unconsciously to ourselves, we are all Spencerians."[34]

Considerable help came from abroad in the person of Henry Drummond,

lecturer in natural science in the Free Church College of Glasgow, who
devoted much of his forensic and literary power to reconciliation. His
Natural Law in the Spiritual World (1883), which supported both evolution
and evangelical theology by judicious argument from analogy, remained
popular for many years. He had modified his positions considerably by the
time of his second major work, *The Ascent of Man* (1894), but he continued
to proclaim the theory of evolution with style and eloquence. Drummond
stressed that evolution involved altruism and claimed that it brought an
"unspeakable exaltation" to humankind. Instead of finding a harsh struggle
for existence, he said that evolution was actually moral. Borrowing ideas
from Lamarck and Prince Kropotkin, he emphasized the unselfish "struggle
for the life of others" as the real key to the evolutionary process. There may
have been strife, he admitted, but it had been more than redeemed by an
infinite amount of mutual aid and self-sacrifice, the latter having been the
key to evolution. This was the theme of his most popular talk, "The Greatest
Thing in the World"—love. "The first chapter or two may be headed the
struggle for life," he noted, "but take the story as a whole and it is not a tale
of battle, it is a love-story."[35]

Another widely read harmonizer was Congregational minister Lyman
Abbott, who began his work along these lines with a series of lectures in
1892–93 before the Lowell Institute. These were published as *The Evolution
of Christianity* (1897). "Adam did not represent me," said Abbott, "I never
voted for him."[36] The popularizing of Abbott's ideas so annoyed Boston
Unitarian minister Minot J. Savage that he responded by writing *The Irrepressible Conflict between Two World-Theories* (1892). Abbott's Lowell
lectures were creating a response all out of proportion to their worth, Savage
stated. Nothing said by Abbott was new; all serious investigators had been
aware of these facts for years.[37] Savage was probably correct as far as scholars
were concerned, but Abbott was bringing the ideas of harmony down to the
public at large.

In 1885, Henry Ward Beecher claimed that the period of controversy
between evolution and Christianity had closed. This claim may have been
premature, but in 1901, in a lengthy series of articles, British journalist W.
H. Mallock admitted that although the religion-science conflict had not
ended, it had entered a new phase. There once had existed an atheistic
theory of evolution based on materialism, noted Newell Dwight Hillis, but
the theory that now reigned was theistic and increasingly Christian.[38]
"Already the time has come," Hillis noted in 1900, "when almost everybody
exclaims, 'Evolution—certainly, why, I always believed in theistic evolution.' "[39] At the centenary of Darwin's birth in 1909, it was widely agreed
that the earlier polemics against evolution had passed forever. In 1911,
Richard E. MacLaurin, president of the Massachusetts Institute of Technology, called the rapid change in the relations between science and religion

one of the unrecognized wonders of the modern world. For both sides, he said, this was the end of the battle.[40]

The victory of the theory of evolution was widely hailed on both sides of the Atlantic, yet in America it seemed an easy triumph. Evolution had conquered, but Darwinism had not. Instead of the celebration of pure chance, the optimistic, purposeful views of Spencer, Lamarck, Fiske, Youmans, Beecher, and Abbott had emerged victorious. If an American believed in evolution, it was most likely to be in a benign, optimistic, theistic variety of the theory. By the 1890s, evolution had become almost a fashionable creed. It was equated with progress, advance, and improvement. Those who opposed it as atheistic had all but disappeared.

From the end of the Woodrow case in 1887 until just before World War I, therefore, those who spoke out against evolution had little ammunition with which to fuel their position. Their arguments were co-opted by a world that fervently believed in progress, and they had no leader capable of bringing their position down to the people. In these years, no opponent of the evolution theory marshaled a concerted popular attack against it, but instead, foes were reduced to sniping from the sidelines. Even the sniping was sporadic. J. W. McGarvey, longtime contributor to the Disciples' *Christian Standard*, spent his career attacking higher criticism of the Scriptures. On the issue of evolution, he was much milder. He cautioned his readers that "development," such as the growth of an egg into a fowl or an acorn into an oak, was not really part of "the doctrine of evolution." He was not entirely convinced of the truth of the theory of evolution, and suggested only that his readers be cautious about accepting it. The only significance he saw in the Darwinian centennial was that Darwinism was losing the standing it once had had in the scientific field.[41]

Shortly after 1900, William Jennings Bryan, then a twice unsuccessful candidate for president, took to the lecture platform with a varied set of public talks. His most successful, "The Prince of Peace," which he delivered thousands of times, contained a brief statement against the theory of evolution. Bryan delivered no speeches specifically against evolution before 1914. In "The Prince of Peace," moreover, he cautioned his listeners that he was not attacking those who believed in evolution; he simply thought that more proof was needed.[42]

Several itinerant revivalists delivered occasional antievolution messages at the turn of the century. William Bell Riley and Billy Sunday gave popular addresses against it, but they had no national impact. The multivolume series published from 1909 to 1914, *The Fundamentals*—often seen as the beginning of the Fundamentalist-Modernist controversy—contained almost nothing against evolution.

Virtually the only figure of national prominence to attack evolution seriously during the latter nineteenth century was the popular Presbyterian editor and clergyman T. DeWitt Talmage. The antievolution theme formed only a small part of his ministry, but when he did speak on the issue, it was always in the strongest terms of rhetorical denunciation. In numerous sermons, Talmage attacked and distorted the idea of "survival of the fittest" by suggesting that it meant that the soldiers who lost their lives in the Civil War were less fit than those who survived. How could one say that the fittest survived, he noted, when President James A. Garfield had died in September 1881, but Charles Guiteau, his assassin, lived several months longer? Herbert Spencer was not present at the Creation, he observed, but God was. Whom should the people believe? "I tell you plainly," he said in *Live Coals*, "if your father was a muskrat and your mother an opossum, and your great aunt a kangaroo, and the toads and the snapping turtle were your illustrious predecessors, my father was God."[43]

Posing as the national interpreter of Darwin, Talmage argued that most people did not have enough time to undertake their own investigations of evolution. Thus it was important for them to understand that evolution was infidelity, scientifically false, and brutalizing.[44] Talmage, however, was unable to make evolution into a national issue. When he denounced it on a trip to Australia in 1894, his audiences merely found him amusing. Darwin had been familiar with such absurd parodies of his ideas and had once written to Sir Charles Lyell that a Manchester paper had argued that "I have proved 'might makes right' and therefore that Napoleon is right and every cheating tradesman is also right."[45]

The comparative study of religion, the second major intellectual trauma for Protestants at the end of the nineteenth century, was partly a result of the increased interest in other countries and faiths made possible by better communications. In 1871, Unitarian minister James Freeman Clarke published *Ten Great Religions: An Essay in Comparative Theology*, originally a series of magazine articles for the *Atlantic Monthly*. The book went through five editions within seventeen years.

Magazines also treated the exotic theme of other faiths, and this scholarly subject slowly worked its way from academic and intellectual circles into the popular literature.[46] In 1902, *Current Literature* remarked that "the science of comparative religion is probably making the most rapid advances of any branch of theological study at the present time."[47] The theme also drew strength from the rise of anthropology and sociology, and by 1914 even conservative theologians were admitting that comparative religion was an acceptable field of study.

Although some people felt that subjecting Christianity to scientific and comparative treatment was sacrilege, others were less fearful. Comparative religion, its proponents argued, showed the unity of the human race and that religious faith grew naturally in human minds and hearts. F. Max Muller of

Oxford claimed that the person who knows only one religion really knows none at all.[48] It is unclear how far this comparative study drifted down to people in the pews. Few seemed to have an opinion on the issue. It is probably safe to say that the scholars' praise for the comparative analysis of other faiths was not shared by ordinary citizens.

Many travelers who took cruises around the world were shocked by the poverty and degradation they found in China, India, the Near East, and Africa, which they saw as the practical results of the indigenous religions. One visitor declared that the chief burden of Egypt was Mohammedanism. The Reverend Francis E. Clarke, who traveled over forty thousand miles in 1892–93, reported that "Christianity is absolutely superior in its motive power, its purifying influence and its uplifting inspiration from any and all other religions with which it comes in competition." Joseph Cook, in his popular *Boston Monday Lectures* (1877), agreed: "The false philosophies of the Occident must be judged as the false religions of the Orient, by the true philosophy, the Christian scheme of thought."[49] Comparative religion was for these people little more than the comparison of Christianity with other religions, to their disadvantage. Eventually it became touted as a means by which Christians could counterattack assaults from other faiths.[50]

The study of comparative religion, moreover, did not have the predicted adverse effect on foreign missions. Ironically, the high point of interest in other faiths overlapped with a major crusade for missionary activity: the Student Volunteer Movement for Foreign Missions (SVM). The SVM grew out of a gathering held at Dwight L. Moody's Mount Hermon School in Massachusetts in 1886, at which a small group of college students listened to inspiring talks about the deplorable conditions overseas and were offered an opportunity to render service to others. "Missions became the absorbing topic of conversation wherever the students gathered," John R. Mott later recalled, "in the rooms, in the dining hall, at the swimming wharf, and on the athletic field. Each volunteer became an enlister of others."[51]

Under the able leadership of Mott and Robert P. Wilder, these young people began a campaign to enlist other men and women in the enterprise. Taking as their motto "the evangelization of the world in this generation," the SVM crusaders were soon knocking on the doors of thousands of colleges, seminaries, and churches. With traveling secretaries continually in the field and widely publicized district, state, and national conventions, the SVM crusade helped awaken a national interest in foreign missions. The organization spawned two other related mission groups and in fifty years sent over thirteen thousand men and women into the mission field.[52] As a consequence of this activity, when ordinary churchgoers heard about the other faiths of the world, it was more likely from an advocate of foreign missions than from a student of comparative religion.

The manifestation of interest in comparative religion that attracted the most attention, however, came with the staging of the World's Parliament of

Religions in Chicago, as part of the Columbian Exposition of 1893, under the leadership of Chicago educator and jurist Charles C. Bonney and Presbyterian minister John Henry Barrows. Concerned that the Chicago World's Fair would provide only a display of the century's material progress, the two men wished also to illustrate its intellectual and moral progress. To this end, they invited representatives from all the major faiths of the world, and a surprising number agreed to come.

All the faiths were represented by their most distinguished spokesmen, and the major theme was common points of belief. The goals of the gathering, said Bonney, were to unite all religion against all irreligion and to make the basis of this union rest on the principle of the Golden Rule.[53] "The Parliament," noted a bishop from Catholic University, "was to be an object lesson in the comparative study of religions."[54] Only in America of that time, Congregationalist Washington Gladden boasted, could such a parliament be assembled.[55] A British rabbi suggested the phrase that became the official motto: "Have we not all one father? Hath not one God created us?" Religious and benevolent societies, especially the Evangelical Alliance, joined in the hope that the gathering would mark a new era of understanding. The parliament was to be, they said, "a turning point, or at least a starting point, in the history of humanity," "the new era in the history of mankind," and "the greatest event so far in the history of the world."[56]

Although none of these hopes were realized, the parliament provided a magnificent attraction. It rivaled the numerous other exhibits of the fair, even the midway with its infamous belly dancer, "Little Egypt." Beginning on September 11, 1893, and continuing for seventeen days, over 150,000 people crowded the parliament's halls to witness the colorful costume displays and hear talks from the dignitaries. The Chicago press gave the events generous coverage, and the major addresses were later published in two large volumes. In general, the speeches stressed the unity of the world's faiths and told little of problems among different religious groups.[57] Any speaker who emphasized that ethics were much more important than doctrinal questions was applauded. The theme of religious unity was so well received that there was talk of forming a new universal religion to absorb them all. Needless to say, this was never accomplished. As Washington Gladden pointed out, a faith cannot be created as can a political party or a social club.

Although the official theme of the parliament was unity, an undercurrent of dissent seemed to increase as the sessions continued. The archbishop of Canterbury refused to support the program because he felt that to place Christianity on the same platform with the other faiths of the world implied an equality he found objectionable. The sultan of Turkey also protested, for similar reasons, regarding Islam. One Asian speaker rebuked his American audience for their ignorance of the life of Buddha. Unfavorable comments on the slums of Chicago by some visitors from India led Dr. George F. Pentecost to assault the character of all Brahmin priests and priestesses; the latter he called prostitutes. Mohammed Alexander Russell Webb, a Yankee convert to Islam, was hissed by his audience when he extolled the virtues of polygamy and suggested that Mohammed was as thoroughly nonaggressive and peaceloving as the typical Quaker. Mormon missionaries complained bitterly that they were not given a fair chance to present their faith. (Ironically, they were excluded because of their teachings about polygamy.) No Freethinkers were present.

The numerous American denominations met separately to transact their own business affairs, and these gatherings provided opportunities to vent strong feelings. Disciples of Christ minister H. W. Everett attacked every other faith present at the parliament when he gave the opening address to a Disciples audience. Reverend E. K. Bell of Cincinnati reminded a group of Lutherans that they had a mission distinct from that of any other church. Reverend T. DeWitt Talmage viewed the fair as a grand opportunity for the evangelization of all nations. Dwight L. Moody and Reuben A. Torrey engaged in a six-month World's Fair city evangelization campaign, held when the parliament was meeting, to convert the fairgoers to their brand of evangelical Christianity.[58]

Few of the nation's religious editors lost an opportunity to comment on the gala display, and the comments were often critical. The Disciples' *Christian Evangelist* noted that although "other religions contain some gleams of the light of eternal truth, Christianity is radiant with the light of the Sun of Righteousness."[59] True tolerance was intended to be of man for his brother man, noted the *Methodist Review*, not of man for false religions.[60] W. P. Harrison, editor of the *Methodist Quarterly Review*, declared that the parliament had brought together the greatest variety of cranks the world had ever seen. Outside of Bedlam, he suggested, there had never been a greater exhibition of "absurd ideas and unprofitable enterprises."[61]

On another level, Episcopal Reverend Morgan Dix of Trinity Church, New York, suggested in a sermon (often repeated and later published as a pamphlet) that the chief result of the parliament would be simply to spread agnostic views across the nation. Other Episcopalians agreed. "The Parliament of Religions is itself a thing of the past," noted the *Episcopal Recorder*, "but we fear its evil influence will long be felt in the land, promoting, far and wide, an 'agnostic indifference' to the great verities of the Christian Faith."[62]

Charles Bonney's hopes that the parliament would produce a "universal fraternity of virtue and morality" came to naught, and none of the succeeding World's Fairs continued the theme. The International Exposition at Paris in 1900 lacked a parliament of religions, and the St. Louis Exposition of 1904 heard only papers from American religious figures.

Assessing the overall impact of the parliament is difficult, but it must have caused at least brief interest in other faiths. It offered sustained publicity for Mary Baker Eddy's Christian Science, Madame Helena Blavatsky's Theosophy, and for the Baha'is. Nowhere else could one have witnessed all the major religions of the world: all types of theism, Judaism, Islam, Hinduism, Buddhism, Taoism, Confucianism, Shintoism, Zoroastrianism, Roman Catholicism, Greek Orthodoxy, and all the varieties of Protestantism. Perhaps the parliament should best be remembered for the providing of a marvelous show.

Comparative religion came and went with a minimum of dispute; evolution was absorbed with little controversy. The same could not be said, however, for the rise and spread of the higher criticism of the Scriptures.

2
The Rise and Spread
of Higher Criticism:
The Old Testament

Of all the intellectual currents within American Protestantism in the late nineteenth century, none was more controversial than the higher criticism of the Scriptures. The movement that submitted the Bible to historical analysis proved to be one of the most crucial challenges the American churches were to face.

The Bible played a vital role in the early development of the nation. As Henry Otis Dwight noted, the Bible became *"the* Book of the New World."[1] Often the only volume a family possessed, the Bible was a record book for births, marriages, and deaths as well as a source of inspiration. Moreover, it was everywhere. In 1916, the American Bible Society boasted that it had distributed sixty-nine million Bibles, Testaments, and portions of Scripture in eighty-five languages during its ninety-nine year history.[2]

Antebellum Americans believed the world was about six thousand years old. Historian Perry Miller has argued that the American settlers often felt as familiar with the characters in the Old Testament as with their own neighbors.[3] The frequency with which children were named Mary, Abigail, Rebecca, Ruth, David, Jacob, Isaac, Daniel, John, Israel, and Ebenezer bore eloquent testimony to this familiarity.

The Old and New Testaments provided the major images and metaphors for nineteenth-century statesmen, poets, and authors. After Daniel Webster supported the Compromise of 1850, Quaker poet John Greenleaf Whittier termed him "Ichabod." This reference to 1 Samuel 4:21 may be lost on modern readers, but it was once common parlance. Abraham Lincoln's "house divided" image came from Mark 3:25, and the cadence of his second inaugural clearly reflects the influence of Hebrew poetry. Scholars have found that Lincoln's writings contain references to at least twenty-two books of the Bible. Herman Melville's most famous character was Ahab, and *Moby Dick* opens with the words, "Call me Ishmael."

Biblical imagery was also a linguistic bridge among people. Even those who heard no preachers or speakers and read no poems or novels did not escape the Bible's influence: it was embodied in the language. "Now it is not to be forgotten that the King James's translation has *made* the English language what it is," noted Methodist minister Alfred A. Wright, "almost as much as Luther's Bible made the German language what *it* is—impressing characteristics upon it which are ineffaceable."[4] Consider, for example, the phrases "the apple of his eye," "a still small voice," "the salt of the earth," "a land flowing with milk and honey," and "a pearl of great price." The biblical implications of these phrases supplied meaning that extended far beyond the words themselves.[5]

As a source for common metaphors, images, and inspiration, the King James version was unsurpassed. It was an integral part of the lives of ordinary people. But exactly how it was interpreted by American readers before the arrival of higher criticism is a question that can never be answered with precision. All that can be done is to sketch some broad outlines.

Medieval Christianity developed a sophisticated, elaborate response to the question of biblical interpretation. For the scholars of the early Christian era, the Word lay incarnate in Scripture, and, like humanity, it had both body and soul. The body lay in the letter of the Word, the soul in the spiritual meaning. Medievals tended to look through the text rather than at it, and allegory served as their key to interpretation. Origen (182–251) argued that Scripture had several layers of meaning: literal, moral, and allegorical. The first two were for simple believers, the third for initiates.[6] Saint Thomas Aquinas attempted to simplify this interpretation by noting that human writers expressed their meaning through words, but God expressed His meaning through things (that is, historical events, which the human author's words describe).[7]

The literal interpretation of the Bible did not become widespread until the Reformation. As Bible reading spread to ordinary people allegorical interpretation was forgotten. The American Puritans, for example, relied heavily upon a literal interpretation of Scripture during their early days in New England. They based their concept of the state on the Old Testament story of ancient Israel and borrowed part of their early law code verbatim from Deuteronomy 21:20–21.[8]

The ideas of literalism spread to the majority of the country in the aftermath of the first Great Awakening (1740–45) and were continued into the early years of the nineteenth century by the second Great Awakening (1800–ca. 1815). A personal and literal reading of Scripture seemed to form part of the democratic framework of the republic, wherein all people were responsible for their own salvation. "The Bible is a plain book, addressed to the common sense of man," said a Methodist minister in 1851, "and the arrogant pretense that the common people cannot be trusted with its mysteries is an insult to its author."[9]

The authors of many nineteenth-century memoirs recall this literal reading among their families. William A. Stone, governor of Pennsylvania, noted that in his backcountry boyhood no one ever apologized for any saying in the Bible—they simply believed it as stated. Disciples of Christ minister Herbert L. Willett noted that his parents made no allowances for allegory, legend, or myth when they read biblical stories. Narratives that in any other literature would have instantly been recognized as figures of speech were taken as valid history.[10] In *Sixty Years with the Bible: A Record of Experience*, William N. Clarke noted that when his family read from Scriptures, they accepted the words as truth. There were no contradictions, for there could be none. How could God contradict Himself?[11] For everyone over fifty, Washington Gladden observed in 1894, every word in their childhood Bible was absolute truth. Even the suggestion of error would have been shocking.[12] R. Heber Newton caricatured this stance, but perhaps not too wildly, when he noted in 1883: "A book let down out of the skies, immaculate, infallible, oracular—this is the traditional view of the Bible."[13]

Scientists despaired at the prevalence of such views, Freethinkers scoffed at them, and liberal theologians tried their best to modify them. But the literal reading persisted. In 1906, Willard C. Selleck observed that although the old view of plenary inspiration and absolute infallibility had been somewhat modifed by recent events, it still was probably the dominant view of most American Protestants.[14]

To exchange this fixed conception of Scripture for a historical-critical perspective was to undergo a genuine revolution in thought. This revolution took place first in the seminaries and from there reached into congregations. Indeed, as Lyman Abbott remarked in 1911, the change in the popular conception during the last half century was so great that the Bible might properly be called a genuinely new book.[15] This change came about because of the spread of higher criticism.

In the early nineteenth century, scholars began to use literary analysis, archaeological discoveries, and comparative linguistics to gain a better understanding of the Old Testament. The new view of the composition of the Old Testament was usually termed the Graf-Wellhausen, Kuenen-Wellhausen, or simply Wellhausen theory, after its originator, Julius Wellhausen.[16] It argued that the parts of the Pentateuch that had traditionally been assigned to Moses were actually drawn from many sources and telescoped together by later authors. The sources numbered at least four: J (from the use of the term "Jehovah"), E (from the use of the term "Elohim"), D (from Deuteronomy), and P (from the Priestly code, found mainly in Leviticus). As Presbyterian observer M. B. Lambdin noted with irony, "The Pentateuch is thus not Mosaic; but a mosaic."[17]

In addition to declaring the composite nature of the Pentateuch, the German critics raised other issues: the idea that the Book of Isaiah had at least two authors, the second of whom wrote the last twenty-seven chapters; serious questioning of David's authorship of the Psalms; doubt as to the time when Daniel was written; questioning if Job and Song of Solomon were really historical; and questioning if the fifty-third chapter of Isaiah and the second Psalm were indirectly or directly prophetic.

Although the general public remained ignorant of the German theories, most American scholars kept abreast of work being done in European universities.[18] Moses Stuart of Andover had translated some of the German works as early as 1822. Theodore Parker translated Wilhelm DeWette's studies and reviewed David Strauss's radical *Life of Jesus* in the *Christian Examiner* in 1840. This controversial book was available in an English translation by George Eliot in 1846. By the mid-nineteenth century, most of the New England theological schools had accepted the new critical approach.[19] Yet, it was not until these theories shifted to the British Isles that their effects began to be felt by the American public. The shared language and the close connection between American church bodies, especially the Episcopalians and the Presbyterians, with those of Britain brought the unrest caused by the new scholarship to American churches.

The publication of several volumes brought the issue to the attention of American audiences. One of the most important of these was *Essays and Reviews*, published in 1860 and composed of essays by seven contributors from the Church of England (nicknamed by their enemies as "Septem contra Christum"). The book, perhaps the first popular presentation of the critical findings of the Germans, sold well on both sides of the ocean.[20] In America, however, it was read largely by Episcopalians, and the outbreak of the Civil War the next year muted their response.

In 1876, Scottish Presbyterian theologian W. Robertson Smith published several articles using higher criticism in the *Encyclopedia Britannica*. This approach shocked some scholars and provoked several replies that were circulated among Presbyterians on both sides of the Atlantic. As a result of these and several other of his articles, Smith was tried by the General Assembly of the Free Church of Scotland. He was accused of holding that the Pentateuch had been written by more than one author and of writing articles that contained speculation that tended to awaken doubt as to the truth of the inspiration and authority of the books of the Bible and the doctrines as set forth in the Westminster Confession of Faith. The much-publicized Smith heresy trial took two years; in 1880 he was acquitted.[21] The thorough coverage of the trial given by the *New York Times* alerted Americans to the important religious controversies in Britain.[22]

From 1881 to 1883, higher criticism was discussed in the *Presbyterian Review*. In April 1882, Henry Preserved Smith propounded "The Critical Theories of Julius Wellhausen" there. In 1888–90, William Henry Green and William Rainey Harper held a long but polite debate on the Pentateuch question in *Hebraica*.[23] Theologians at the Newton Theological Institution, Oberlin College, the Episcopal Theological School, Union Seminary, the University of Chicago, and others became strong supporters of higher criticism.[24]

After about 1880, the general public awakened to the scholars' disputes, and the Old Testament became the storm center for American higher criticism. Alluding to the famous Civil War battle, some termed the problem of the authorship of the Pentateuch the "bloody angle" of the critical conflict in America. In 1893, Edward L. Curtis remarked that this question had become almost as famous in the religious world as the problems of the high tariff or free trade in the world of politics.[25]

Higher criticism received its first sustained publicity with the furor surrounding the revision of the Bible in the early 1880s. In 1870, scholars from all leading Protestant denominations in Great Britain and America met to plan the proposed revision. Dividing into committees, they set to work on a task that would take eleven years. The American committee, headed by Philip Schaff, published a volume of essays by nineteen of its twenty-seven members stating the reasons for revision and the principle of its execution.[26] The *New York Times* noted that it was "chiefly the progress of Biblical Science, geographical, archaeological, chronological, philological, etc., which has made a revision of the King James Bible almost a necessity."[27] Enthusiasm over the proposed changes was high, but there was fear that many might be uncomfortable about a new translation to correct older mistakes and would respond as if "the axis of the earth had become unsettled."[28] Millions of Americans had shaped their lives not merely around the subject matter but also "the actual wording of the King James version."[29]

When the Revised Version of the English New Testament was nearly ready, Oxford Press alone had orders for a million copies. Interest was high on both sides of the Atlantic, and several American publishers tried unsuccessfully to bribe their way into having the first view. The day sales opened in New York—May 21, 1881—the book was hawked on the sidewalks, and the streets were blocked with vans and wagons. Two Chicago newspapers telegraphed the New Testament from New York to Chicago, a message of 118,000 words, the longest dispatch ever sent. With the aid of ninety-two compositors and five correctors, it was printed entirely in the *Chicago Times* for Sunday, May 22. Other newspapers printed the New Testament as a supplement. Over thirty editions came out during the year.[30] One publishing house in New York sold 365,000 copies before the end of 1881; fifty separate editions were issued within a short time. The revised Old Testament appeared four years later, but the committee had published many of their changes beforehand, so it was greeted with less uproar. The Apocrypha finally was published in 1895. None of the later major revisions of the Bible (American Revised version, 1901; James Moffatt translation, 1913; Revised

Standard version, 1946) caused so much commotion. The first break from the King James version proved the most startling.

The new translation project brought many questions of biblical history to public attention. The fact that this translation was made from numerous fragmentary documents, many of them with variant wordings, was widely publicized. Because no one possessed the original documents, the question was raised of the accuracy of the over 2,600 Hebrew manuscripts containing parts of the Old Testament and the over 3,000 manuscripts containing parts of the Greek New Testament.

After the initial flurry, however, controversy over the new Bible died down. Catholics and Episcopalians did not plan to use it, and several publishers lost money on the venture. In 1897, eight copies of the Revised Version sold for every one hundred of the King James; its chief virtue appeared to be as a scholarly textbook. Two unpopular changes, Matthew 6:13: "And bring us not into temptation, but deliver us from the evil one," and, the Gloria in Excelsis: "Glory to God in the highest, and on earth, peace among men in whom He is well pleased," decided the fate of this version with the public.[31]

Among those who criticized the new translation, British evangelist C. H. Spurgeon said that the revisers were more careful of their reputations as Greek scholars than they were to represent the mind of the Holy Spirit. Reverend T. DeWitt Talmage wholeheartedly denounced the new version and urged his congregation to keep their old Bibles. He attacked the thirty-eight scholars as practicing ecclesiastical "bossism." "D.D. and Ph.D. and LL.D.," he noted, "are often only the heavy baggage of a very slow train." When he suggested that 999 out of every 1,000 considered the revision a desecration and outrage, he was greeted by applause.[32]

With the new translation providing the backdrop, American awareness of higher criticism began to grow rapidly. In the period from 1888 to 1906, the critical ideas were popularized and distorted to such an extent that by the latter date few educated people could have been unaware of the broad outlines of the issues involved.

Charting the means by which these complicated and often esoteric views came to be shared by ordinary people is difficult. It is also clouded by the fact that no single dramatic event served to focus attention on the subject. Instead, numerous small incidents gradually combined to bring these ideas to popular attention: several works of fiction; some controversial publications from England; hundreds of local talks; numerous newspaper articles; sustained efforts by dedicated liberals, especially Lyman Abbott, Washington Gladden, and Herbert L. Willett; and heresy trials. An isolated book, talk, or newspaper article might, by itself, mean little, but added together they formed a movement of considerable importance. Moreover, a presentation of critical discoveries was often followed by a rebuttal of equal or greater magnitude. The eventual result was to draw up two distinct points of view on the issue of higher criticism.

The year 1888 marks a peak in the growth of the nation's awareness of higher criticism because in that year two significant novels on religious issues appeared: *John Ward, Preacher* by Margaret Deland and *Robert Elsmere* by Mrs. Humphrey Ward. Although much of Protestantism had long frowned on novel reading, this view had pretty well collapsed by the late nineteenth century, and the religious novels produced offer a good way of viewing the problems of the day.

Deland's *John Ward, Preacher* is not a great novel, but it points to a great theme in American life: the decay of Calvinism and the vacuum its disappearance seemed to leave. The character John Ward is an old-fashioned Presbyterian minister who firmly believes in the infallibility of the Bible and the reality of Hell for those dying unconverted. His wife, Helen, is a liberal and rejects most of the principles for which he stands. His petty congregation accuses her of spreading her system of unbelief, and reluctantly she leaves her husband. After terrible moral agony, John decides to stay with his congregation. He conveniently dies at the end, and Helen is left to seek her salvation in the helping of others.[33]

The sympathies of the author are evident. There is much about escape from "this hideous shadow of Calvinism," and several sections of the book discuss the infallibility of the Bible. John holds to this view, but Helen does not. Eventually they conclude that discussion between them is impossible. "Don't you see, dear," Helen says, "we cannot reason about it. You take all this from the Bible because you believe it is inspired. I do not believe it is. So how can we argue?"[34] The religious press reviled the book, and many librarians refused to purchase it. But the thin edge of the wedge had been driven in—the crisis in American religion had reached the popular novel.

Mrs. Humphrey Ward's *Robert Elsmere* is a much better book. Her name is not well known in America, but in her native England she was recognized as a leading antisuffragette, founder of an evening play center for city children, and charming hostess. As late as 1909 she was praised as one of the most interesting and important literary figures in the world.[35] Although she wrote many other works, none ever achieved the fame of *Elsmere*. It is difficult for a modern reader to comprehend the reasons for the success of this tome, which was marketed in three volumes in Great Britain and as a six-hundred-page one-volume version in America, yet it sold widely everywhere. Mrs. Ward estimated that half a million copies were sold in the first year of publication. At first, a free copy was given with the purchase of a case of Balsam Fir soap. Clerical denunciations seemed only to excite interest, and small-town libraries could not keep enough copies on hand.[36] It remained in print until 1934, and in 1967 the University of Nebraska Press published a paperback edition with an introduction by Clyde de L. Ryals.

Church reviews were frequently unfavorable—one referred to it as "Robert L. Smear." William E. Gladstone reviewed it in a ten-thousand-word critical essay in the British journal *Nineteenth Century* in May 1888, which the *North American Review* reprinted verbatim for American readers in January 1889, when it ran a symposium on the book. Henry James called *Elsmere* "a beautiful book," and Julia Ward Howe said, "I know of no story since *Uncle Tom's Cabin* whose appearance had excited so much comment [and] intellectual interest of so high a character."[37] Oliver Wendell Holmes agreed. Today one can scarcely find a copy in a used book store, but in the late 1880s and early 1890s *Robert Elsmere* was a major best seller.

The story centers on the trials of a clergyman of the Church of England and his lovely Christian wife, Catherine, with a subplot about her sister Rose, who moves slowly into the world of art for art's sake. All subplots, however, are lost in the mental struggles of Reverend Elsmere. Filled with faith after taking a small parish with his wife, Elsmere meets wealthy Squire Wendover, whom he finally but reluctantly convinces to take better care of his neglected tenants. But the squire more than gets his revenge, for he invites Elsmere to use his library whenever convenient, and this eventually proves to be the minister's downfall. Elsmere begins to read heavily and, in so doing, loses his faith. After great agony, he decides to found another religion, "the New Brotherhood of Christ," that will work among the lower classes; at the end, he dies in the attempt. Catherine and their young daughter, left bereft and bewildered, decide to attend regular services on Sunday mornings and work at the New Brotherhood in the afternoons. The books that destroyed Elsmere's faith are carefully left unmentioned, but it was clear that the author meant German higher criticism.

Elsmere was not the first popular novel to touch this theme, but it was the first best seller to raise the question of the authenticity of the Scriptures.[38] Says Catherine: "If the Gospels are not true in fact, as history, as reality, I cannot see how they are true at all, or of any value."[39] Mrs. Ward noted in one of the many articles that followed the publication of the book that "the supernatural element connected with the life of Jesus must be eliminated from the *New Testament* in the interests of historical veracity."[40]

More than *John Ward, Preacher, Robert Elsmere* raised the question of the authority of Scriptures and the role of the supernatural, and it concluded with a resounding question mark. The mechanical, industrial world of the late nineteenth century seemed to offer little comfort to the traditional world of faith. From the sales figures, it seems obvious that Reverend Robert Elsmere's mental struggles were widely shared by his American contemporaries. The issues had become public property.

The next year (1889) brought another shock with the publication of a British volume entitled *Lux Mundi*. A book of twelve liberal theological essays by eleven Church of England clergymen, *Lux Mundi* raised a storm comparable to *Essays and Reviews* almost thirty years earlier. It, too, argued strongly for higher criticism. The book went through ten editions in two years, and one of the numerous sermons against it, *The Worth of the Old Testament*, also went through several editions. *Lux Mundi* also was widely circulated in America. William T. Stead, editor of the transatlantic *Review of Reviews*, ran a condensed version of it for his May 1890 issue. William Croswell Doane, Episcopal bishop of Albany, devoted much of his 1890 bishop's address to its implications.[41] This concern was combined with the rumored heresy trial of Rector R. Heber Newton and the actual trial of Howard MacQueary by the Ohio Episcopal diocese on the issue of the Virgin Birth and physical resurrection of Christ. *Lux Mundi* was also clearly responsible for the 1895 bishops' pastoral letter in which they restated their doctrines of faith.[42] After these publications, no Episcopalian could have been unaware of higher criticism.

Again, the issue raised was that of inspiration and the Bible's historical accuracy. In discussing *Lux Mundi,* the *New York Times* correctly saw that it would cause much less problem to Episcopalians, who could rely on the church as having equal authority to Scripture. But for evangelical Protestants, who had no church, as such, the issue would be much more complex.[43]

Higher criticism also reached the American people through numerous speeches by liberal popularizers. The scenario was repeated over and over again: a liberal scholar would give a talk; an angry exchange would follow, sometimes covered by the press; at times a pamphlet or two would appear in response. This occurred in almost every denomination, with considerable effect. In October 1889, for example, Professor Edward L. Curtis of McCormick Theological Seminary shocked the congregation of the Rockford, Illinois, Westminster Presbyterian Church by declaring that Job was a poem and meant to be understood as a parable.[44] In New York in 1894, a crowd of 375 Methodist clergymen heard Boston University Professor H. G. Mitchell speak on "Profit and Loss: A Reckoning with Biblical Criticism," in which he presented the Wellhausen theory of the Pentateuch. An angry audience poured derision on his talk.[45] In February 1897 in Chicago, a Metropolitan District Association heard a paper by a Drew Theological Seminary professor on "The Authority of the Bible," which evoked a similarly fierce discussion of biblical infallibility.[46] In 1892, a Baptist conference in New York was thrown into disruption by a paper on the different biblical views of the parousia, which conservatives claimed was impossible.[47]

The popular magazines also picked up the issue. Articles entitled "When Were the Gospels Written?" "The Nature and Method of Revelation," "Higher Criticism as Viewed by a Liberal Scholar," "The Higher Criticism," and "The Present State of Old Testament Criticism" were very popular in the early 1890s. A surprising number of popular magazine articles on the recent archaeological and linguistic biblical discoveries carried the title "The

New Old Testament." The church press also gave the subject wide coverage, but here much of the comment was critical. In fact, William Rainey Harper once accused the church press of waging a negative war against higher criticism. Slowly it became obvious to many that two conceptions of biblical interpretation were fighting for supremacy in the various Protestant denominations.[48]

The most steady means of spreading higher criticism to the American public, however, came through the pens of three popularizers: Washington Gladden, Lyman Abbott, and Herbert L. Willett.

Washington Gladden, a popular Congregationalist pastor in Columbus, Ohio, is most widely remembered today as a proponent of the Social Gospel, but he should also be recalled as a major popularizer of the theories of higher criticism. He first became acquainted with critical studies in 1875 when he served as pastor at Springfield, Massachusetts, and became convinced of the value of these studies to theology. But when he tried to expound some of his readings from the pulpit—especially that Acts 8:37 was not in the original manuscripts—he found himself in trouble with his congregation.[49]

Moving to Columbus, Ohio, in 1882, then a city of fifty-three thousand, he agonized over the growing contempt for the Bible spread by freethinker Robert G. Ingersoll and the embarrassing dilemmas raised by men such as Dwight L. Moody, who replied by insisting on its literal accuracy in all fields of knowledge. In a popular series of Sunday evening lectures, later collected into *Who Wrote the Bible?* (1891), Gladden tried to steer a middle course between the two.[50]

Subtitled *A Book for the People*, *Who Wrote the Bible?* was not the only manual available, but it soon became the most popular.[51] It received wide circulation, and the collection of newspaper reviews in the Gladden papers shows that it was universally welcomed. The *Congregationalist* praised it for making higher criticism understandable by the common people. The *Chicago Standard* claimed that because the question of the authorship of the Bible was much in public discussion, Gladden's moderate views would be very beneficial. Only a few papers, such as the *New York Examiner* and the *Portland* (Maine) *Christian Mirror*, felt the book would do more harm than good.[52]

Actually, *Who Wrote the Bible?* was very moderate. Accepting the multiauthor version of the Pentateuch, Gladden confessed that there probably would never be exact agreement as to the extent of the compilations. And he felt that much had been written in the time of Moses, if not actually by him.[53] He felt that Daniel had been written after the close of the Babylonian Empire, and he doubted if David wrote many of the Psalms. Regarding the New Testament, however, he was much more cautious. Conservative newspaper reviews praised this part of his book because Gladden accepted most of the New Testament as authentic.[54]

As to theories of inspiration, Gladden hedged. He argued that the Bible was partly divine but also partly human and historical. Revelation was "not the dictation by God of words to men that they may be written down in books; it is rather the disclosure of the truth and love by God to men in the process of history, in the development of the moral order of the world."[55]

In over 114 articles and 38 books, Gladden continued to spread his message of liberal Christianity. His chief enemies always remained the rationalists on one hand and the literalists on the other. Although he was never a profound or original thinker, few others could match Gladden's impact. He was one of the most effective popularizers of his era.

A recent biographer of Lyman Abbott has called him the outstanding figure in the liberalizing of American theological thought. Others were perhaps more scholarly, or wrote better books, but Abbott always had at his disposal a vital organ for expressing his views in the magazine *Outlook*, which he edited from 1876 to 1922.[56] His contemporary, Herbert L. Willett, has credited him with doing more for the interpretation and vindication of the teachings of evolution and higher criticism than any other man in the country. Willett recalled that as *Outlook*'s editor, Abbott "led multitudes of all communions out of the wilderness of confused and obscurantist ideas regarding the Bible and the Christian faith." As a result, they held a "hospitable attitude toward the broader interpretations of theology, the psychology of religion and the social implications of the gospel."[57] Although Abbott wrote no books on higher criticism, as pastor of the popular Plymouth Congregational Church in Brooklyn he gave a series of lectures on the Bible as literature in 1896, and these caused considerable reaction among New York conservatives. The talks were later printed as pamphlets and spread to other denominations.

Willett was less well known than Gladden or Abbott, but perhaps more important in the long run than either. Although he wrote several books, none had the same impact as *Who Wrote the Bible?*; although he wrote numerous articles, he had no steady voice at his command such as the *Outlook*. Nonetheless, he affected thousands of listeners, for he spent many years traversing the nation giving talks on the Lyceum and Chautauqua circuits. In over twenty-five years of such speaking, he traveled to every part of the country. On his death in 1944, the *Christian Century* referred to him as "the most effective and fruitful interpreter of the Scriptures which the American church has produced."[58]

Born near Auburn, New York, to a Disciples family, Willett went to Bethany College in Kentucky and from there to Yale, where he fell under the influence of William Rainey Harper. Willett followed Harper to the University of Chicago, where he finished his graduate work and later became professor of Semitic languages and literature. In his thirty-four years there, he founded the Disciples Divinity House of the University of Chicago and founded and served as pastor of the University Church of the Disciples. He held three successful pastorates, and until 1941 he served as minister of the Union Church of Kenilworth, a Chicago suburb. He was also very active in the Federal Council of Churches and at the time of his death was president of the Disciples Commission on Church Unity. He wrote several works, *The Daily Altar* being the most popular, and had he not been troubled by arthritis in mid-career, he might have accomplished even more.[59]

While involved in all of this activity, Willett also was engaged in an extensive program of giving biblical lectures across the land, which he began in his first years at Chicago under the urging of Harper. Harper believed passionately in university extension courses, and he encouraged members of the Old and New Testament departments to develop religious programs. Thus Willett joined such stalwarts as Edgar Goodspeed, J. H. Breasted, Shailer Mathews, and Richard G. Moulton on the speaking circuit. He soon discovered that the Bible offered a very attractive field for popular presentation and that his speeches aroused the interest of average people. What began as a sideline eventually turned into a crusade. As he said in 1905, "I am only trying to save the Bible for the parents and teachers of this generation."[60]

Shortly thereafter, Willett began speaking on two very controversial areas—miracles and New Testament criticism. Such irresponsible newspaper headlines as "Pastor Hits Miracles—Calls Them Fairy Tales—" and "[Jonah and the Whale] just a Child's Yarn" attracted attention. Reporters loved such stories, and Willett was given much publicity when he discounted the miraculous crossing of the Red Sea as having no basis in fact, the hurling of stones down on the Canaanites as probably a stream of meteors, Joshua's demand that the sun stand still as a figure of speech, and the plagues of Egypt as mere natural disasters. He lectured on Old Testament fiction and was quoted as saying, "No man ever lived who could perform a miracle."[61]

At the same time, he boldly moved into the New Testament. Casting aside his cautious early lectures on the miracles of Jesus, he called the Virgin Birth "non-essential" and "esoteric" in Los Angeles in August of 1908. He then took on all comers in the pages of the *Christian Century*. Playing down the question of the personality and teachings of Jesus, he hedged only on the raising of Lazarus and the Resurrection; he said he hoped that science might in the future be able to explain all miracles. Many years later, he noted to his Kenilworth congregation, "We believe in Jesus today rather in spite of the miracles than because of them." If there were no miracles and predictions in the Bible, he said, many would find it easier to believe in its inspiration and in Jesus' divinity.[62] Willett was one of the major popularizers of these views.

The final way by which the issues of higher criticism reached the American public was through the numerous heresy trials that plagued Protestantism from 1870 to 1908. During this time, most of the denominations experienced problems over the views expressed by their more liberal thinkers. Not all of these, however, reached the trial stage. In 1877, Dr. Augustus Blauvelt was forced out of the Dutch Reformed church for his advanced views. Two years later, Southern Baptist Crawford H. Toy fled his denominational seminary at Louisville for the more amenable theological climate of Harvard. Although the Chicago Presbytery upheld David Swing's liberal theological position in the early 1880s, eventually he was forced to leave the Presbyterian church.[63] Baptist Nathaniel Schmidt was pressured to leave the Hamilton Theological Seminary without any specific charge, but his friends declared that his acceptance of higher criticism was the real cause.[64] Methodist minister H. W. Thomas of Chicago was excluded from his denomination because of his liberal views on the Atonement, and Presbyterian A. C. McGiffert eventually left that church because of conservative reaction to his views on the New Testament. Even the Unitarians had difficulty. In 1880, a Cincinnati minister who had renounced supernaturalism and advocated that all hymnbooks be sold as waste paper was forced to leave the church.[65] Episcopal conservatives were long unhappy over the liberal views of prominent Bostonian Phillips Brooks, but no action was taken against him. In the early years of the century the Northern Methodists brought heresy proceedings against H. G. Mitchell of the Boston University School of Theology and his colleague, Borden P. Bowne, but this, too, came to nothing. "The spread of heresy," remarked the *New York Times* in 1882, "is one of the conspicuous characteristics of the times."[66]

All these controversies disrupted the churches immediately involved, of course, and the more important of them soon spread across denominational lines. Because they made such good copy, the newspapers frequently gave the heretics' views considerable coverage, but heresy trials seemed anachronistic, and sympathy usually went to the accused.

The heresy case that did the most to spread the views of higher criticism to the public and had enormous impact in popularizing critical views was the trial and eventual conviction of Presbyterian Charles A. Briggs. The case kept the Presbyterians in turmoil from 1891 to 1893, and the *New York Times* often gave it front page coverage. Virtually every denomination discussed the Briggs case, and references to it can be found from New York City to the Iowa countryside. The trial caused Union Seminary to split from the Presbyterian church. When Briggs joined the Episcopal church in 1897, the issues flared up again. Finally, on Briggs's death in June of 1913, the obituaries raised the questions one last time.

The furor began when Briggs set forth his critical position in an inaugural address on January 20, 1891, upon assuming the Edward Robinson Chair of Biblical Theology at Union. His enemies were outraged by this talk, and he was quickly charged with heresy. Union Seminary was vulnerable because, under the terms of the Presbyterian reunion of 1870, the General Assembly had the right to rule on the appointment of Union professors. After a long and bitter trial, Briggs was acquitted by the New York Presbytery.[67] The *New York Tribune* of November 6, 1891, claimed Briggs's acquittal as a great victory for higher criticism. Had the Presbytery been a secular tribunal, the affair would have ended there for only the aggrieved party could appeal. Church law, however, worked differently, and the prosecutor continued his appeal up to the General Assembly. This body declared by a vote 383 to 116 against Briggs, and he was suspended from the Presbyterian ministry. Henry P. Smith's strong support of Briggs eventually cost him his position at Lane Seminary.[68]

The charges raised against Briggs were complex. Briefly, he was accused of teaching that Moses was not the author of the Pentateuch and Isaiah not the author of the book that bears his name; that human reason, the church, and the Bible were equal avenues of divine authority; that the original biblical autographs (now lost) may have contained errors; that sanctification was not complete at death; and that many of the Old Testament predictions had been reversed by history.[69]

The uproar raised by the Briggs case almost split the denomination in two. Out of two hundred Presbyteries polled, ninety reacted negatively to his inaugural address. The *New York Times* predicted that prosecution of the case before the New York Presbytery would be "one of the fiercest theological contests that the country has ever witnessed."[70] The *New York Observer* noted that even if his opponents could not read Hebrew or Greek, they knew what was hostile to their faith.[71]

With Presbyterian thoroughness the prosecution spent over six months preparing its case. Once the trial began, the discussion moved from scholarly fencing to outright shouting. On the floor of the General Assembly, where speeches were finally limited to three minutes, one opponent cried out: "Whom will you believe—Christ or Dr. Briggs?"[72] While this august body was meeting, a Reverend Smith of New York preached a guest sermon at the First Presbyterian Church in Washington, where he pleaded for unity in this matter. Afterward, his host, the aged conservative Bryon W. Sunderland, arose and said: "I am sure we have all enjoyed Dr. Smith's sermon this morning. But there is one important omission. He neglected to state the cause of the dissension and distraction in the Presbyterian Church at this time—the reason why the Church has failed to accomplish what it ought to. I want here and now to state the cause. That cause is Dr. Briggs. I would not be in that man's shoes to-day for all the world. Let us sing Hymn No. 533."[73]

The Briggs case quickly moved beyond the Presbyterian realm to affect other main line denominations. The *Times* felt that the issues raised affected all churches that boasted an intelligent, thinking membership.[74] The *Boston Congregationalist* argued that the biblical questions raised by Briggs could never be settled by heresy trials. The *New York Evangelist* noted that the Bible and truth were forever in harmony and that the march of truth could not be stopped. The Presbyterian General Assembly, it said, "had brought Christianity into more disrepute than 100 Ingersolls."[75]

The Savannah, Georgia, *News* named the real issue—the growing gap between scholars and clergy on one hand and the people on the other. "The great majority of Christians regard the Bible as the inspired work of God, and, therefore, cannot contain errors," it said. "An admission that it does contain errors opens the door to doubts, and when doubts are once entertained, it is a difficult matter to place a limit upon them. Professor Briggs's doctrines may be entirely satisfactory to those who clearly understood them, but it is about impossible to make them understood by the masses. To the average mind the whole Bible is true, or it is not the inspired work of God."[76]

Terms such as "Briggism" and "Briggs bacillus" were common in ecclesiastical circles in the early 1890s and were revived in 1899 when Briggs took orders in the Episcopal church. Episcopal conservatives rose in union against his admission. Reverend Benjamin F. DeCosta, long an opponent of liberalism in his church, said that New York's Bishop Henry C. Potter should be impeached if he allowed this to happen without investigation. The New York area divided again into pro- and anti-Briggs factions, and the old issues were rehashed. Briggs was ordained an Episcopal priest on May 10, 1800, and thus became the first non-Presbyterian ever to teach at Union.

A new Episcopal monthly, *Church Defence*, began publication in September, edited by William M. Mills, largely to carry on the fight against Briggs and higher criticism. Briggs's new status brought forth similar comment from other denominations. Reverend Isaac M. Haldeman of New York City's First Baptist Church preached on the subject: "Ought the Church to admit into its ministry a man who does not believe that the Bible is the infallible word of God?" The *Methodist Review* also wrote against him.[77] When Briggs died on June 8, 1913, the same issues were aired one last time in his obituaries. Thus did Charles A. Briggs, through his writings, his stubbornness, his conversion to Episcopalianism, and even his death, bring higher criticism to the public's attention.

Although heresy did not disappear after the Briggs case, spectacular heresy trials did. The various denominations still had their problems, but they handled them more quietly. Heresy trails seemed to be a thing of the past, noted the *New York Times* in 1896; the churches were devoting their attention to philanthropy and slum work instead of creedal distinctions.[78] This proved true for almost fifteen years.

3

The Rise and Spread
of Higher Criticism:
The New Testament and
the Formation of Liberal
and Conservative Arguments

Critical studies of the New Testament paralleled those of the Old, but seem to have had less popular impact during the late nineteenth century. David Strauss penned his radical *Life of Jesus* in 1835 and Ernest Renan his equally radical *Life of Jesus* in 1863, but neither caused much commotion in the United States, the Freethinkers being the only group to take much notice of them. Americans seemed not particularly susceptible to such biographies of Jesus. They wrote only a few themselves, and those that sold well, such as the studies by Lyman Abbott and Henry Ward Beecher, were very conventional.

The New Testament was being subjected to considerable scholarly scrutiny, however, and some of the most important discoveries were made by Ferdinand Baur of Tübingen and the famous Tübingen school of criticism. In 1847, Baur published his work on the origin of the Gospels. Deeply influenced by Hegel, he saw in the apostolic age a fierce fight, lasting well into the second century, between the followers of Peter and those of Paul. He saw the points of view of one or the other of these parties in the New Testament books. According to this so-called tendency theory, New Testament history became not so much historical as dogmatic. The Hegelian scheme of thesis, antithesis, synthesis then became Jewish Christianity, Paulism, and the reconciliation of Catholicism. Moreover, Baur dated all the books late in time: Matthew (Jewish-Christian), A.D. 130; Luke (heathen-Christian), A.D. 150; Mark (neutral), A.D. 160; John (separate category), A.D. 165. This late dating was significant because it meant that several generations had elapsed before any words of Jesus were recorded, thus again bringing into question the literal authority of the Gospels. Baur tended to see the New Testament as chiefly the product of human struggles, and he denied traditional authorship of all the New Testament books except four letters of Paul and Revelation. Bishop Stephen Neill later claimed that Baur's greatest permanent contribution lay in his assertion of the differences between John and the other three Gospels.[1]

Yet this radical theory caused few ripples in America because by the time it arrived, in the early 1890s, the works of Albrecht Ritschl and his followers had overthrown Baur's dating system. They argued that the relative unity of New Testament writings would have been impossible had they not all been written within a relatively short time period. They also established the basic order for the Gospels now generally agreed upon. Mark is placed as the earliest, not one of the latest, and Ritschl suggested that Matthew and Luke drew upon Mark. Adolph Harnack also dated the Gospels much earlier than did Baur. He put the latest almost seventy years before Baur's earliest: Matthew, A.D. 70; Mark, A.D. 65–70; Luke, A.D. 90; John, A.D. 80–100. American conservatives rejoiced at this dating, for it seemed to strengthen the historical accuracy of the Gospel accounts. Many conservatives anticipated a similar overthrow of Old Testament criticism in due time. This, however, was not to be.[2]

Conflict over the Old Testament receded with the coming of the new century, however, and popular concern moved increasingly to the New Testament. On the scholarly level, questions revolved around the "Johannine problem," the multiauthorship of the letters of Paul, and the theories of form criticism (the attempt to recover the oral tradition that was in circulation before the Gospels were written down). On the popular level, however, the key issues centered around the figure of Jesus of Nazareth, especially the miraculous events surrounding His birth, teachings, and resurrection. One could hold different views on the composition of the Pentateuch, Isaiah, or David's authorship of Psalms and still maintain a traditional view of Christianity, but if one changed opinions as to the role of Jesus, could one remain traditional? Here lay the most vital question for American Protestantism, and it came to a head in the 1906 heresy trial of Episcopal priest Algernon Crapsey.[3]

Born in 1847 in Ohio, Algernon Crapsey rose from a childhood of poverty to enter the Episcopal priesthood. In 1880, he moved to Rochester, New York, where he headed St. Andrews Church, a Protestant parish in a fiercely Roman Catholic neighborhood, for twenty-eight years. A small, gentle, but firm man, he gained a local reputation for great generosity. Many years afterward, Crapsey's daughter-in-law recalled him as "the most Christlike man" she had ever known.[4]

Facing declining attendance at evening services in 1903, Crapsey began a series of lectures on the relationship between religion and politics. In one of these he declared that he found Jesus the Man more inspirational than Jesus the God and denied that Jesus ever knew of the Virgin Birth. He also urged the church to become more "scientific" in its approach to the world. The local papers ran numerous columns on his sermons, and eventually a committee of five was appointed by the church hierarchy to investigate his position. Meanwhile, he published his work under the title of *Religion and*

Politics (1904). The committee was satisfied, but several denominational conservatives demanded blood. Shortly afterward, Crapsey was indicted by a standing committee of the diocese on charges of heresy. Eventually, he was brought before the court of the Diocese of Western New York for trial.

Unlike most of the heretics discussed in chapter 2, Crapsey was neither a deep thinker, a theologian, nor an academic. A full-time parish priest, he had arrived at his views through a desultory reading of Darwin, Marx, Spencer, W. Robertson Smith's articles in the *Encyclopedia Britannica*, and the biographies of Jesus by Strauss and Renan. As had Thomas Jefferson, he removed the supernatural element from Jesus' life and argued that the meaning of His message should take precedence over the nature of His person. He denied the Virgin Birth and bodily resurrection. As one critic bluntly put it, "There is no more divinity in Crapsey's Christ than there is in that telephone pole."[5]

The issues of the historicity of the Virgin Birth and of higher criticism in general had often been discussed in the Episcopal church press in the early years of the century. In 1906, a group of prominent lay and clerical figures had published a declaration asking the church to help solve the problems posed by critical studies of the New Testament. The accusations against Crapsey helped bring all this concern to a sharp focus. The trial was long and complicated. The charges were, essentially, that Crapsey's *Religion and Politics* and his other sermons contained statements about Jesus' birth, resurrection, and Incarnation that were contrary to the church creeds. The decision asked that Crapsey be suspended from the priesthood unless he changed his views.

For a man once described as having "a wing on one shoulder and a chip on the other," such a change was impossible. On November 26, 1906, Crapsey resigned from the priesthood in a lengthy letter that received wide publicity. Afterward he took upon himself the role of martyr. Although he had no further connection with any church, he spent much time in his later years lecturing on the Chautauqua circuit, further spreading his ideas. In his somewhat self-serving autobiography, *The Last of the Heretics*, Crapsey claimed to be the first American to publicly apply the principles of higher criticism to the New Testament.

Like the Briggs trial of 1893, the Crapsey case had an impact that extended far beyond his own denomination. Most of the religious press discussed it at some length. The issues raised were crucial, noted the Disciples' *Scroll*, for Crapsey's position went to the heart of theistic belief.[6] The questions Crapsey raised concerning Jesus' birth, miracles, and resurrection were not limited to the Episcopalians.

Thus, by 1906, the activities of Gladden, Abbott, Briggs, Willett, Harper, Crapsey, and others had moved the issue of higher criticism of the Old and New Testaments from the cloistered halls of the university to the public at large. A confirmation of this popularization came in 1909 in a series of articles by Harold Bolce in *Cosmopolitan*. Bolce quoted the president of Cornell University, Jacob Gould Schurman: "History and criticism have made the Bible a new book, or rather a new collection of books, written, for the most part, we know not by what authors or at what dates, and put together as a Bible we know not on what principle. All the landmarks, Moses, Solomon, Job, are gone, and a restless sea of criticism threatens to engulf religion with the records it adored." As long as higher criticism remained in the Old Testament, the public was not much affected, but when it moved into the New and concerned itself with the life of Jesus, this was something else. Bolce noted that the crucial issues of the time rested not on the conflict between science and religion but on vital faith versus antiquated creeds.[7]

With the issue of higher criticism now in the public realm, both liberals and conservatives began to develop their arguments. The liberals, however, had the upper hand. Regardless of their original denominations, the burden of their argument remained much the same. They felt assured that with the tools of higher criticism they had discovered the key to biblical truth. They awaited the next discoveries with anticipation. They used the phrase "the assured results of scholarship" or its equivalent so frequently that conservatives hurled it back at them with derision. The liberals clearly envisioned scholars as "problem settlers" and not, as Ved Mehta would argue later, as engaged in an "argument without end." Such disagreements as did exist were so temporary, they felt, that they would all be settled in the future.

Except for those books and articles that deliberately set out to shock, most liberals took the older view into consideration and tried their best to assuage the conservatives. The critical method was leading to a deeper appreciation of the Bible, they insisted, and it held no dangers for those who used it.[8] Nevertheless, most also admitted that the critical method would eventually destroy the traditional view of biblical interpretation because with higher criticism, the older method of Bible reading could not long stand. Although the devotional power of the Bible might be weakened temporarily, most liberals were optimistic for future generations. Surprisingly, no one forecast conflict "even though many of the old notions once held essential to Christianity seem to be crumbling away."[9] Liberals held out little hope for the literalists and accused them of being the "real assassins" of the Bible.[10] Advocating "the verbal theory of inspiration," said Washington Gladden, "comes perilously near to the sin against the Holy Ghost."[11]

The burden of their message was twofold: that the Bible should be studied just like any other piece of literature, using the methods of literary criticism, and that it should be studied and understood within its historic context. Abbott's lectures and pamphlets on the Bible as literature offer a good example of this method. Arguing that the traditional view began with the assumption that the Bible was the Word of God, he suggested that a new day was at hand: "The literary method takes up the Bible without any preconceptions whatever. It takes it up exactly as it would take up any other collection of literature, to see what kind of a book, or what kind of a collection it is. . . . It assumes nothing. It leaves the conclusion of the questions, whether the Bible came from God, how far and to what extent it came from God, all to be determined by examination of the book itself."[12]

Disregarding a priori assumptions, liberals felt they were using the objective methods of science to uncover biblical truths.[13] Theology, they proudly acclaimed, had become science. Oberlin president Henry C. King noted that higher criticism "stands squarely opposed to the *a priori* attitude on either side—both to the *a priori* abstract supernaturalism which assumes that a record of the divine revelation must be without touch of human error, and to the *a priori* abstract antisupernaturalism which assumes that the supernatural is impossible."[14] To unravel a difficult biblical passage, Harvard professor Joseph Henry Thayer had one simple formula: "Interpret *historically*. Remember that Palestine in the first century is not America in the nineteenth."[15]

Thus were Americans introduced to historicism, the idea that events can be fully understood by knowing the historical circumstances that surrounded their origin. Gone were the idle fights of the Ingersolls versus the Moodys, the skeptics versus the literalists. A real historical interpretation of the Bible, which they considered the only true interpretation, was now possible. Because the Bible was written by men, they must have shared the outlook of their historic times. The flood appeared universal, but it was only local; Ecclesiastes merely offered a cynic's view of life; Jonah, read afresh, should be seen as a parable and not as history or magic; and Job was a great narrative poem. They also stressed the composite character of the Pentateuch, the double authorship of Isaiah, and the postexilic date of Psalms. Some of the more radical American interpreters, such as Crawford H. Toy, professor at the Harvard Divinity School, stressed the prevalence of myth in the Bible. "[T]he march from Egypt through the wilderness, and the exploits of Moses and Joshua must be regarded as a mass of legend," he said, "whose kernel of history, if there be any, we are not able to extract."[16]

Although the liberal popularizers were convinced that they now had a new Bible, they were also certain that nothing spiritual had been lost. Although they downplayed supernaturalism (simultaneously denying any rationalist approach), they insisted that their views led to a more enlightened view of Scripture, whose claim to Divine authorship was not diminished.[17] "A man does not usually spend the best years of his life in propagating the teachings of a book in which he does not believe," noted Herbert L. Willett sarcastically.[18]

Americans might be reading their Bibles less than they had before, but the spread of the historical-critical method of understanding convinced most critics that people were reading them more accurately and with more understanding. For every person whose faith was lost because of higher criticism, noted one critic, ten would have been lost for lack of it. Only a few liberals, such as William Rainsford, suggested that perhaps too much was lost in the change. Rainsford agreed that practice of religion was more sincere now than when he was younger, but in his youth religion had been so clarified and popularized that ordinary people could understand it. Now it had become the prerogative of experts.[19]

In 1902, Professor George Adam Smith declared in his Yale lectures that the war between criticism and the traditional views of Scripture was over.[20] Six years earlier, Professor Angus Crawford of the Theological Seminary of Virginia had concluded, in an Episcopal Church Congress debate, that "we are all critics, I trust, and higher critics too."[21] As the new century dawned, liberals were convinced that the time of disagreements had passed. Everywhere they looked their views were gaining ground. Most of the major denominations had strong liberal voices within their ranks. Baptist, Episcopal, Presbyterian, Methodist, Congregationalist, and Disciples scholars all contributed to the chorus in approximately equal numbers. Through magazines, books, speeches, and lectures, these men spread their version of the Gospel and called it "traditional Christianity," always assuring the public that there was nothing to fear.[22]

Response from conservatives to this spread of theological liberalism was not long in coming. Bewildered at first, they soon began marshaling their reactions to the new views. Many of the scholarly conservative voices rose from within the Presbyterian fold, both in the United States and in the British Isles. With a strong tradition of scholarship and a zest for cantankerous argument, Princeton long remained the bastion of the conservative position. In his monumental *Systematic Theology* (1873), Presbyterian Charles Hodge defined orthodoxy: "That the Scriptures of the Old and New Testaments are the Word of God, written under the inspiration of the Holy Spirit, and therefore infallible, and of divine authority in all things pertaining to faith and practice, and consequently free from all error, whether of doctrines, fact, or precept."[23]

With the death of James McCosh, William Henry Green became the most notable scholarly spokesman for American conservatives. Professor of Oriental and Old Testament literature at Princeton, he headed the Old Testament Committee that brought about the Revised Version and served as moderator of the Presbyterian General Assembly in 1891. Incensed by W. Robertson Smith's *Old Testament in the Jewish Church* and Abraham Keunen's *Prophets and Prophecy in Israel*, he wrote *Moses and the Prophets*, *The Unity of the Book of Genesis*, and *The Higher Criticism of the Pentateuch*, as well as several other works, to counter what he felt were pernicious influences. He took on William Rainey Harper in debate in the pages of the *Princeton Review*. "With his death [in 1902]," noted Herbert Willett, "it may be said that almost the last of his type of conservative scholar has disappeared."[24] This was not quite true. In 1906, Robert Dick Wilson became professor of Semitic philology and Old Testament criticism at Princeton, and he continued the attack along similar lines for many years. His *Is the Higher Criticism Scholarly?* (1922) used linguistic evidence to support the negative position, and his views saw wide distribution through numerous publications by the *Sunday School Times* of Philadelphia. At Princeton he joined the eminent conservatives Benjamin B. Warfield and later J. Gresham Machen; the result was to make the school a bastion of the older position.

Conservative views from abroad bolstered their position. William Binnie of Free Church College, Aberdeen, wrote *The Proposed Reconstruction of the Old Testament History* (2d ed., 1880), which saw wide circulation here as did James Orr's *The Problem of the Old Testament* (1906). Both were balanced attacks on the Graf-Wellhausen thesis. Said Orr, "Is [the Old Testament] a natural product of the development of the human spirit, as scholars of the distinctly 'modern' way of thinking allege; or is it something more—a result of special supernatural revelation to Israel such as other nations did not possess?"[25] Orr's passing was greatly mourned by American conservatives, but Baptist minister W. H. Griffith-Thomas of Toronto attempted to pick up his mantle.

Conservatives drew on sources wherever they could find them, but many were unable to meet the liberal scholars on academic grounds and turned to other types of evidence. First came the argument that higher criticism was not really new, but was simply revived rationalism. Conservatives argued that higher critics began with an a priori assumption against miracles and against inspiration; consequently, they found what they were searching for. Voltaire, Thomas Paine, and Robert Ingersoll had often criticized the Bible from such a rationalistic basis—the alleged discrepancies, Moses' account of his death, and scientific misstatements—and the critics were accused of simply reviving the rationalists' arguments. Higher critics, said one opponent, "are engaged in the business of threshing old straw, straw that has been threshed a thousand times and that yielded only chaff at the first threshing."[26] The argument that higher critics were simply deists in modern garb became standard.

This view was dramatized by an incident that occurred in 1895 at a Baptist congress in Detroit. Two liberal professors from Brown University were arguing that the last twenty-one chapters of Isaiah were written by a different man. After the talk, Howard Osgood of Rochester Theological Seminary rose and read a lengthy statement, by another "higher critic," that gave a similar view of Isaiah. He then asked the audience to name the author.

When they could not, he triumphantly announced him as Thomas Paine.[27] "Infidelity has frequently denied the Mosaic authorship of the Pentateuch," said the *Methodist Review*, "the infallibility of the Scriptures, the predictive element in prophecy, the Christian conception of Messiahship as founded on the Old Testament, the authorship of Peter's epistles and of several of Paul's epistles, the Johannine structure of the fourth gospel and the general importance and value of Christianity as taught by its founder."[28] The only difference, conservatives argued, was that now the rationalists were appearing within the various Christian denominations.

After painting the critics with the rationalists' brush, conservatives went for support to the Bible itself. They argued that the Bible testified to its own infallibility (a charge hotly denied) when the prophets said, "Thus saith the Lord." If the books did not bear the names assigned to them, argued conservatives, the authors were forgers.[29] If they did the writing after the times they were supposed to be talking about, they were liars, not prophets. God would surely write history as accurately as any other historian, conservatives said, and if errors appeared in His historical work, then why not in the plan of salvation or in the doctrine of atonement?[30] The Presbyterian *New York Observer* noted that the writing of passages supposed to be predictive after the events they described was pure and simple fraud: "Now we distinctly and emphatically object to any view of Christ which makes him the culmination of men who did their predicting after events had occurred and endeavored to gain credit as prophets."[31] If Daniel did not write his formal book, noted a Disciples editor, then he was not a prophet, but a deceiver. Everything rested on the historicity of the events described. If the dates of events and the statements regarding science were wrong and the historical section misleading, said Baptist George C. Lorimer, is it possible that God had much to do with it? A corollary to this argument concerned the fact that Jesus had borne witness to the Pentateuch. Surely He would not have been mistaken as to its authorship. If Moses had not written the books, why did Jesus assume that he had?[32]

Conservatives often criticized the contradictory conclusions of the liberal scholars. Bishop Doane found thirty different theories as to the authorship of the first five books of the Old Testament.[33] During the Briggs trial, someone claimed to have found eight hundred. The multiplication of sources that occurred from 1890 to 1910, when every book in the Bible became more and more subdivided, gave weight to their argument. From two Isaiahs, a host more appeared, placed all the way from 640 B.C. to 160 B.C. One author found the following components in the Hexateuch: J1, J2, J3, E1, E2, D, Dh, Dp, P1, P2, Px (indefinite number of writers of the P School).[34] Many liberal critics also disliked these radical "hypotheses of embarrassment," but conservatives felt they clearly illustrated the inadequacy of the critical method. New discoveries about the Bible were being made almost daily, announced one author in 1897. How could they all be true? At the Chicago World's Fair of 1893, a group of Lutherans said they would refuse to accept higher criticism until all of the critics came to the same conclusion.[35]

One study of Romans, which argued on the basis of doctrinal and linguistic considerations, noted the different references to "Jesus Christ" and "Christ Jesus" and concluded that Romans was the work of a compiler who used at least four original sources: G1, G2, JC, and CJ.[36] This wild multiplication of sources did not inspire confidence in the so-called "assured results of scholarship." Several parodies emerged. Bishop Doane urged ordinary people to stand aside and let the combatants, after the manner of the frogs and mice, dispose of each other. Such confusion among liberals gave conservatives hope. Many felt that the Pentateuch stood unscathed as the inspired Word of God.

The only important turn-of-the-century conservative to denounce higher criticism on a popular level was T. DeWitt Talmage.[37] He, too, blamed Ingersoll—"the champion blasphemer of America"—as the chief source of these ideas. In "The Splendors of Orthodoxy," one of his most popular sermons, he warned "advanced thinkers" of the dangers inherent in their path. Before the Washington City Bible Society in 1896, he bemoaned the spread of the theories that the Creation story, Adam and Eve, the flood, and the miracles were not true.[38] "My idea is that Higher Criticism is lower religion," he said. "The Bible is good enough for me, and it seems to be a satisfactory book for most people. After all the higher critics have got through with their criticism the old Book will stay just as it is—doing the great work for the world's evangelization."[39]

Although most historians of this period have ignored the gradual spread of higher criticism, its importance was clear to contemporaries. One Scottish opponent of W. Robertson Smith said he felt the church was entering its most significant battle since the Reformation. Many others agreed. Alfred Benn compared the arrival of higher criticism and the attack on it to the previous generation's denunciation of Darwinism.[40] Others equated the new discoveries with those of Copernicus. One minister confessed in 1900 that his parish duties forbade much original study, but that he believed the higher criticism issue to be the greatest question currently facing his church.

In 1899, the *New York Times* said that two topics of widespread interest among clergymen and church people involved the resurrection of the physical body and verbal inspiration of the Bible. The greatest problems of the day, according to a 1900 Baptist sermon, were the critical forces at work denying the inspiration of the Bible and weakening and destroying the power of the church.[41]

Conservatives feared that if one part of Scripture were found to be in error, the rest would also be endangered. "If the Bible is not all inerrant," Methodist clergyman Alexander McAllister asked liberal professor Hinckley

G. Mitchell, "what parts are inerrant?" Mitchell said that was yet to be determined. "How am I to be assured that I have the truth?" McAllister asked. "If we have no infallible standard, we may as well have no standard at all."[42] Three years later, Reverend Junius B. Remensnyder, pastor of Saint James Lutheran Church on Madison Avenue in New York City, responded to a series of sermons by Lyman Abbott with one on Jonah and the whale. He insisted:

> This story of Jonah and the Whale stands in just the same category as all the miracles narrated in the Holy Book. They belong in the domain of the supernatural, and will be accepted or rejected according to our faith in the inspired Word of God. If we reject Jonah, what about the parting of the Red Sea, the fall of Manna in the wilderness, the fall of Jericho when Joshua blew his horn? Not only this, but what shall we do with the miracles recorded of our Lord, and indeed, what becomes of that crowning miracle of miracles, most momentous and incredible of them all—the death and glorious resurrection of Christ? How is the story of Jonah more difficult to believe than any or all of the others? We must accept or reject them as a whole.[43]

George Adam Smith told the following story of his discussion with Dwight L. Moody: After an evening meeting at Northfield, Moody, at whose house Smith was staying, said to him, "Now, Mr. Smith, I wish you would tell me just what it is about this higher criticism." "This was my opportunity," Smith noted. "For an hour or so I did my best to put into a form that would appeal to a man of Mr. Moody's antecedents a plain statement of the assumptions and methods of historical treatment of the Bible. He listened attentively, asking here and there a question which gave me pointers about what to say further, and he seemed to receive what I said in a thoroughly kindly spirit. After we had talked ourselves out, there was a pause, during which I had time to wonder what impression I had made. Presently Mr. Moody said, with the air of having satisfied himself, and of giving me the upshot of his reflections: 'I think I see your point, Mr. Smith—but after all, what's the use of telling people there were two Isaiahs, so long as most of them don't even know there was one?' "[44]

No denomination completely escaped the controversy. With Herbert L. Willett serving as a focus, the Disciples' *Christian Standard* subjected all liberal doctrines to the most vicious attacks.[45] The Episcopal bishop's pastoral letter of 1901 warned the faithful not to be afraid of any criticism of God's Word and urged that all scholarly discoveries make more manifest the indwelling truth.[46] The *Methodist Review* under James W. Mendenhall's editorship (1888–1902) maintained a steady crusade against Old Testament criticism that slackened only slightly under his successors.[47] The *Methodist Quarterly Review* was criticized severely by Reverend A. T. Watkins of the Mississippi Conference for printing a large number of articles on higher criticism. The editor, Dr. Gross Alexander, was urged to be more careful in the future, and he promised to do so.[48] Methodist Charles Cardwell McCabe, who died in 1906 after thirty-eight years of service as an apostle at large for religion and patriotism, regarded all critics as "the common enemy" and waged unceasing warfare against them whenever he could. He equated a critical examination of the Bible with the testing of a mother's love by acid or blowpipe.[49] In responding to the fight in his own Episcopal church, Benjamin F. De Costa remarked that to say Noah and the flood were fictitious would cast doubt on Jesus' promises about being the Resurrection and the Life.[50] By destroying what had been traditional authority for most of the Protestant denominations, higher criticism opened a genuine Pandora's box.

Many people were honestly perplexed by the ramifications of the controversy. The result of higher criticism, complained English scholar Robert F. Horton, was "Plymouth Brethrenism [literalism] on one hand, and infidelity on the other."[51] Some felt that the spread of the critics' views had led to a reaction in favor of revived bibliolatry.[52] Charles A. Briggs felt the two great religious movements of the age were higher criticism on one hand and the growth of Sunday schools on the other, but these two were on vastly different, even opposing, courses.[53]

On a popular level, the term "higher criticism" quickly became a scare word, often equated with "German rationalism" or free thought. Seminary students therefore found it an ordeal to pass through and still keep their faith. At Princeton Theological Seminary in the late 1880s, the "higher critic" was depicted as an enemy lurking in ambush. In fact, within a few years, higher criticism became a symbol for many for what was wrong with the nation. In 1899, Methodist evangelist Leander W. Munhall shocked a Methodist ministers' meeting by blaming higher criticism for intemperance, licentiousness, infidelity, agnosticism, theosophy, Christian Science, and spiritualism.[54] In 1908, Southern Presbyterian M. B. Lambdin credited it for the breakdown of the Sabbath, the rise in divorce, the declining tone of the nation, and widespread graft, crime, and murder.[55]

For many Protestants, higher criticism brought up the question of the role of experts and their expertise in a democracy. It seemed to imply that the average person was no longer competent to read the Bible. Some subjects, such as science and technology, might be given over to experts, but religion and ethics had ever belonged to the common realm. Authors worried about the tendency of biblical scholars to assume the exclusive right to dictate to the people what they should believe and disbelieve about the Scriptures.[56] One theologian confidently told his readers that all they had to do was leave everything to the experts.[57] Conservatives rebelled at this directive. Ordinary Christians might depend upon scholars for a true text and a true translation. "[B]ut once these are obtained," said W. H. Griffith-Thomas, "every Christian, according to his own equipment or knowledge and mental power, has a responsibility which he cannot escape."[58] Only the South seemed safe. No church had less to fear from the Old Testament critics than the Southern Methodists, said one observer proudly in 1899. Shortly thereafter, the Southern Presbyterians declared that the destructive higher criticism was itself coming to destruction.[59]

By the end of the first decade in the new century, however, the lines had been firmly drawn. Little new would be added in the ensuing years, but the bitterness, intensity, and distortion of the arguments would increase markedly. The surface was calm, but it was the calm that precedes the storm. Critical observers were well aware that two distinct bodies existed within most of the main line Protestant denominations.

William Hyde, writing in the *Atlantic Monthly* in 1900, found two theologies, two types of ministers, and two policies of theological education struggling for supremacy within the Protestant churches.[60] Arthur T. Pierson wrote in 1900 that many people were afraid of another "irrepressible conflict" in a few years.[61] Henry C. Vedder, in his *A Short History of Baptists* (1907), noted that two parties—progressive and conservative—existed within his denomination.[62] This was also true for the Episcopalians, Disciples, Presbyterians, and Methodists. "In every evangelical church," noted Albert C. Knudson in 1911, "we have representatives of both the old and the new view."[63] From 1900 onward, however, concern over such distinctions seemed to go underground, where it remained for two decades during the interlude known as Progressivism.

4
The Triumph of Evangelical America, 1901–1917: The Liberals

The American generation that has come to maturity since 1960 has the distinction of being the first not to have a blind faith in progress. In the late nineteenth century, however, evidence of progress was apparent wherever one looked. From as early as 1881 to as late as 1914, observers joined in a loud chorus of praise for the century's accomplishments. With the start of the new century, this chorus reached a crescendo. More good had come to humanity in the nineteenth century, everyone agreed, than in any other period in the history of the world.

An excellent example of this attitude is Lyman Abbott's address to the Clark College graduating class of 1912. He described the four great burdens of human society, noting that his generation had abolished famine and gone a long way toward abolishing pestilence. He called upon the graduating seniors to abolish poverty and war.[1] Credit for this moral advance was most frequently given to the churches, and few entertained doubts that it would continue. This optimistic spirit gave its name to an era in American life from 1901 to 1917: Progressivism.

The origins of Progressivism have long perplexed historians. Scholars such as George E. Mowry and Samuel P. Hays, have seen it as largely directed from above, imposed on the nation by the middle-class, "better" elements of society. The newer interpretations of J. Joseph Huthmacher and John D. Buenker, however, have stressed the working-class, ethnic contributions to the reform tradition.[2] Still others have seen it as an attempt by big business to rationalize and control the emerging economy.[3]

Obviously the Progressive mind was not all of one piece. Reform had different meanings to different people. Some reformers, for example, crusaded for women's rights, public health, protection of immigrants, more democratic politics, workmen's compensation, housing regulations, and child labor laws, while their comrades worked equally hard for immigration restrictions, stronger divorce measures, and stiffer blue laws. Although the National Association for the Advancement of Colored People (NAACP) was founded in 1909, Progressive reformers generally ignored the issue of race, and Woodrow Wilson resegregated the federal bureaucracy.[4] Progressivism contained a diversity that has only recently been recognized.

But Progressivism meant more than those specific, even contradictory, reform measures. Behind all of them, and the cement that held the numerous programs together, was the Progressive mood—one might almost say theology—of moral commitment to social causes. Although this moral-evangelical approach to society has often been criticized, it could just as well be praised, for often it provided the major impetus for reform activities. From 1901 to 1917, the evangelical ethos emerged triumphant in American life. Religious metaphors provided the essential framework for Progressive thought.

A direct connection existed between American Protestantism and the rise of American Progressivism. The vitality of the churches from 1901 to 1917 was integral to the reform movement. Without the former, the latter would have been much less effective. Working with people from all areas of life, the clergy helped to create an atmosphere that encouraged social reform.

Studies by Samuel P. Hays, Roy Lubove, and Samuel Haber have shown that one critical component of this mood of reform came from professional expertise.[5] For the first time, people possessed the social skills to make their dreams at least partially come true. Not only was there a desire to alleviate misery in the urban slums, there was also a growing group of professional social workers, such as Jane Addams, Lillian Wald, Julia Lathrop, and Florence Kelley to see that it was done efficiently. Likewise, when a mandate arose for better city government, a corps of city managers existed to carry it out. When Theodore Roosevelt popularized the need for conserving America's natural resources, there existed a body of scientific conservationists, such as Gifford Pinchot, who knew where to begin. Much of the strength of the Progressive movement came from these scientific professionals, who might well be termed the "head" of the movement.

Yet it was the "heart" of the movement that provided the impetus, for in large measure Progressivism was a genuine crusade. Like their abolitionist ancestors, Progressive reformers tended to view the world as a kind of moral drama.[6] When historian George E. Mowry studied the numerous reformers in California, he found that the "long religious hand of New England" rested heavily upon them. A 1906 American Institute of Social Service survey, which sought to determine the church preference of a large number of social crusaders, discovered that only 15 percent were not somehow connected with evangelical Protestantism. Alexander J. McKelway, who was both a social worker and a Southern Presbyterian minister, felt that most people who engaged in social work did so because of their religious background. When the moral powers of churches and synagogues were united, he said, there could be no stopping them. He urged that the pulpit make the "anti-social-concern man" as uncomfortable as it had once made the atheist or libertine.[7]

Even those who had left their religious heritage behind with their youth discovered that they were not immune. Colorado lawyer Robert Kerr belonged to no church, yet he argued that unless the Golden Rule and the ethics of Jesus could be put into business and public life, society was in real danger.[8] "Physical escape from the embraces of evangelical religion did not mean moral escape," Frederick Howe noted in his *Confessions of a Reformer*. "From that religion my reason was never emancipated."[9]

This crusading approach to social ills proved short-lived. The rise of scientific expertise (the "head") has continued until our own day, but the moral-evangelical approach (the "heart") went out of favor with World War I. The evangelical appeals of Robert LaFollette in 1924 seemed strangely dated, and those of William Jennings Bryan were comic when they were not tragic. To chart the fortunes of this attitude of mind, then, is to chart the fortunes of Progressivism.

If one were seeking a metaphor to describe the aim of the Progressives, it would have to be creation of the Kingdom of God. The exact nature of the Kingdom was never defined for its meaning seemed obvious to everyone. The vagueness of the Kingdom ideal proved healthy because it allowed for varying interpretations. Some, such as Southern Presbyterian Walter Lingle, could discuss it theologically. Others could interpret it as Christian socialism; still others, as a purified democracy.[10] Its basis, however, lay in the improvement of social conditions. Said Lyman Abbott, "My Roman Catholic brother, and my Jewish brother, and my agnostic brother, and I, an evangelical minister, have started in various quarters, and are going in different directions, but we are all aiming for the same place."[11] That place was the Kingdom of God.[12]

It is clear in retrospect that there were several versions of the Kingdom masquerading as one. Liberal Christians envisioned a merging of Christianity with the world and hoped that the spirit of Christ would permeate all aspects of the secular order. Conservatives, on the other hand, envisioned a Kingdom of converted Christians who would serve as a leaven for the rest of society. The return of Christ alone, they felt, would usher in the true millennium. The merging of these two versions of the Kingdom gave Progressivism its moral, evangelical tone.[13] While they worked together, a moral dimension was added to society, and this proved to be a good atmosphere in which to enact legislation.

Herbert Hoover once recalled that in his youth in West Branch, Iowa, his family had ground their own corn and wheat at the mill, slaughtered their own hogs, woven their own clothing, erected their own buildings, and made their own soap. But this was in the late 1870s and early 1880s, and such independence largely ended with the century. The Progressives were the

first generation of Americans to realize one of the major themes of fin de
siècle society: that all aspects of American life had become interrelated. The
rapid changes in thought and technology had developed a unity never before
realized. The popularity of biology provided a new metaphor: society was an
organism. Everything was related to everything else. "The day of home-
brewed ale, of home-made bread, and home-spun clothing is already past
with us," said David Starr Jordan, president of Stanford, in 1903.[14] Pioneer
sociologist Edward Alsworth Ross in his classic *Sin and Society* (1907)
agreed: "Nowadays the water main is my well, the trolley car my carriage,
the banker's safe my old stocking, the policeman's billy my fist. My own eyes
and nose and judgment defer to the inspector of food, or drugs, or gas, or
factories, or tenements, or insurance companies. I rely upon others to look
after my drains, invest my savings, nurse my sick, and teach my children. I
let the meat trust butcher my pig, the oil trust boil my sorghum, the coal
trust chop my wood, the barb wire company split my rails."[15] This interdependence also extended to the area of social problems. "There is no finest
residential street of the proudest city," said Alexander J. McKelway, "that is
wholly detached from the vice and the disease and misery of the slum."[16]

This new awareness of human interdependence coincided with the liberal
Protestant relaxation of creedal, denominational, and theological distinctions. The result was to downplay man's intimate relationship to God in favor
of "social service." Christianity now began to stress "the deliverance of
human society from disease, poverty, crime, and misery; the development
and perfection of the institutions of men's associated life; and the construction of a social order that is the city of God on earth."[17]

There had been aggressive social action on the part of the churches before
the first decade of the new century, but except for the Episcopalians and (to
a lesser extent) the Congregationalists, it had been sporadic. As historians
Henry F. May and Charles H. Hopkins have shown, winning the Protestant
clergy to causes of social concern was not an easy task.[18] The traditional
teaching of individualism made it difficult to think in social terms.

The realization that the Old Testament prophets and Jesus of Nazareth
had been speaking about society as well as individuals was slow in dawning.
But when it did arrive, it evoked a revolution in the study of Scripture that
was almost as significant as the arrival of the higher criticism. Some Social
Gospel proponents felt that much of Jesus' social message was indirect and
had to be "inferred." Others suggested that His teachings offered a transcendent goal against which the ugly realities of society could always be mea-
sured and found wanting. In this sense, the Social Gospel provided a
legitimate inference from the Gospel writings. Henceforth the Bible became
a whole new book with a very vital, and current, message.[19]

Gradually, the clergy began to awaken to this new emphasis. From about
1890 on, the theological seminaries expressed more interest in social prob-

lems. By 1892, several seminaries had inaugurated professorships in social ethics. The Episcopal Church Association for Advancement of the Interests of Labor was founded in New York in 1887; the first meeting of the Society of American Christian Socialists was held in Boston's Baptist Tremont Temple on February 18, 1899; the Baptist Brotherhood of the Kingdom was founded in Philadelphia in 1892. Radical journals such as the *Kingdom* and the *Dawn* kept the issue in front of a limited audience.

It was not really until after 1900, however, that this social awareness became widespread. Then, slowly but steadily, denomination after denomination saw the light. In 1904, Dr. Charles R. Brown, popular pastor of the First Congregational Church in Oakland, spoke to the National Council of Congregational Churches on "The Supreme Need of the Churches." This need was the application of the social principles of the Gospel to everyday life. Two years later, Brown was asked to deliver the prestigious Lyman Beecher Lectures on Preaching at Yale. Although the lectureship had been established for over thirty years, Brown's message was the first time it was exclusively devoted to setting forth "The Social Message of the Modern Pulpit."[20]

It was generally agreed, however, that the most important popular statements came from Baptist theologian Walter Rauschenbusch. His *Christianity and the Social Crisis* (1907) was often mentioned by both lay and clerical contemporaries as the most significant religious book of the times.[21] Published when Rauschenbusch was forty-six years old and little known outside the academic world, this volume pushed him into the limelight as one of the new century's most creative religious thinkers, a position he retained until his death in 1918.

The essence of Rauschenbusch's message was that Jesus came to save both the individual soul and the human race. Rauschenbusch's "new evangelism" did not seek so much to eliminate the concept of sin as it did to broaden its context. As Edward A. Ross had suggested earlier, modern sin had simply expanded to encompass the interconnectedness of the times. Ross felt that the opportunity for chicanery had so increased that America needed annual supplements to the Ten Commandments.[22] Rauschenbusch felt that a proper reading of Scripture could accomplish the same purpose.

In a series of short popular prayers, *For God and the People* (1910), many of which originally appeared in the *American Magazine*, Rauschenbusch showed how this goal should be achieved. The Lord's Prayer, for example, which he saw as the purest expression of the mind of Jesus, had become so familiar through centuries of repetition and ritual that few had paused to understand it. "But its deepest significance, for the individual," Rauschenbusch insisted, "is revealed only when he dedicates his personality to the vaster purposes of the Kingdom of God, and approaches all his personal problems from that point of view."[23] It was, he insisted, the great charter of all social prayers.

When Jesus bade people to say, "Our Father," Rauschenbusch argued, he did so from the conception of human solidarity that ruled out the possibility of any isolation. All were one in both sin and salvation, and recognition of this oneness is the first step toward praying the Lord's Prayer in the right spirit. The three petitions with which it begins express Jesus' yearning faith in the possibility of a reign of God on earth. One finds here, not an "escape from earth to heaven, but that heaven be duplicated on earth through the moral and spiritual transformation of humanity, both in personal units and corporate life." Thus, Jesus' hope for social salvation was vital. "The desire for the Kingdom of God precedes and outranks everything else in religion," said Rauschenbusch, "and forms the tacit presupposition of all our wishes for ourselves."[24] The remaining petitions deal with personal needs. We stand together when we ask for our daily bread, and this shows, he argued, that Jesus never belittled the elemental need for bread. The place he accords this petition shows a recognition of the economic basis of life. Moreover, Rauschenbusch pointed out, the commonality of the petition should make us shameful if we take more than our fair share and leave others hungry. Spiritual needs were considered, but those, too, make us affirm our common humanity. "Forgive us our debts as we forgive our debtors": we have to be socially right if we want to be religiously right. "Lead us not into temptation" means avoidance of certain situations, but it also means that such situations are often created largely by the social life around us. If society is characterized by sexual dalliance and alcoholism, if business life is such that we have to be cruel and cheat to survive, if our political life demands graft, then society itself frustrates the prayers we offer to God. Although "Deliver us from evil" probably meant "evil spirits" in the first century, in modern times it means the power of organized covetousness and institutionalized oppression. "Thus," concluded Rauschenbusch, "the Lord's Prayer is the great prayer of social Christianity."[25] Here, indeed, was a new interpretation of an old message. In its own way it provoked a revolution in religious thought which some observers considered as significant as the Reformation.[26]

With this new version of Scripture as their guide, most of the main line churches suddenly came to life on social issues. At their December 1908 meeting, the Federal Council of Churches confessed that they had been taken unawares by industrial progress. "Machinery, facilities for transportation, building methods, commercial exchanges, modes of heating and lighting have in a generation created a community life, to which the thought of the Church has not rapidly adapted itself," they noted. This statement, which appeared in a widely distributed pamphlet, also expressed their "profound belief" that the complex problems of modern industry could be interpreted and solved only by the teachings of the New Testament and that Jesus Christ was the final authority for both social and individual life.[27] Here was the churches' official indictment of their own guilt.

More effective than official pronouncements, however, were the activities of the numerous clerical proponents of social action. By 1910, at the latest, few cities and few rural areas were without prominent advocates of the Social Gospel. One of the best examples of the social impact of the clergy during the Progressive era can be seen in the career of Alexander J. McKelway. Raised on a southern farm, McKelway graduated from Hampden-Sydney College and Union Theological Seminary in Richmond, Virginia, where he was ordained by the Albemarle Presbytery in 1891. Although he composed good sermons, he soon discovered he was no orator. In 1897, he moved to full-time religious journalism when he took over the editorship of the North Carolina *Presbyterian,* whose name he changed to the *Standard.* Shortly afterward, he fell under the influence of Edgar G. Murphy, Episcopal rector of Montgomery, Alabama, who had long been an advocate of better working conditions. Murphy arranged for his friend to be considered for the position of secretary of the National Child Labor Committee, which McKelway held until his death at age fifty-two in 1918.

At first, his friends tried to persuade him not to accept this position, but McKelway felt called to champion a social vision in the South that would bind man to God and simultaneously to his fellow men. In McKelway's case, one should probably say "fellow child," for he became the most articulate southern champion for children's welfare. Through his influence with President Woodrow Wilson and Democratic party officials, he was instrumental in bringing this and other social causes to national attention.[28] For example, he virtually wrote the social justice plank of the 1916 Democratic platform. A copy of the official text of the platform, with checks by the statements originally his, is in the McKelway manuscripts at the Library of Congress. McKelway's understanding of Christianity revolved mainly around the theme of social justice. His political connections gave him several opportunities to implement his version of the Kingdom of God.

Perhaps one reason for the urgency of the Social Gospel message as it was expressed during these years was the need to counter the growth of American socialism. The churches viewed the socialists as their chief rival in the heady task of restructuring American life.

The question of whether one could be both a Christian and a socialist was often discussed. In 1908, John T. Stewart and his Epworth League colleagues attended a rally for Socialist presidential candidate Eugene V. Debs. On their way home, they solemnly debated whether their future as social reformers lay within the Socialist party or within the Methodist church. Several churches made it plain that one could not do both, believing the hope of some Episcopal priests and laymen to inspire and Christianize socialism was impossible. In fact, numerous conservative newspapers had religious editors who kept up a steady stream of antisocialist articles in the name of Christian orthodoxy.[29] "Our nation is trembling in the balance, we are not far from some great process of reconstruction," Episcopal Rector Alexander G. Cummins of Poughkeepsie, New York, told the Church Congress audience at Charleston in 1913. "Shall it be Christian reconstruction or godless revolution?"[30]

Many liberal and all conservative Christians stressed that social service, though important, should always be a by-product of the Gospel message. Purely secular agencies were considered both necessary and vital, but it was pointed out that they frequently lacked inspiration that religion alone could provide.[31] Thus did the church hope to inspire and fulfill numerous other functions hitherto seen as chiefly secular. First among these was the expansion of what later came to be known as the "institutional church," a term that reportedly was coined in 1893 by a Boston newspaper reporter, who applied the label to the Berkeley Temple of that city.[32] The institution itself, however, existed long before the name. Born out of the dilemma of how to handle the immigrants in the crowded cities, the institutional church tried to extend its ministry over all seven days of the week and to expand the services offered. The institutional church, said reformer Josiah Strong, tried to undertake certain functions of the home when the home failed to perform them.[33]

The concept of the institutional church stemmed from two main sources. The first was the British example, for as William R. Hutchison has argued, perhaps the Social Gospel was not as exclusively American as has been suspected.[34] Successful institutional church ministers often received their training overseas. The second source, however, was closer to home—the American black churches. The idea of the institutional church was nothing new to the Negro community. From emancipation onward, these churches, especially in urban areas, were simultaneously schools, lecture halls, meeting houses, and centers for entertainment. As the *Atlanta Constitution* noted on June 18, 1882, "the colored man not only takes his spiritual information but also his social information from the pulpit of the church which he attends."[35]

A few post-Civil War black clergymen eschewed politics, but most participated actively. Virtually every urban black minister of any standing took positions on such issues as prohibition, black teachers in public schools, and equal rights. St. John's African Methodist Episcopal church in Nashville sponsored a lecture series on black life in the winter of 1884–85, and the Ebenezer Baptist Church of Richmond heard lectures on African history, art, architecture, and religion. T. W. Walker, pastor of the Shiloh Baptist Church in Birmingham, maintained a strong interest in the lives of his primarily servant-class congregation. He maintained an organization that functioned as a labor union, kept a list of white families who had treated their servants unfairly, held a day school in the basement, founded a sick fund, and stressed the virtues of savings accounts and good appearances.[36] When the white churches began to expand their services in a similar fashion, they had both foreign and domestic examples to draw from.

"The frontiers of modern civilization are in the great cities," the Southern

Methodist bishops reminded their audience in 1906, "and America expects Methodism to man the frontier."[37] This the Methodists and most of the other denominations tried to do with their institutional church experiments. Wesley Chapel in Cincinnati in 1894 had a kindergarten, day nursery, and young ladies' benevolent society. Their bureau of justice called on the services of four lawyers for free legal aid to the poor. They also boasted an association that taught people to save money and a visitation society. Bethany Memorial Chapel of Madison Avenue Church in New York contained reading rooms, assembly halls, club rooms, a good gymnasium with shower facilities, and a large day nursery. In 1893, New York's Grace Episcopal Church constructed a laundry to employ fifty women at higher wages than could be had elsewhere. By 1897, an institutional church quarterly, *Open Church*, under the editorship of Reverend E. B. Sanford, was available to all denominations. Soon thereafter nearly every major institutional church employed a full- or part-time visiting nurse.[38]

Such activity, however, was limited to the larger cities and, because the South had fewer cities, it involved mostly northern denominations. By 1906, New York City was said to have had 112 such institutional churches, Chicago about 25, and every other major city at least one. Although the Episcopalians, Congregationalists, and Presbyterians seemed to be more actively involved than the Baptists or Methodists, the issue was less denominational than personal. The success of a good operation often hinged on the personalities of the people involved.

One successful practitioner of this ideal was Samuel Parks Cadman, an English-born Methodist pastor who came to New York in 1890 and in 1895 took over the Metropolitan Temple (Methodist) on West Fourteenth Street. Like all downtown New York churches, it had been declining for several years, but he revived it so that by 1900 his efforts were receiving nationwide acclaim. In 1900, he went to the Central Congregationalist Church of Brooklyn, where he remained until his death. Cadman had great impact on numerous young seminary students, many of whom served an apprenticeship with him.

Another man whose dynamic personality catapulted a rundown church into a nationally known success was William Rainsford, rector of St. George's Episcopal Church, Stuyvesant Square, New York, from 1883 to 1906. Like Cadman, Rainsford was a native of the British Isles. When he first crossed the Atlantic, he pastored St. James Church in Toronto, remaining until 1883, when he received the call from St. George's. When he moved to St. George's, it was very old-fashioned, and though its membership still included such wealthy parishioners as J. Pierpont Morgan and Seth Low, president of Columbia University, it had begun to decline, as had most churches of the area. When Rainsford arrived, New York below Twentieth Street had seen forty churches move uptown at the same time that 300,800 people had moved into the area. It was estimated that 50 percent of all New York Protestants were without a church.[39]

At first, Rainsford used every technique at his disposal to rebuild the church. He engaged speakers from Jerry McAuley's Waterfront Mission for mission Gospel services. He held extensive meetings and prayer sessions, some of which lasted all night. For six years he stressed the old-fashioned Gospel preaching on Salvation Army lines. The results, however, were disappointing, for despite his work with the "down and outers," he never convinced a single one to join. He did get some response from children, however, and this encouraged him to move into children's work.

Dancing classes, a dramatic society, Sunday youth meetings, places for wholesome recreation, billiard halls, gymnasiums, and clubs suddenly became subjects of concern. "The greatest need in our city today is places of recreation," he said. "They are far more needed than libraries. Good wholesome recreation is first cousin to religion: the rest and refreshment of the body goes a long way towards giving the soul a show [chance]."[40]

By the middle 1890s, St. George's had grown from seventy families to over four thousand. It held daily services, sponsored numerous organizations, and boasted the largest physical plant in the city. Rainsford also had considerable influence on theological students, for many of them served an apprenticeship with him.

Most of the institutional churches were churches first and social settlements second, but some operated in reverse. The New York City People's Institute, begun in 1897 by Columbia Professor Charles S. Smith, was one of these. Smith had decided to use the Cooper Union Hall as a popular forum for discussion of economic, social, and ethical problems. The series was so successful that someone suggested a Sunday evening series, and gradually, as the format changed, it came to be called a church. Addresses, poems, music, and sermons all characterized this gathering. All denominations except Roman Catholics, who refused numerous invitations, shared the Institute's platform. Its congregation included Catholics, Jews, Protestants, agnostics, Democrats, Socialists, and anarchists. All claimed allegiance to the common spirit of brotherhood.[41]

This "Church of the People" maintained that its only article of faith was the brotherhood of man. Its rules were equally simple: no proselytizing by any creed and no attack by one creed on another. Its congregation was heavily non-Protestant, and many entertained revolutionary thoughts. The Institute thus served as a peacekeeping force. "This is our church," a socialist said proudly, "a church wide enough to welcome Catholic, Protestant, and Jew, atheist, agnostic and infidel—and its creed is the Golden Rule." To this statement a 1905 crowd applauded and cried out, "That's right."[42]

Probably the most famous of such organizations was the remarkable Presbyterian Labor Temple, founded on the lower east side of New York by the even more remarkable Charles Stelzle. Eldest son of a family of German immigrants, Charles was forced by his father's death to enter the factories at age eight. He left school at age eleven, and his years at R. Hoe and Company, New York's large manufacturer of printing presses, supplied the bulk of his education. "That big machine shop actually became my training school, my university, my seminary," he noted later.[43] After deciding to enter the ministry, Stelzle applied to Princeton, Union, Drew, and McCormick seminaries, only to be refused by each because of his lack of formal education. Moody Bible Institute in Chicago accepted him, however, and his ten months there provided the extent of his formal religious training.

He began his career as a lay worker in a downtown Minneapolis mission, and from 1892 to 1903 he worked in similar operations in New York City and in St. Louis. Finally ordained a Presbyterian minister in 1900, he received national attention the next year by his widely publicized series of letters written to leaders of the country's unions. While serving at Menard Street Mission in St. Louis, he sent out over two hundred letters to union leaders, asking them four frank questions: (1) What is the chief fault workingmen find with the church? (2) What takes the place of the church in the life of the average workingman? (3) How do you regard Jesus Christ? (4) What should engage the activities of the church? Stelzle regarded his questionnaire as the American public's first major confrontation with a scientifically based survey. The results, published by Lyman Abbott in the July 27, 1901, *Outlook*, were chilling to many church supporters. Workers saw the church as a largely hypocritical institution, existing solely in the interest of the capitalists. They thought it overemphasized pomp and show and that it tried to close public places of recreation, galleries, and concerts on Sunday, begrudging the worker all harmless pleasures. Why pay pew rent to be told that you were going to hell, remarked one respondent. The strife among denominations and the arguments over Scripture seemed meaningless when compared with larger social issues.

By general agreement, the saloon had replaced the church as a gathering spot for rest and relaxation. The more articulate argued that socialism served as the new theology. Although union leaders admitted that over two-thirds of the workers probably did not understand socialism, nevertheless, it was growing rapidly. Jesus was really a socialist, they said, and His mission was largely here and now. Had there been a carpenter's union at the time, one man remarked, Jesus would have been among the first to join.[44]

The answers to Stelzle's questionnaire hit home, and in 1903 the Presbyterian Board of Home Missions appointed him to a special mission to workingmen. Thus he launched a career that, for over a decade and a half, made his name a household word to both laborers and church goers. He became America's "Apostle to labor."[45]

During the same period, Stelzle also turned out a steady stream of books and articles. After 1906, he provided a weekly column to 150 labor papers on the church-labor question, of which one editor remarked, "Their influence has been to change the attitude of the entire labor press toward the church."[46] Moreover, he frequently appeared on the Chautauqua circuit, and one season he delivered the same lecture, "The Church and the Men Outside," in sixty-nine cities. He pioneered in perfecting noon religious meetings at factories. In 1905, he convinced many denominations to observe Labor Sunday and to exchange delegates with the major labor organizations. He spoke often and well to both labor unions and clerical meetings and at times addressed crowds of ten to fifteen thousand. For years, he was present at every major strike, and he interviewed people as diverse as John D. Rockefeller, Samuel Gompers, and Big Bill Haywood. In his ten years of social service, he estimated that he had contact with ten thousand American ministers. "Charles Stelzle," said William T. Ellis in one of the numerous articles written about his work, "is a machine-shop graduate who is teaching organized Protestantism in America that its biggest task at the moment is to understand, serve, and co-operate with the workingman."[47]

His message during these years was both simple and complex: the church had ignored the workers far too long. They were essentially religious people, but socialism had, in effect, become their religion; the labor movement had become their substitute church. The system Jesus taught was essentially a socialist system, and were He here today, he would surely side with labor. The saloon served the workers as a gathering spot for social exchanges, an aspect middle-class reformers too often ignored. Child labor was the darkest blot on American civilization. Cities, clearly, were about to dominate the nation, and because most city pastors were country-bred, they were woefully ignorant of the situations with which they had to deal. The major Protestant churches had left the downtown areas to the chapels and missions, but even they could not do the job.[48]

When Episcopal Bishop Henry Whipple had asked the head of a railroad yard how to interest his men, the chief replied, "Study a locomotive"; when a country minister asked a Cornell professor how he could fill his empty church, he was told, "Take a course in agriculture."[49] Stelzle was delivering essentially the same message to the middle-class churches: study the factories and cities. The church had been spending far too much time studying the life of the "Israelites, the Jebusites, the Hivites, and the Hittites," he said, and had ignored the "social life of the Pittsburghites or the Brooklynites, or the Chicagoites."[50] True religion, he reminded countless audiences, was always service.[51]

Simplistic, uncomplicated, and more than a little naive, Stelzle's vision also contained a unique perspective. He maintained that employers were human, too, and that wealth did not necessarily equate with evil. Although he saw the saloon as serving a necessary social function, he eventually became a prohibitionist (which cost him a good many labor votes), but he always defended bartenders and the Bartenders Union. He was also aware of class distinctions among workers, for he well remembered how full machinists had scorned mere journeymen. Over and over he preached the message of Jesus as he understood it: "Workingmen increasingly recognize that Jesus the Carpenter belongs to them."[52] Brotherhood, peace, democracy, liberty, equality, fraternity, and justice were the key words in his message. He argued that though the church should not commit itself to any economic system, it should apply Christ's great principles of justice, love, and service to every social problem. He saw class division, which he detested, as the major source of unrest, and he argued that any social movement based purely on class would be certain to fail. "[M]ost of the bitterness of the world," he said, "is due to misunderstanding."[53]

Stelzle's institutional attempt to erase this misunderstanding, and perhaps his most creative accomplishment, was the New York Labor Temple. After several months of badgering, he finally convinced the Board of Home Missions to take over financial support of a lower East Side Presbyterian church and turn it into a labor church. Similar proposals had been tried in Brooklyn, Chicago, Minneapolis, and St. Louis, and the board hoped to help solve the problems of the city by this novel means.[54] They would bring the Gospel to both worker and immigrant, who, as Abraham J. Muste later noted, had "in the past studied Marx more assiduously than Jesus."[55]

The old church was located in one of the most densely populated areas in the world. In three-quarters of a square mile lived one-quarter of a million people. Only one-half of 1 percent owned their own homes, and only 2 percent had native-born parents. Saloons, cheap dance halls, and houses of ill repute abounded. All previous attempts to improve conditions had met with failure. In 1896, Alfred T. Schauffler, then head of the New York City Mission and Tract Society, had called Dwight L. Moody to the church to try his methods for a month. Typical of the reception he received was the question by a man playing cards in a saloon: "Who the ——— is Moody?" Moody was unsuccessful. When he went uptown, however, he had no trouble filling the seats. As had Rainsford, the Presbyterians discovered that revivalist methods often had little or no effect in slum areas.[56]

Stelzle threw himself into the task of involving these people, and on a budget of $12,000 a year, he tried to run the Labor Temple as a church-oriented settlement house. Clubs, health activities, movies, choirs, and a Friday religious night where everyone spoke formed the core of his program. Over 50 percent of the audience was Jewish, and because of their fears of the intentions of Sunday schools, Stelzle recommended, in 1911, that no church be established: "We must demonstrate to the people that the church is simply a means to an end and not an end in itself; that Christianity is more concerned about building up the people than it is in building up the church."[57] Eventually, a gymnasium, pool, and school were established, the latter run in the early 1920s by Will Durant. A Labor Temple Fellowship was organized with a membership of several hundred, but it was short-lived. The people were asked to promise: "I accept the purpose of Jesus. I will help bring in the Kingdom of God."[58] An American International Church was organized in 1915, and it functioned as a Presbyterian church.

One of the most popular features of the Labor Temple was the Open Forum, which offered large halls to controversial speakers. More than any other gesture, the Open Forum confirmed the Temple's commitment to freedom of speech. Among its speakers were Theodore Roosevelt, Leon Trotsky, Norman Thomas, Anthony Comstock, Emma Goldman, and Samuel Gompers. At a time when union halls were small and when few other places existed where literally anything could be said, this open platform performed a vital function. Theodore Roosevelt supported the organization, and his widely read article "The Church and the People" in the January 27, 1912, *Outlook* helped stave off an early collapse.[59]

In the winter of 1914–15, when over four hundred thousand were unemployed in New York City, several radical organizations began a campaign to invade the churches and use them as hotels. Stelzle challenged the leaders of this movement (mostly Industrial Workers of the World) to a debate in the Open Forum. He believed that his arguments helped convince both audience and leaders to end the occupation of the churches. In 1920, the Temple threw open its doors to striking women workers.

In 1912, Stelzle turned the Temple over to Jonathan D. Day, and under his and others' leadership it lasted until 1958, when its purpose had disappeared. Stelzle himself turned to other interests. In 1911–12, he served as the dean of the Social Service Department of the Men and Religion Forward Movement and in 1916–18 as field secretary for the Federal Council of Churches. In the 1920s, he began his last career as a public relations expert. He died February 28, 1941. One observer noted that "Stelzle just missed being a great man."[60]

Thanks to the activities of Rauschenbusch, McKelway, Cadman, Rainsford, Stelzle, and countless others, social Christianity was much in the ascendant from 1901 to 1917. The liberals had forged a viable framework for social thought. But, as will be shown in the next chapter, the conservatives were also much involved with social issues.

5

The Triumph of Evangelical America, 1901–1917: The Conservatives

The contribution of the liberal wing of Protestantism to the Progressive reform movement has generally been acknowledged. What has not been acknowledged, however, is that the other wing of Protestantism—the conservatives (many, but not all, would later be called Fundamentalists)—were often also involved. Historians' traditional separation of the clergy between those concerned with the Social Gospel and those concerned only with individual salvation is not accurate for this period. From 1901 to about 1917, both liberal and conservative Protestant groups worked to alleviate social ills, each in its own way. This parallel interest, in large measure, supplied the moral-evangelical fervor to Progressivism. The Christian Endeavor Society, for example, was concerned with both the individual and society, holding personal experience meetings as well as forming committees to investigate local slum conditions.

The literary work that best illustrates the union of conservative and liberal forces is Charles Sheldon's *In His Steps* (1896). Sheldon arrived as pastor of the Central Congregational Church in Topeka, Kansas, in 1888. To bolster his sagging Sunday evening services, he began reading to his congregation from chapters of a novel he had written. Like the later movie serials, he left his audiences hanging in suspense when he broke off his narrative for the night. This technique worked well, and in October 1896 he began reading chapters from *In His Steps*—the seventh of an eventual total of twenty-five such novels. As with his six previous ventures, he sold *In His Steps* to a religious magazine, the *Advance*, which later published it in book form. Because of a technicality—the publisher of the *Advance* filed only one copy with the proper copyright department, instead of the necessary two—the copyright was nullified, and the book was thrown into the public domain. There it has remained, and it is still in print in numerous editions.[1]

The plot is simple. A poor wanderer (clearly not an ordinary tramp)—"not more than thirty or thirty-three years old, I should say"—collapses and dies before the astounded congregation of Reverend Henry Maxwell. This so unnerves the pastor that he asks his congregation to make a vow that for one year they will ask themselves, "What would Jesus do?" before they act. The plot then revolves around how a newspaper editor, businessman, singer, college president, and clergyman use their talents in this new light. Sheldon presumed to know exactly what Jesus would have done in a wide variety of circumstances: Jesus would run a special type of newspaper. He would not print accounts of prize fights or society gossip, or run liquor or tobacco ads. He would use a girl's beautiful voice for Gospel singing rather than opera performances. He would try to bridge social classes and clean up the slum district (called here "the Rectangle"). And he would urge the college president to leave the ivory tower to enter politics.

The little book sold incredibly well. Exactly how many copies were sold will probably never be known. In 1930, Bruce Barton estimated twenty-three million, about the same number Sheldon himself claimed. Literary critic Frank L. Mott lowered the estimate to around six million. It was referred to as "the second best seller to the *Bible* alone." *In His Steps* appeared in an English penny edition, was produced in a lantern-slide version, acted as a drama, and translated into several languages, including Russian and Arabic.

Sheldon lived until 1946 and continued to write books on similar themes. *The Narrow Gate* (1903) was a short temperance tract; *The Reformer* (1901) called attention to the housing problem; *The Heart of the World: A Story of Christian Socialism* (1905) and *Jesus Is Here* (1914) followed the same pattern. None of these achieved great prominence, however, and *Jesus Is Here*, which described Jesus as someone who "looked like an average man—only different" must rank as the worst of the lot.

Fads such as the immense popularity of *In His Steps* are far easier to describe than to explain. Yet surely one reason lay in the fact that both conservative and liberal Christians could read this tale with approval. Eric Goldman in his list of books that changed America credits the book's large sales primarily to the social gospel message it carried.[2] But this is only half correct. The conservative evangelical approach to society is also an integral part of Sheldon's message. As *In His Steps* shows, revival meetings go hand in hand with the establishment of institutional churches and settlement houses. There is no conflict between them.

Moreover, perhaps the book may be more sophisticated than it has been credited with being. The mysterious workman was technologically unemployed (he was a printer forced out of work by a linotype machine). The newspaper that tried to run on purely Christian principles collapsed financially (it was saved only by a sympathetic heiress). A "socialist" stands up at a public meeting and gives a cogent summary of his position. But the ultimate touch of sophistication lay in Sheldon's realization of the partnership between conservative and liberal Christianity—they were working together to usher in the Kingdom of God.

Other evangelical speakers and writers also exhibited this combination of

efforts. At a late 1880s Atlanta revival, led by evangelists Sam Jones and
George R. Stuart, Stuart once stepped to the platform with Bible in hand. "I
hold in my hand the Word of God," he said, "and it is the source of the
Wisdom of God on all subjects: moral, social, business, and political."[3]
Following their belief in the literal interpretation of the words of Scripture,
these revivalists sought concrete ways to apply their faith. "The world wants
practical illustrations of our Christianity," Stuart told the crowd, "and we
will never reveal Christ to this old world until we mix our preaching and our
prayers with bread and meat and clothing for the poor."[4] These words were
spoken in the midst of a message urging temperance!

Conservative literature also kept the theme alive. In *Chicago by Gaslight*
(1909), the chief investigator for the Douglas Neighborhood Club, Samuel
Paynter Wilson, denounced the evils of the big city. In addition to warning
youths about the evils of gambling, social clubs, dancing, fashions, ice cream
parlors, "chop suey joints" (which, presumably, served more than chop
suey), cigarettes, and alcohol, he reminded his audience that sin was all-per-
vasive. Moreover, he said, it was not just limited to individuals—entire
communities could be infected by its myriad forms. Wilson denounced love
of wealth, political corruption, and the low wages paid by department stores
($5 to $7 a week) that drove women into sordid lines of work to avoid
starving. Only the church, he believed, held the balance of power to change
the situation.[5]

In *Save the Girls*, reformed gambler Mason Long warned young ladies of
the dangers of society, dancing, poverty, and big city life. But he, too,
blamed poverty on the system, not the individual, and denounced the
capitalists for paying starvation wages to working girls.[6]

Mark A. Matthews of Seattle, John R. Straton of New York City, and
William B. Riley of Minneapolis were prominent conservative ministers. All
came from conservative evangelical backgrounds, and during the Progressive years all were involved in promoting social reform measures. Yet during
the 1920s, all three dropped their social concern to become spokesmen for
the aggressive wing of Fundamentalism.[7] It is highly probable that their shift
in outlook was shared by many other conservative evangelicals, whose
defection from social issues is crucial in explaining the decline of Progressivism.

Mark A. Matthews came to Seattle to head the First Presbyterian Church
in 1901 when the church had four hundred members and the city a popula-
tion of around eighty thousand. At his death in 1940, he had seen the city
grow to over half a million and the church to the largest Presbyterian church
in the world. Although he periodically preached on the virtues of Calvinism,
he was not a Calvinist except in the sense that he believed in the reality of
sin. The devil was at work in the world, he often said, and it was the church's
duty to stop him. He considered Christianity the only power able to solve

the problems of society, and he urged that it be applied to all avenues of life, both individual and social. To find the true answer of a question, one had only to discover what view Christ would have taken on it.[8]

His sermon collection at the University of Washington Library shows that from 1905 to 1912 he expressed considerable social concern. "In preaching the gospel," he said in 1909, "every true preacher is compelled to be a reformer in the community and in the world in which he lives."[9] In 1911, he vigorously campaigned against the bête noire of Progressivism, the special interests—in this case the companies that controlled Seattle's coal supply. No man has the right, he said, to monopolize natural resources such as water, air, light, and coal and then sell them to the people at a profit. During the same period, he preached sermons declaring that women should have wages equal to those of men and that every child should have the opportunity to go to college. In addition, he established an open-air camp, from which the city's first tuberculosis sanitarium later grew, opened Seattle's first kindergarten, started its first day nursery, and, as a member of the bar, helped write a bill that established the first city juvenile court. He was also active in the Red Cross and the White Cross (an antinarcotics society). At his most radical, he urged that Seattle build a hospital with a free clinic for the poor.[10]

Matthews also used his pulpit to denounce Seattle's graft and corruption. In his 1905 New Year's sermon, he attacked the city council for "graftitis" and later appeared before them with a list of "nineteen symptoms of graft." This act elicited much publicity but few results. In 1910 and 1916, he personally led two widely publicized crusades to clean up the city. In the first, he helped uncover enough evidence of collusion between city officials and the local red-light district to recall the mayor and send the chief of police to jail. After this, he boasted that Seattle was "the cleanest town in the country."[11] Six years later, he began another crusade, this time accusing several city officials of involvement in a bootlegging racket. Again he was successful, and again there were convictions. "During the seven years from 1910 to America's entry into the World War in 1917," said the *Seattle Star* in 1940, "the Rev. Mark A. Matthews was almost continuously in Seattle's political limelight, actively waging war on Mayors, police chiefs and bootleggers."[12] During this time, he closed every sermon with a plea for personal repentance.[13] Although always very conservative in theology, Matthews was an integral part of Seattle's Progressive reform movement.

John R. Straton pastored Baptist churches in Baltimore from 1908 to 1914 and in Norfolk from 1914 to 1918, when he moved to the Calvary Baptist Church in New York City, where he remained until his death in 1929. His Baltimore and Norfolk pastorates were marked by concern for the society around him. Although theologically conservative, he, too, was very much a part of the Progressive reform crusade. He shocked his more conservative parishioners by wide advertisement of his sermons, catchy titles, and a wholesale verbal assault on political corruption, alcohol, and prostitution. He also spoke out against child labor, women's labor, low wages, and bad working conditions.

When addressing a Washington ministers' conference in 1908, he argued that individual salvation comes when man gets into the right relationship with God, and social salvation comes when man gets into the right relationship with man. "We are led to believe," he continued, "that Christianity is a means of *social* salvation as well as a means of individual salvation."[14] He felt that a major portion of Christ's mission was to establish an ideal social order on earth, and in one sermon he viciously attacked those who perverted Christ's words by using them as an excuse for not abolishing economic injustice.[15] He compiled a thick file folder on socialism, and his early writings show that he had read Henry George and Karl Marx even if he had not always understood them thoroughly. While serving as the executive secretary of the Social Service Commission of the Interchurch Federation, he said that the emphasis in religion seemed to be shifting from individual as individual to individual as member of society. Consequently, he declared it essential that legal changes concerning factory workers, fair housing, sanitation, and prison redemption follow immediately.[16]

Straton's social concern is most evident in his little booklet, *The Scarlet Stain on the City* (ca. 1916). In these pages he attacked the laws he considered unjust and argued that an economic issue could be discovered at the base of every form of immorality. Laws were needed, he argued, to equalize opportunity. He scorned the idle rich and attacked them for paying pauper wages to their servants. He advocated minimum wage laws, mothers' pensions, public ownership of utilities, and heavy taxes on incomes and inheritances; he predicted that the wrath of God would descend upon any social order that allowed such economic injustices as he had described to continue.[17] In advocating such a program, Straton touched on many of the Progressive causes, for example: "The minister and the church of Christ are traitors to their trust, they are recreant to their duty, unless they battle heroically against such evils as unjust wages, especially to women workers, child labor, and the hell-black social evil, lawlessness, and the awful shame and disgrace of the liquor traffic."[18] The life of Jesus Christ, he felt, had clearly shown the way by which man could come into the right relationship to man.

William B. Riley pastored the Calvary Baptist Church in Chicago from 1893 to 1897 and the First Baptist Church in Minneapolis from 1897 to 1940. Riley was aware of the challenge the city posed to the Protestant churches, but he refused to make any concession to the methods of the social gospel in meeting it. He had one answer—the conversion of individuals—for the problems he saw around him. "The answer is in one name—Christ," he wrote in 1900. "He alone is sufficient for the city-center."[19] He remained committed to this idea throughout his life.

During the Progressive years, however, Riley was more than willing to work with the other agents of social reform. He carried no antagonism toward the groups that were using other means to clean up the city, he said. He claimed in various sermons that there was no disharmony between the premillennial pastor and the social reformer and that the church could be spoken of in connection with social reconstruction without putting an undue strain on the word. Moreover, he periodically engaged in sermon crusades against prostitution, gambling, political corruption, and alcohol. In one talk he stated: "We need a federation of these forces that shall bring down the whole hand of better public opinion upon the lawless and criminal classes to teach those who have no regard for moral truth, a sense of obedience to law, who their masters are."[20]

Other conservative clergymen carried on similar social crusades in their various cities. In Fort Worth, Texas, the Reverend J. Frank Norris frequently accused city officials of involvement with local prostitution and alcohol rings. Itinerant revivalists, such as Sam Jones, J. Wilbur Chapman, William E. Biederwolf, and Billy Sunday, portrayed themselves as champions of "social service," as they attacked various forms of "vice." Denver's Jim Goodheart, a reformed alcoholic and a Baptist minister, supervised a downtown mission that functioned as an institutional church, distributing food and lodging and providing an orphanage and an employment bureau for Denver's poor. Simultaneously, however, Goodheart put his emphasis on a change of heart, and his annual reports always noted conversions by the hundreds. As he told his audiences, "What God has done for me, no one else could do."[21]

"Parson Tom" Uzzell also manifested the conservative concern with social reform. A Methodist-turned-Congregationalist, Uzzell ran the People's Tabernacle of Denver from 1884 until his death in 1910. During those years, he helped establish the city's first night schools and kindergartens; he also ran a free medical dispensary and a legal aid clinic for the poor. In addition, Uzzell maintained an active employment agency, which was well respected by Denver's business community. After he was elected city supervisor and county commissioner, he distributed jobs to the needy like a ward boss. Simultaneously, however, he and the Tabernacle placed much emphasis on the conservative evangelical message. Tom Uzzell reportedly always "had one evangelist coming in the front door and another going out the back."[22]

In a recent study, historian Norris Magnuson has argued that some of the most extensive social gospel activities were conducted by evangelical slum workers. The Salvation Army, the various rescue missions, shelters, and homes for women that emerged in virtually every major city all combined an active social involvement with a traditional evangelical message. Because the dedicated men and women who ran these institutions often had extensive personal knowledge of slum conditions, they were able to offer insights the middle-class reformers often missed.[23]

Nowhere was the combination of conservative theology and liberal social concern more clearly illustrated than in the most orthodox section of the country—the South. Considering the role evangelical Protestantism played in southern society, it is surprising that the role of the southern clergy during the Progressive period has not been given more emphasis by historians. For years, it was believed that the southern churches avoided most of the northern currents, but recent studies by Kenneth K. Bailey, Rufus B. Spain, and Wayne Flynt have shown that southern Protestantism differed only in degree from that of the North on social issues.[24]

Excluding certain Catholic areas such as New Orleans, evangelical Protestantism and the South have had a long, intimate connection. Southern thought was largely shaped by the symbols of pietistic revivalism. These symbols, moreover, proved remarkably flexible: sometimes they supported change; sometimes they supported the existing order. Appeals to Scripture could go either way.

For much of the late nineteenth century, however, the conservative position prevailed. Historian Robert C. McMath, Jr., has described this as a time when "most leading churchmen of the South were using the received religious tradition to support the economic and political status quo."[25] Reformers and southern liberals, such as Walter Hines Page, who had gone North to pursue his career as a journalist, despaired over such a relationship.[26] They decried the fact that the church viewed its role as solely to "preach the Old Gospel."

Yet appeal to scriptural authority could also provide a means to critique the existing social order. The Southern Alliance lecturers clearly used the language of Zion as a focus for social change, and in the 1890s the Populists often used Scripture to condemn the churches. In 1895, Dr. Cyrus Thompson shocked an Alliance-Populist crowd in Cary, North Carolina, when he stated: "The church today stands where it has always stood—on the side of human slavery."[27] Such criticisms often hit home, and not infrequently churches split because of them. Historian Frederick A. Bode has argued that such attacks caused many fin de siècle Protestant church leaders to ally themselves with the emerging business community, in part to preserve their "traditional" influence.[28]

The flexibility of the evangelical appeal to Scripture became even more apparent after the turn of the century. The Southern Baptists, for example, were considerably behind their northern brethren, but when compared with their earlier position, they had made many advances. In 1870, the churches were concerned with Gospel preaching alone. By 1900, they were also heavily involved in temperance reform, antigambling crusades, campaigns to eliminate political corruption, the promotion of public morality, care of orphans and the aged, and attacks on child labor. Under the able leadership of Edgar Y. Mullins, the Southern Baptist Seminary in Louisville adopted a moderate social gospel stance from about 1904 to 1915. The students became so excited over social questions that in 1910 they petitioned Mullins to make sociology courses mandatory for them. Charles S. Gardner's *The Ethics of Jesus and Social Progress* (1914) was a major treatment of social Christianity by a Southern Baptist. He argued that one could adopt liberal social thought without accepting a liberal theology.[29]

In the ten years before World War I, the Southern Methodists and Southern Presbyterians both affiliated with the liberal northern Federal Council of Churches, and the Southern Methodist General Conference later officially adopted the 1912 council's social creed. Although it avoided the council, the Southern Baptist Convention in 1913 established a social service commission, and two years later it officially condemned crowded tenements, child labor, women's labor, sweatshops, corporate greed, and political graft.[30] The traditional evangelical appeals still used the rhetoric of individual salvation. But now one was "saved for service," and "service" in southern life began to take on a wider set of meanings.

Clerical roots can be found in the southern Progressive impulse. Prison chaplains (who were usually conservative evangelicals) were always in the forefront of the southern prison reform movements. They played a significant role in reducing the use of chain gangs, convict labor, and cruel and barbarous punishments. They were also instrumental in establishing prison farms. Frank W. Barnett, who became editor of the *Alabama Baptist* in 1901, used the pages of his paper to express social concern on labor issues, convict abuses, child labor, and prohibition. He urged a Christianity that would make a man vote right. "If the preacher was heard oftener on political questions that effect [sic] the moral welfare of the community, it would be better for the State," he said in 1905.[31]

This was also true in mountain work, as shown by the career of Southern Presbyterian Edward O. Guerrant, who for years preached only the "Old Gospel Story" in the highlands of eastern Kentucky. In the years from 1886 to 1896, he argued that the Gospel was the driving force in effective social service. His sermon in Whitesburg, Kentucky, converted Jonathan D. Day, who later became superintendent of the Labor Temple in New York City. Yet while telling the old story around the mountains, Guerrant also set up the first hospital in Breathitt County, Witherspoon College, Highland College, and Highland Orphans' Home (later consolidated into Highland Institute and numerous grade schools). In 1917, he turned over to the Executive Committee of Home Missions seventeen schools and mission stations, an orphanage, and thirty-four buildings, having a total property value of $50,000.[32]

Robert F. Campbell, pastor of the First Presbyterian Church in Asheville, was another conservative who engaged in significant mountain work. He served as president of the Lord's Day Alliance of North Carolina, which attacked Sunday newspapers and Sunday mail. He also denounced the abuses of animals for the SPCA in 1907 and read a paper before the Asheville Pen and Plate Club that quoted from John Spargo denouncing child labor.[33]

These southern clergymen who spoke out on social issues could not have been called liberals. They supported blue laws, stricter divorce measures, and temperance legislation. They denounced immigrants and the continental Sunday and avoided movies as temptations of the flesh; they eschewed the race question entirely. Yet for several years they formed an integral part of southern Progressivism. Their concern, moreover, was not long-lasting. When Charles H. Nabers collected a series of sermons for the *Southern Presbyterian Pulpit* in 1928, no one mentioned social concerns.[34] Their interest had lasted only twenty years.

Perhaps the best example of the liberal-conservative alliance in the South can be seen in the religious sessions of the Southern Sociological Congress, a large, general conference held annually from 1912 to 1919 to discuss common problems. The conclusions of those attending these meetings clearly illustrate the new social outlook of the southern churches. Speakers from all sections of the country gave addresses urging that the community had a soul and that the gospel of pure individualism be replaced by the gospel of social commitment.[35] "The Son of Man did not come—"said Samuel Z. Batten, general secretary of the Social Service Commission of the Northern Baptist Church, "how plain it all is now—the Son of Man did not come merely to save a few individuals out of the world, but to make men citizens of the Kingdom of God."[36] "It is strange," noted Reverend John A. Rice of Fort Worth, Texas, "that we should so long have read the Bible with the eyes of the individualist, that we should have failed to see in the Old Testament the germs of a great social order in which the spiritual should be supreme."[37] Reverend Charles S. MacFarland, secretary of the Federal Council of Churches, spoke several times to these southern congresses. He reminded the delegates that evangelism and social service were inseparable, if not one and the same. "True social service," he said, "is simply evangelism a hundred or a thousand fold."[38] In his 1914 address, he borrowed evangelical rhetoric for his social gospel message: "Let us determine to know nothing save Jesus Christ and him Crucified. The cross of Christ is the symbol of our faith; let us lift it up as the solitary hope of mankind and of its social salvation."[39]

The most inclusive social question for conservatives during the Progressive years was that of prohibition. If they favored no other social reform, all evangelical Protestant ministers could become involved with the campaign to prohibit the sale of alcohol.[40] The prohibition movement during this period extended beyond the desire to regulate the consumption of alcohol by the individual to include a view of the ideal social order. The advocates of prohibition saw it as the chief cure for poverty, crime, and prostitution. To destroy alcohol would in large measure destroy the others.

William B. Riley referred to the liquor industry as the "mother" of gambling and prostitution. He served as a member of the Civic Federation while in Chicago and helped found a similar organization when he moved to the Twin Cities. In one of his early battles he attempted to force the saloons to obey the legally established closing hour. He organized mass meetings, wrote several polemics, and set up a strong pressure group, all of which finally forced the mayor of Minneapolis to tighten enforcement of the law. In addition, he fought hard to retain an old city law that limited the selling of alcohol to certain areas of the city, and in the midst of this battle debated two wet politicians before a crowd of twenty thousand in the Minneapolis streets.[41] As he noted in his *Messages for the Metropolis* (1906), "Two well-defined movements have characterized these first years of the twentieth century. For six years 'evangelism' has been the watchword of Evangelical Christendom. For the same length of time 'reform' has been the shibboleth of every successful politician. It is most natural that these movements should come together."[42]

Both conservatives and liberals had ample grounds on which to unite. The trust served as the bête noire for liberals and alcohol served the same role for conservatives. George R. Stuart blamed liquor for the anarchist riots in Chicago, corruption in city, state, and national government, 90 percent of American poverty, and 90 percent of the country's divorces.[43] Evangelist Billy Sunday leveled his most vitriolic attacks against "booze."[44] The Methodists suggested that temperance might form the issue for Christian unification. They hoped that all clerics, even Catholic priests, could unite on this issue.[45] A few, in fact, did so. From North and South, from liberals and conservatives, lectures and books poured forth the new message of social salvation and the Kingdom of God. The journals of the period also devoted numerous articles to such concerns. Although the various denominations arrived at the Social Gospel at different times, from different paths, and with different degrees of conviction, by 1910 every major denominational publication was discussing social concerns. In 1899, the Disciples' *Christian Standard* labeled François Millet's painting and Edwin Markham's poem, "The Man with the Hoe," as products not of America but of the Old World.[46] By 1912, no denominational paper would have been so complacent about American poverty. Shortly afterward, even conservative Union Seminary in Richmond was nodding in the direction of the Social Gospel.[47]

The evangelical rhetoric of these years, moreover, reached far beyond the bonds of organized religion. The Progressives extended their biblical imagery to all aspects of society. Biblical rhetoric had always had a great impact on American life, but suddenly it reached massive dimensions. In 1896, William Jennings Bryan gave his "Cross of Gold" speech. In 1912, Theodore Roosevelt, who stood at Armageddon to "battle for the Lord," gave his followers a "Confession of Faith." The theme song for the ensuing Bull Moose or Progressive party was "Onward Christian Soldiers." In supporting the party platform of 1912, Lyman Abbott found precedent in Isaiah, Amos, Hosea, the Christian Fathers, and St. Francis of Assisi. He saw the crusade to prevent the concentration of wealth and extension of poverty as the greatest political theme for centuries.[48]

Evangelical rhetoric also played a part in the conservation movement. Gifford Pinchot's *The Fight for Conservation* (1919) urged that everyone should help bring in the Kingdom of God and that such public spirit was simply the application of Christianity to the commonwealth. John Muir cast his fight to prevent the damming of California's Hetch-Hetchy Valley in the same terms. The socialists used biblical rhetoric. So, too, did single taxers and prohibitionists.

The spread of evangelical Christian rhetoric proved crucial to Progressivism. As Reverend Sidney Strong pointed out in an 1893 address on capital and labor, ministers often have no more expertise than others in solving economic or social problems. "Perhaps the most useful work of the ministry," he noted, "will be to emphasize the moral factor which must come into the problem before solution is possible."[49] "And if the preacher can awaken in his people the desire to promote justice in the school and library facilities, the parks, the taxation, the control of corporations, the adjustment of wage scales," noted James H. Tufts of the University of Chicago in 1908, "he may well decline to pose as the universal expert in the details of all these difficult matters."[50]

The clergy were urged never to become too specific. Walter Rauschenbusch and others warned them against becoming involved in political campaigns and taking political stances. Instead, they were instructed to supply the spirit needed to fuel the reform movement. "The preacher is not here to preach ethics or sociology," said Samuel Z. Batten in 1902, "he is not here to preach on the rights of labor or the rights of capital; he has nothing to do with platforms of parties and the programs of reformers. But he is here to witness for righteousness and love in all the relations of life."[51]

The social function of the church, noted Professor Graham Taylor at an 1899 symposium, was to supply the power of reform. Without the ideal form, he noted, there could be no actual reform. Gospel ideals had borne their best fruits whenever they had given the initiative to a higher conception of national life.[52] It was the duty of the church to form the conscience of its people, said Batten two years later. No democratic state could rise higher than its public conscience. If the conscience of a people is high, he said, it matters not who makes their laws. Without this, they would fall dupes to demagogues and bosses. No single, isolated reform could ever create the ideal society because reforms are, by their nature, partial and limited. The all-around conscience, the desire for the Kingdom of God, must always be left to the church.[53]

Even though time may have dimmed their accomplishments somewhat, the Progressive generation was well aware of the role they played in awakening the nation's moral sense. Not since the antebellum reform era had the notion of change so swept the country. Moreoever, it produced results in the fields of conservation, child labor, unemployment laws, social justice, and city reform.

The clergy have not been given the credit they deserve for these accomplishments. Seldom, if ever, did they actually sit in the legislatures to vote for the various reform bills. In some states clerics were barred by the constitution from sitting in the state legislature. Consequently, when historians have examined and analyzed the makeup of the various state legislatures and the Progressive wings of the major parties, they discovered few clergymen. They found doctors, journalists, real estate and insurance men, professors, immigrants, professionals, and middle-class businessmen of all types, but because of the separation of church and state, the ministers were often missing.

Yet their absence should not be discounted, for the Progressive years found the clergy at the height of their power. They were an important moral force in their communities. They were listened to on all subjects. Never had they been so admired; seldom would they be so again. Working, each in his own way, to bring in the Kingdom of God, they brought in, instead, an atmosphere that made numerous reforms possible.

Although the social reform emphasis of American Protestantism did not collapse entirely, it did undergo considerable change during the 1920s.[54] Never again would the social question have the undivided church support of the years before World War I. In large measure it declined when liberal and conservative pastors began to see each other as more dangerous enemies than the social evils around them.

6
Seeds of Conflict, 1901–1917

At the same time that both liberals and conservatives were attempting to usher in their different versions of the Kingdom of God, forces were also at work to make sure that the Kingdom never became even a remote possibility. Growing conservative awareness that the "new" theology was appreciably different from their position, the belief that the liberals were running the denominations as a minority faction, and the rise of new militant interdenominational Fundamentalist organizations all were potential threats to denominational stability.

No one doubted that the theological positions of the various churches were changing, but few were certain as to precisely what these changes would mean for the future of Protestantism. Most of the great historical religious movements either were associated with a towering figure such as St. Francis, Luther, Calvin, Zwingli, George Fox, or John Knox, or embodied themselves in impressive official documents such as the decrees of the Council of Trent or the Westminster Confession, or resulted in formation of a new sect, such as the Quakers or Methodists.

But the rise of Protestant liberalism in both America and Europe had none of these results. It produced no Luther, Calvin, or Zwingli. The major thinkers of the movement were essentially secondary figures. The early nineteenth-century Unitarians as well as such later figures as Horace Bushnell, Theodore Munger, Phillips Brooks, Washington Gladden, Lyman Abbott, and Henry Ward Beecher all had been forerunners of change. The tenets of the new position were far from clear, but basically Protestant liberalism revolved around several affirmations: (1) God was immanent in the affairs of men, and progress toward the realization of His goals came through His participation. (Darwin had raised doubts as to God's participation in the world of nature, but most liberals still held to some kind of immanence.) The natural world may have evolved by the process of evolution, but the question of initial origins was still considered God's handiwork and the bailiwick of theologians, not scientists. The idea of God's immanence was emphasized far more than the corollary idea of God's transcendence. (2) "Love" was stressed over "Justice" and "Character" over "Grace." (3) The Bible was to be understood by judicious application of the results of the scientific method. (4) Most, but not all, liberals believed in the Social Gospel.[1]

The liberals were dismayed by the creedal restrictions existing among the Protestant denominations. As had the early Unitarians, liberals hoped to bring all the old mysteries and creeds to the bar of reason and make Christianity "more easily digestible."[2] William R. Hutchinson, in *The Modernist Impulse in American Protestantism,* credits the Unitarians with having originated many liberal ideas.[3] The liberal ideology slowly spread from the scholars to ordinary churchgoers, entering the different denominations at different times until by 1917 liberals were represented in all the major denominations.

John A. Faulkner of Drew Theological Seminary charted the momentum the process gained in Northern Methodism:

> The new theory of atonement by Dr. Miley in 1879, the revolutionary series of little books by Dr. Bowne in 1898–1900 (gathered into *Studies in Christianity* in 1909), the almost complete passing of the emphasis on holiness and perfect love, of which the first note was the remarkable book of Dr. J. T. Crane (father of the novelist Stephen Crane) in 1874, the substitution of the "liberal" Baptist divine's book on Theology (Dr. W. N. Clarke) for our own Dr. Curtis' in 1916 in the Course of Study for Preachers, and the many recent books and articles by Methodists of a radical or Unitarian trend—these are signs of a disintegration of that solidarity of testimony which was once our glory and the spring of our worldwide conquests.[4]

When Baptist historian Norman H. Maring surveyed the Northern Baptist seminaries in 1880, he found no trace of liberalism. In 1914, however, liberals were on the staffs of all the major institutions.[5]

In 1906–7, the *American Journal of Theology* ran a lengthy series of articles on how theology had changed within the various denominations. Most of the major figures of the period presented their opinions, each noting the rise of some variety of liberalism within his denomination. Denominational journals picked up this theme, and it was not long before "liberalism" became a major topic for discussion.[6]

The rise of theological liberalism also began to undermine many of the old creedal certainties. Calvinism, backbone of Congregationalists, Presbyterians, and some Baptists, came under severe attack in the post–Civil War period. The Congregationalists found it easy to revise their creed in 1883, but the question of revising the Westminster Confession troubled the Northern Presbyterians for over a generation. Although many voices urged the church to modify its Calvinist heritage, when the 1902 creedal revision finally occurred, the changes were moderate. Nevertheless, many Presbyterians had moved quite far from Calvin's original ideas. One spokesman identified the elect with "whosoever will" and the nonelect with "whosoever will not." Baptist liberal William H. P. Faunce noted that social surveys had become the modern equivalent of self-examination.[7]

Theology was changing, the popular understanding of Jesus was changing, and denominational creeds no longer held the certainty they once did. For many people, the very heart of their faith was in question. God was no longer the transcendent judge; He had become the benevolent, immanent Father. Jesus was no longer the divine intercessor; He had become the "perfect man." The Bible was no longer the Word of God; it had become a book of "great literature." Creedal positions were no longer firm statements of denominational truths; they were historical attempts to define the undefinable. Here was a major conceptual revolution, and it had suddenly become widespread. In 1915, sociologist Albion W. Small noted that Christendom had but one principal line of division, and it ran not between the various denominations but through them.[8]

Several incidents focused attention upon the growing uneasiness among the churches. Ray Stannard Baker's popular *The Spiritual Unrest* (1910), originally published as a series of articles in the *American Magazine,* exposed the sins of Trinity Episcopal Church in New York City and presented a decidedly gloomy picture of the entire religious community. Discontent and discouragement were rife among all the churches and missions of New York City, said Baker. Low vitality, fulminations against minor evils, and the collapse of sincere faith were obvious to all. The Episcopal Cathedral of St. John the Divine in New York was contrasted with the thirteenth-century cathedrals built of, by, and for the people. The churches had become wealthy, educated, and amusing, but they no longer led, or even stirred, the masses. Revivals were a dismal failure. Baker thought that most of the genuine power and vision of Christianity lay outside the churches: in settlement houses, charity organizations, civic groups, and among the socialists. "The Roman Catholic has his Modernist, the Protestant his higher critic and the Jew his Reform Movement," he noted. "It goes deep—this spiritual unrest."[9]

Charles W. Eliot, president emeritus of Harvard University, agreed. A Boston Brahmin famous for his educational reforms, Eliot sparked the last great controversy of his career when he delivered a closing address titled "The Religion of the Future" for the 1909 Harvard Summer School of Theology. Eliot spoke of the faith of the future with Brahmin confidence. The religion of the future would not be based on any authority, either church or Bible, he said. It would have only one commandment—love of God, shown through service to others by contribution to the common good. Ideas about God would change greatly in the future and would "comprehend the

Jewish Jehovah, the Christian Universal Father, the modern physicist's omnipresent and exhaustless Energy, and the biological conception of a Vital Force." God would become absolutely immanent in all aspects of life, so much so that no mediation would be needed between Him and any part of His creation.[10]

This new faith, predicted Eliot, would have no dealings with sin or the Fall, and its saints would be "the discoverers, teachers, martyrs, and apostles of liberty, purity, and righteousness." In the future there would be nothing "supernatural." Nor might there be any further need for worship. He admitted that many of the religious comforts and compensations of the past would be lost amid these changes, but he was basically optimistic: "The new religion cannot supply the old sort of consolation; but it can diminish the need of consolation, or reduce the number of occasions for consolation." The new clerics would be surgeons and social reformers—those who make positive social gains. The new religion would be in harmony with the great secular movements of the day: democracy, individualism, education, social idealism, preventive medicine, the spirit of research, and the advance in business and industrial ethics. Moreover, its results were certain.[11]

At another time, such an address might have evoked little response. In 1909, however, church tensions were such that Eliot's address was given heavy coverage in the popular press and caused alarm within the churches. Protestants were astonished by his comments, and several Roman Catholics attacked his predictions. Yet, Dr. George W. Knox of Union Seminary in New York claimed that Eliot had made "a very able summary of what the intelligent men of the present day think, whether they are in or out of the churches."[12]

In the fall of 1913, novelist Winston Churchill gave his lecture, "The Modern Quest for a Religion," to several West Coast audiences and responded to its popularity by having it printed for distribution. The lecture set forth the major religious dilemmas of the day. Sensing a "divine discontent" among Americans, he noted that "we are unable to say with the conviction of our fathers, 'This is the absolute truth.' "[13]

The hundreds of books published on the subject furthered the diffusion of liberal ideas. How much effect these volumes had on the American reading public, of course, is open to conjecture. But the variety of works available and the large number of editions printed of the more popular ones would suggest that it was considerable. Clearly, there was a market for books that combined solace for the passing of the old faith with an explanation of the arrival of the new.[14] Thus, although no such radical an act as the nailing of liberal theses to American church doors occurred, a number of books and dramatic incidents helped to spread liberal ideas to ordinary citizens.

The conservative response to the spread of liberalism eventually took many forms. One of these came to be known as Fundamentalism, although the name was not coined until 1920. Two recent books have done much to further our understanding of the rise of Fundamentalism: Ernest R. Sandeen's *The Roots of Fundamentalism* (1970) and Timothy P. Weber's *Living in the Shadow of the Second Coming* (1979). Sandeen provided the framework, and Weber amplified many of his points.[15] Distinguishing between the Fundamentalist *movement* and the Fundamentalist *controversy* Sandeen argues that each existed independently of the other. He credits the rise of the movement to an alliance between the theology taught at Princeton Seminary and the post–Civil War revival of premillennialism.[16]

Princeton Seminary was probably the Presbyterian church's most prestigious institution, and from the early nineteenth century onward Professors Archibald Alexander, Charles Hodge and his two sons, and Benjamin B. Warfield developed a sophisticated, scholarly argument for biblical inerrancy. Casting themselves as the sole heirs of Reformation theology, these learned men insisted that all mystical feeling, natural theology, and church teachings be subordinated to the theological science of the Scriptures. The Scriptures, they insisted, were the infallible Word of God. Although they were willing to tolerate disagreement as to the means God used to convey His truth to the ancient writers, they all insisted that the end product be regarded as authoritative. Eventually they were forced to adopt the position that verbal inerrancy belonged only to the Bible as it came from the hands of the writers—the original autographs (now lost)—but this qualification was often overlooked in appeals to existing English translations.[17] Historian Lefferts A. Loetscher has pointed out that by 1894 the Presbyterian church required all ministers to affirm belief in the inerrancy of the original manuscripts of the Bible.[18]

The impact of the Princeton theology, however, was limited mainly to Presbyterians. Far more important to the rise of Fundamentalism was the revived interest in millennial thought after the Civil War. Unlike the Princeton theology, it appeared in virtually every Protestant group. The millennium is the period of a thousand years during which Christ will rule on earth, as promised in Revelation 20:1–7. Although there are many varieties of millennial thought, the main distinction lies between the pre-'s and the post-'s. Postmillennialism holds that human effort must establish the thousand years of peace, and only then will Christ return to judge the earth. Premillennialism maintains that Christ will return bodily to begin the process. This distinction was to have considerable impact on American church life.

The American Puritans were largely premillennial, but by the middle of the eighteenth century many thinkers on the subject, such as Jonathan Edwards, had adopted the postmillennial position. Several early nineteenth-century groups, including the Oneida Community, the Shakers, and the Church of Jesus Christ of Latter-Day Saints (the Mormons) held strong millennial views. The premillennial activities of William Miller and the Millerites of the 1830s and 1840s, however, are probably the most famous. Twice Miller actually set dates for the end of the world (1843, 1844), and when Christ did not return as predicted, millennial thought went into an eclipse.[19] A small, dedicated group of Miller's followers became the Seventh-Day Adventists.

After the Civil War, a new variety of premillennial thought began to gain followers. These people tried to disassociate themselves from the now discredited Millerites and maintained that they were little different from the main line Protestants.[20] One distinguishing aspect of this new approach was its reliance upon dispensationalism, a complex set of theological ideas that stresses that all time is divided into separate ages or dispensations. God demands different responses from mankind during each separate age, and each age is brought to an end by divine intervention. The listing of these dispensations varied somewhat, but all believers in this ideology felt that late nineteenth-century America was in the last age. Conditions were certain to worsen until Christ returned to bring earthly existence to a close. This theme was promulgated in the post–Civil War period by the Englishman John Darby and his followers on both sides of the Atlantic. Cyrus I. Scofield, a Kansas lawyer, developed an elaborate chronology of eschatalogical events that received wide distribution through his popular *Scofield Reference Bible*. Even more important than the millennarians' charting of the final days, however, was their insistence that all passages of the Bible be taken literally. Their ideas gradually became incorporated into many of the conservative colleges, Bible schools, and seminaries.[21]

These schools were very concerned with premillennialism and especially with the introduction of the "pretribulation" secret rapture of the church. This latter idea was a nineteenth-century innovation, but it gradually came to be seen as indistinguishable from premillennialism in general.[22] The rise of dispensationalist thinking after the Civil War greatly aided the growth of American premillennialism. As it grew, it merged with and extended far beyond the older Adventist tradition. As a consequence, premillennialism, which had been peripheral to the main body of Protestantism, gradually came to be seen as more and more essential. Several commentators noticed the rapidly growing interest in the doctrine of the second coming.[23] Radical millennialism forms a variety of social protest, similar to the writings of the utopians, and post–Civil War America was sufficiently removed from the ideal state the country was earlier thought to be to produce much interest in the subject.[24] Increased concern with premillennialism might well be seen as the religious counterpart of *Looking Backward* and *Progress and Poverty*.

A series of conferences served as the chief avenues for popularization of such views. With the rapid decay of social reform following the Civil War, the churches had less and less need to gather together for joint causes. The relatively new phenomenon of Bible conferences arose to fill their place. According to Leander W. Munhall, who was present, the first Bible conference held in America took place at Swampscott, Massachusetts, July 19–26, 1876. Thereafter, a conference was held annually for twenty-five years, excepting only 1884. In 1890, these meetings took on the name of the Niagara Bible Conference. Other, smaller conferences were held in Indiana, Pennsylvania, and Colorado.[25]

Closely paralleling these Bible conferences and often involving the same people were the so-called prophetic conferences that developed during the same period. These meetings were devoted exclusively to the study of biblical prophecy, especially the books of Daniel and Revelation. The first one was staged by Nathaniel West in October 1878 in New York City. Others followed in Chicago (1886), Brooklyn (1890), London (1891), Allegheny, Pennsylvania (1894), Boston (1901), and Chicago (1914).

The conference of February 1914 was the largest to that date. All the major denominations were represented, and the audiences heard John T. Stone, moderator of the Presbyterian church, Cyrus I. Scofield, Arno C. Gaebelein, Reuben A. Torrey, William B. Riley, and James M. Gray, whose addresses were later published as a book. Several smaller prophetic conferences were held in Minneapolis, St. Paul, St. Louis, and Los Angeles. The Moody Bible Institute, Northwestern College, and the Bible Institute of Los Angeles (BIOLA) hosted the conferences in their cities.[26] The sudden outbreak of the European war in August of that year confirmed the participants' expectation that the world was, indeed, drawing to an end. These conferences were the forerunners to the 1918–19 New York and Philadelphia prophetic meetings that led to the World's Christian Fundamentals Association.[27]

These conferences were vitally important to the rise of Fundamentalism. They gave conservatives of similar views from all the various denominations and from all parts of the nation and abroad a chance to meet and exchange ideas, especially on premillennialism, which led to a consciousness of their numerical strength. Leander W. Munhall, one of the founders of the original Bible conference, was still alive in 1922, and Reuben A. Torrey lived until 1928, thus establishing a continuity between men, ideas, and organizations.

The aggressive premillennial position produced enormous effects. The Adventist position suddenly gathered strength. "No doctrine has come to the front of Christian thought more prominently," said Nathaniel West, "than the pre-millennial return of Christ."[28] This twentieth-century emphasis avoided William Miller's errors of attempting to fix dates, but it did stress that Christ might return "at any moment."

The popularization of the Adventist doctrine led to increased study of the murky books of Daniel and Revelation, and such study carried with it an absolute insistence upon biblical literalism. It also harbored the seeds of fatalism. Like Marxism and Calvinism, however, this fatalism evoked great activity. Nor was it hard for conservatives to find evidence that the world was getting worse and worse: the war in Europe, the spread of higher criticism (the "theological forerunner of Anti-Christ"), and the successes of Mormonism, Christian Science, and the Jehovah's Witnesses, all were blatant examples.[29]

How should people confront this time of trouble? The conservative answer was simple—preach the Gospel. They had decided that it was not necessary to convert the world before the end of time. It was only necessary to present the Gospel to everyone.[30] All the evidence indicated that the "last days" were at hand, and their belief in this fact carried with it renewed stress on the literal authority of Scripture. "We always demand an authority in religion. The world always has," said Baptist Cortland Myers, pastor of Boston's Tremont Temple. "We will have no Pope, infallible or otherwise, for our authority; we will have only the Christ of the Book for our authority."[31] Premillennialism was not so much a doctrine or scheme of future events, noted Professor J. M. Stifler of Crozer Seminary in Chester, Pennsylvania, as it was an attitude toward Christ and His word that meant one would read the Bible exegetically and accept its plain statements in a common-sense fashion.[32]

Stifler was correct when he said that premillennialism was an attitude. Adoption of such an attitude, moreover, led directly to a new view of life and the world, as its adherents soon testified. When the truth of this view grips a person, believers noted, it makes time seem short and such worldly concerns as stocks, railroads, and business affairs less important.[33] At the 1914 conference, Charles G. Trumbull, editor of the *Sunday School Times*, compared accepting the premillennial view of the Bible with a second conversion. After reading William E. Blackstone's *Jesus Is Coming*, Trumbull noted, "God gave me not only a new conception of Christ, but a new Christ on that Sunday morning."[34] Howard W. Pope, superintendent of men at Moody Bible Institute, agreed. Pope noted that though the world could not be converted in his generation, it could be evangelized in that period of time. When he discovered this fact, he noted, "I was converted to the premillennial view as quickly as Saul was converted to Jesus Christ."[35]

Experience meetings now took on a new gloss. "How I became a pre-millennialist" became a standard theme among many conservatives. As James M. Gray wrote in 1895: "I know that I am a different man today from what I was twenty-five years ago prior to my conversion to Jesus Christ, and I attribute the change to that conversion; and I know I am a different Christian today from what I was say ten or twelve years ago, when the doctrine of our Lord's coming began to take hold of my spiritual consciousness, and I attribute the latter change to that fact."[36]

The series of conferences also provided opportunity for what would be one keynote of Fundamentalism in the 1920s—the formulation of creeds or confessions. Creedal statements of faith have played a large role in the Christian tradition. As a rule, they were created in regal splendor by assemblies of worthy divines and quickly became susceptible to a literalistic interpretation. The creeds were rarely biblical, and reformers have traditionally delighted in attacking them. The Northern Presbyterians were content to stick by the Westminster Confession, hammered out by the English Puritans in the seventeenth century, and in 1910, 1916, and 1923, the General Assembly simply reaffirmed its major points. For the Baptists, however, who had carefully avoided creeds in their turbulent history, this issue became crucial. The 1878 conference was one of the first to compile a list of points which the assembled deemed essential to Christianity.[37] The World's Christian Fundamentals Association formulated a nine-point creed, the Baptist New Hampshire Confession of Faith had eighteen points of belief, and BIOLA held fourteen points essential. The Northern Presbyterians reaffirmed five points of belief. The compilations all varied slightly, especially on the millennial question, but the doctrines of the infallibility of the Bible, Christ's Virgin Birth, His vicarious sacrifice, and His physical resurrection were almost always included.[38] In a day when liberals tended to scoff at creeds, another group had begun to stress them more and more.

Paralleling the development of the various conferences, and often connected with them through shared men and ideas, was the rise of the Bible school. The first to be established may have been the lay college adjunct of T. DeWitt Talmage's Tabernacle. Another claimant was the Nyack, New York, Missionary College set up by Albert B. Simpson in 1882. The most famous, Chicago's Moody Bible Institute (MBI) had roots back to 1873, but became firmly established only in the late 1880s. The usually accepted date of origin is 1886, although it was formally opened in 1889 and not named until 1900. Perhaps only a dozen evangelical liberal arts schools existed when MBI was founded. It sparked numerous others, however, and as William S. McBirnie has noted, became known as "the mother of most Bible institutes."[39]

MBI began when Dwight Moody found difficulty in getting enough trained pastors to aid him in his city evangelism efforts. Consequently, he came up with an ingenious solution: "I believe we have got to have gap-men," said Moody, "men to stand between the laity and the ministers; men who are trained to do city mission work."[40] Moody founded his school in the midst of fierce labor troubles in Chicago, and there was a sense of urgency in his scheme. "Either these people are to be evangelized," he said in March 1886, "or the leaven of communism and infidelity will assume such enormous proportions that it will break out in a reign of terror such as this country has never known."[41]

William Bell Riley's Northwestern Bible School (later Northwestern College) also became a bulwark of the Fundamentalists. It was founded in 1902, when 92 of Minnesota's 185 Baptist churches were without pastors, for the purpose of supplying the small towns in Iowa, Minnesota, North Dakota, and South Dakota with ministers. In 1946, Northwestern claimed over 1,700 graduates and 60 Baptist pastors in the area. The peopling of the state with his school's graduates eventually enabled Riley to gain control of the Minnesota Baptist Convention and to dominate many other Midwestern conservative organizations.[42]

Another important school was the Bible Institute of Los Angeles, established with Lyman Stewart's oil money. Thomas C. Horton, BIOLA's superintendent until 1925, and Reuben A. Torrey, who moved from the Moody Bible Institute and served as dean from 1912 to 1924, founded and provided the inspiration for the institution. When he heard about the proposed founding of BIOLA in 1907, James M. Gray, president of Moody Bible Institute, noted in a rare snatch of sardonic humor, "Why not make a trust of all these institutes and set ourselves up as Bible Barons?"[43]

The fortunes of BIOLA are intimately connected with the career of the Stewart brothers, Milton, and especially Lyman. Lyman Stewart was born in 1840 in Pennsylvania. He served in the Civil War and had both made and lost a fortune when he arrived in the Los Angeles area in the winter of 1882–83. There he struck one of the first oil wells in the region and in 1890 formed the Union Oil Company of California. Convinced that the Lord had allowed him to prosper for a purpose, he began to devote himself to conservative evangelical work. Although his name is not widely recognized today, he played a crucial role in the history of American Protestantism, becoming the main financial backer of the early Fundamentalist movement.

Lyman Stewart supported virtually every worthy cause in the Los Angeles area for many years. Of the hundreds of letters in the Stewart papers requesting funds, few indicate complete refusal. But his prime interest was evangelism, and he gladly supported oil-field evangelistic teams, China mission enterprises, the YMCA, a Gospel wagon, a Gospel boat, and even chapel railroad cars. Although he seems to have had some connection with Social Gospel issues during the depression of 1893–97—he once gave away food—toward the end of the decade he became extremely concerned over what he saw as the rise of apostasy.[44]

By 1906, he was badgering local YMCAs to exclude books written by such liberals as William Rainey Harper,[45] often making his contributions contingent upon these requests. Founder and financier from 1906 to 1916 of the chair of biblical literature at nearby Occidental College, he frequently pressured the president of the institution, John William Baer, to withdraw certain books. He attacked volumes of the Hastings *Encyclopaedia* and damned (without reading) several books by Baptist liberal Rush Rhees and others.[46] Eventually he excluded the Y from his contributions; by 1909, he was refusing to support any work except that following premillennial lines.[47] A college professor who once boarded with his sister and allegedly turned her sons into infidels made him especially suspicious of academics.[48] His financial power was so great that he was able to swing considerable weight in the area until he turned most of his attention to BIOLA.

Although Bible schools were originally set up to train "gap men," they soon became a short road to missionary service and to the ministry. Placing less emphasis on educational requirements than on a sincere profession of faith, they sent thousands of men and women out into the field. At a time when the theological seminaries were in trouble and the small, country churches were crying for ministers, the Bible schools filled the gaps. Within four years of BIOLA's founding, it was serving about a thousand students. By 1929 MBI alone had graduated over four thousand people. Baptist conservative Jasper C. Massee suggested that the latter school probably saved the evangelical churches from extinction.[49]

In addition to contributing to the rise of the Bible schools, conservatives expanded their publishing efforts. The *Sunday School Times* began its career as a children's paper but soon left that genre to become a strong voice for the conservative position. In 1903, the American Bible League chartered the *Bible Student and Teacher*. Numerous books also appeared. The most significant literary manifestation, however—the one that contributed most to popularizing the conservative cause—was the publication of twelve small paperback volumes, *The Fundamentals*, intermittently from 1909 to 1914. They appeared when the Social Gospel was at its height, but the real impetus to their publication came not from the Social Gospel but from conservative fear of higher criticism and theological liberalism.

Lyman Stewart had been toying with the idea of such a project for some time, and after hearing an especially impressive sermon by Amzi C. Dixon, then pastor of the Moody Church in Chicago, he decided to act.[50] He hoped that a conservative publication might help to stop the spread of heresy. In urging his brother Milton to support the cause, Lyman suggested that it was necessary for the welfare of both national and foreign fields. "It is for us to send out the 'testimony,' " he wrote Milton, "and leave the results to God."[51] He bemoaned the millions from the Rockefeller fortune that had gone to the University of Chicago to support liberalism, especially among the Baptists, and believed the Methodists suffered from the same liberal infection at Syracuse University, financed by John B. Archibald. The Presbyterians were equally troubled. But some instructors might have been teaching error out of ignorance; thus he believed the remedy would be a publication setting forth the truth. For this purpose, he put up $300,000 in securities. "This will be such a testimony," he said, "doubtless as has never before been presented simultaneously to the English speaking churches, and will tend to temporarily check error and purify the streams through which the gospel is to be given to the heathen. But the *influence* of this testimony would be much greater if it could be sent also to the Protestant preachers and teachers of the other leading languages of the world."⁵² Thus were created the twelve booklets called *The Fundamentals*. As they were printed, these books were sent "to every pastor, evangelist, missionary, theological professor, theological student, Sunday School superintendent, YMCA and YWCA secretary in the English speaking world, so far as the addresses of all these can be obtained."⁵³

Amzi C. Dixon, a Baptist who was prominent internationally, accepted editorship of the project. He did a good job as head of the editorial committee and in compiling the first five volumes. When he was called to the pastorate of Charles Spurgeon's London Tabernacle in 1911, Louis Meyer became editor and published another five volumes before his sudden death. Reuben Torrey edited the last two volumes. The original plan was to issue twelve books, one every two or three months, but the interval between the later volumes was longer. Over two and a half million copies were issued, and with demands for back numbers pouring in, the total publication ran to nearly three million, one-third going outside the United States, chiefly to England.⁵⁴

Many respected conservative scholars from all over the world argued their positions in the first volumes. Professor James Orr of the United Free Church College in Glasgow, Charles R. Erdman of Princeton, Professor Benjamin B. Warfield of Princeton, Amzi C. Dixon, Reuben A. Torrey, George F. Wright of Oberlin, Phillip Mauro, a New York lawyer, James M. Gray of Moody Bible Institute, and Edgar Y. Mullins of Southern Baptist Theological Seminary were only a few of the men who expressed their views in the early volumes. The first books show a positive approach to the question of religion, and only in the later volumes can traces be seen of the invective that became characteristic of the movement in the 1920s. Attacks against the Roman Catholic church as "the antagonist of the nation," against the Mormons, the Christian Scientists, and the Millennial Dawnists did not emerge until the later volumes. This change could be interpreted as a shift from the offensive to the defensive position during the five-year period, but it more probably resulted from the change in editors.⁵⁵

The arguments presented in these volumes include virtually all of those touched on in the 1920s. It is interesting to note, however, that evolution was the sole topic of only two articles. Instead, higher criticism came under the heaviest attack, and articles on that subject clearly illustrated the dilemma confronting the conservatives. Robert Anderson noted that the higher critics too often began with rationalistic presuppositions, whereas true higher criticism maintained an open mind. James Orr and W. H. Griffith-Thomas agreed. One commentator noted, "No study perhaps required so devout a spirit and so exalted a faith in the supernatural as the pursuit of the higher criticism." Without faith, he continued, no one can explain the Bible, and without scholarship no one can investigate its origin.[56] A few of the arguments were on the level of "the old is better," but most were fairly sophisticated. One reason for their high level was that higher criticism was a very difficult topic and discussing it intelligently demanded considerable knowledge. One could easily devote a lifetime to the study of the Gospels alone. When dealing with higher criticism writers seldom conducted irrational tirades, for the critics' goal—understanding the Bible—was also the goal of the Fundamentalists. But both sides clearly saw the importance of the critical studies. When Julius Wellhausen was asked if he felt the Bible could keep the same position in church life if his critical views were accepted, the German replied, "I cannot see how that is possible."[57]

The files of BIOLA contain numerous replies from the people to whom the booklets were sent that give an understanding of the need they met. The voices were almost all united in praise. A man from Canada said that the books were a major help to him, for he had been fighting the destructive effects of higher criticism for years. A Baptist minister from Massachusetts urged Stewart to get copies into the hands of every preacher and Christian worker of the land. Were he to do so, the minister said, "you will be rendering one of the greatest services that you could possibly render to this generation."[58]

The Fundamentals project cost several hundred thousand dollars and clearly helped to polarize the existing factions in every denomination. Liberal authors were convinced that the majority of those who received the books threw them away, but they did admit that some people might like them and that their dissemination would only make the liberal task harder.[59] One letter from two laymen noted, "As soon as we see them come in, we fire them into the stove! They are out of date, outgrown seventeenth century in thought, an impertinence to this age, and an insult to any thinking clergyman who wants to live in and think in today."[60]

The liberals underestimated the response. Over one hundred thousand people wrote to request copies of issues they had missed.[61] Letters of praise continued to come in until 1916. An Illinois pastor said that the booklets had set liberal Christianity back a full generation. "Truly," wrote Reverend John H. Burrows, "the Lord is using the little volumes widely."[62]

Union Oil was worth nearly $25 million in 1916 and had profits of between $6 and $7 million; a surprising amount of these profits was spent on religious affairs. Lyman Stewart was deeply convinced of the truth of premillennialism and therefore never contributed to any endowment fund because he expected the world to end at any time. In 1916, he reasoned that this time was, indeed, drawing near. He began selling stock and increasing his publication efforts, and for aid he turned to his old friend, William E. Blackstone.[63]

Born into a New York Methodist family in 1841, Blackstone served with the United States Christian Commission during the Civil War and then migrated to the Chicago area to make his fortune in construction and investments. Convinced of the literal truth of prophecy, he became one of the first Americans to advocate the return of the Jews to Palestine. Accordingly, in 1890 he organized and chaired the first conference between Christians and Jews in Chicago and sent the czar a resolution expressing sympathy for the plight of the Russian Jews. The next year he sponsored a "memorial" on behalf of the Russian Jews. Signed by 413 prominent Americans (including Cyrus McCormick, John D. Rockefeller, and J. Pierpont Morgan), the memorial, which urged that Palestine be given back to the Jews, was forwarded to President Benjamin Harrison. In 1916, Blackstone sponsored another memorial to Woodrow Wilson with the same message. Although he always advocated conversion of the Jews, Blackstone has nevertheless been acclaimed as one of the fathers of the Zionist movement.[64]

In 1878, Blackstone published a small volume, *Jesus Is Coming*, that saw modest distribution among premillennarians. Filled with biblical verses and complicated eschatological charts, it argued that the "perilous times" were imminent. This book might have dropped into oblivion except that in 1906 Lyman Stewart decided he wanted to help distribute a good study of the Second Advent. Choosing Blackstone's work, Stewart helped fund a special 1908 edition that was sent free to thousands of theological students and missionaries. As a consequence, *Jesus Is Coming* eventually received the most widespread distribution of any piece of premillennial literature. By the time of Blackstone's death, November 7, 1936, at age ninety-four, the book had been published in forty-eight languages, and over one million copies were in print.[65]

Lyman Stewart credited this volume with conveying the truth of premillennialism to him, and in 1916–17 he gave over to Blackstone's care several trusts totaling over $5 million. Although the trusts had advisory committees to offer suggestions, Blackstone retained the final decision on allocation of the money. The fund produced and distributed conservative literature both at home and abroad. Stewart carefully instructed Blackstone to spend the money only to promote premillennial enterprises. Blackstone managed the fund so well that he earned an extra million dollars, and for twenty years this money was spent as Stewart had directed. Needless to say, it became the bête noire of the liberals.[66]

Material in the William B. Riley manuscript collection at Northwestern College suggests that conflict between conservatives and liberals might have come much earlier had World War I not diverted the growing theological antagonisms. In 1908, only one year after the Northern Baptist Convention was formed, Riley publicly advocated that Baptists contemplate a split. He noted that the Presbyterians seemed to have destroyed any seeds of heresy by swift disciplinary action and thereby had strengthened themselves considerably. He urged that the Baptists follow their example. "The fact is, the day is not far away when there will be a division in the Baptist denomination over the question of theology," he wrote, "and I, for one, believe it desirable." Others also felt that a division might soon be in the offing.[67]

The events of 1910, however, fully aroused Riley's consciousness concerning the menace of creeping liberalism. The Northern Baptist Convention for that year was scheduled to be held on the campus of the University of Chicago, which Riley felt was an insult to all conservatives. Of the voluminous correspondence that must have crossed his desk, there remains only one small file drawer, but the letters there are very revealing concerning this incident. Riley sent out many letters to his conservative friends and urged that the time had come for swift action. Were there hesitation, he said, the convention would become a tail of the University of Chicago. As he stated in one letter, "If we sit still, not even taking a positive stand in this matter in any organized or co-operative way, at the rate we are not driving, fifteen years more will see every organization we have in the Northern states in the hands of the destructive critics."[68]

The plans he suggested laid out the form that the actual Fundamentalist break followed nine years later. Riley carefully compiled lists of men of whom he was suspicious and those he felt to be solid in the faith. He believed that most of the Baptist journals—the *Examiner*, the *Journal* and *Messenger*, the *Christian Herald*, the *Pacific Coast Baptist*, and the southern papers—would support such a move. He was suspicious only of the *Standard* and the eastern papers. "The time has come for the Baptists of America to declare themselves," he wrote in a letter to the *Examiner*, "unless we are willing to surrender our honored heritage to Unitarian heretics."[69] He proposed that a group of fifteen to twenty conservative pastors sign a statement attacking the current theological drift and protesting holding the convention in Chicago. He hoped to get Baptist leader J. Whitcomb Brougher of California to sign the document but decided himself to remain in the background and asked conservative pastor John M. Dean of Seattle to put pressure on Brougher. He was convinced that a well-reasoned, widely published statement in Baptist journals would have many benefits. He also urged that the conservatives all gather together a few days before the convention in Johnston Meyer's Chicago church. They might not accomplish anything, but the fact of their gathering would show the Modernists they were not alone and would give the conservatives an idea of their allies.

Riley apparently was the originator of the idea of a conservative preconvention conference, but, because he was based in Minneapolis, he felt that the call would have more effect if it came from Chicago. Riley wrote the call and suggested that similar meetings might be held concurrently in such cities as Philadelphia, New York, Seattle, Portland, Los Angeles, and Denver. He believed that conservatives all over the nation were simply waiting for a chance to make known their views. Had he been content to issue the call by himself, the Fundamentalist controversy might have erupted in 1910, for the program he suggested was the same as that which was carried out after the war. But his insistence upon having the call come from Chicago, where the convention was to be held, doomed it. Meyers favored the idea, but did not want to be held responsible for it, and by the time the other arrangements had been made, a preconvention meeting no longer seemed relevant.[70]

Indecision, the lack of coordinating power, and personal hesitation all seemed to be reasons for the failure of the 1910 call. These problems were not lost on Riley. For the next few years, however, he seems to have diverted his energies to other affairs. In 1911, he received an invitation from his good friend Amzi C. Dixon to come to London to speak, and he did so in the following year. The *Minneapolis Tribune* reported that he took a year's leave of absence in 1914, and he also held some of his most extensive revivals during that period. The Northern Baptist Convention seemed to go smoothly, and when the war broke out in 1914, it provided an issue that drew attention away from the traditional denominational difficulties, and the controversy brewed for another few years.

7
World War I and
The Rise of Aggressive
Fundamentalism

The outbreak of World War I severely shocked all elements of American Protestantism. Before 1914, it was widely believed that future wars, if they occurred at all, would be limited to underdeveloped countries. In 1912, in a widely publicized prayer, Congregationalist minister Washington Gladden expressed his belief that the Lord was closer to that age than to any other. Yet, scarcely two years after Gladden's prayer, the most widespread disaster since the Black Death had engulfed the most civilized area of the globe. Although America was not drawn into the conflict until 1917, the tensions preceding that decision produced such a change of atmosphere that historian Henry F. May has called the period 1912–17 "the end of American innocence."[1]

America's entry into the conflict produced a strong display of solidarity from all elements of Protestantism. From the moment the Northern Presbyterian church told President Woodrow Wilson they would support him, both liberal and conservative Protestants rallied behind the allied war effort. The nation witnessed the rise of what John M. Mecklin termed "militant ecclesiastics."[2] Stories of German atrocities frequently were aired from the pulpit. Henry Van Dyke of the Brick Presbyterian Church in New York City, Newell Dwight Hillis of the Marble Collegiate Church in Manhattan (both liberals), and conservative evangelist Billy Sunday were especially guilty of such excesses. One minister wore a naval uniform when preaching to his congregation.

The war dampened enthusiasm for all things German and made "German theology" even more an anathema than before. Many calls were made for an American response to "German thought." Germany "has methodically insinuated herself into every type of educational institution in America, and has so *kulturized* our thinking at its formative sources," complained E. W. Thornton in the *Christian Standard*, "that, until recently we turned up our noses at our own achievements and swallowed everything 'made in Germany,' from limburger cheese to theology."[3] Charles Stelzle warned the nation that it had to reckon with "Kaiser Bill Hohenzollern" as well as "Kaiser John Barleycorn." The *King's Business* joined "Kaiser Bill and Kaiser Beer."[4] Reverend George F. Pentecost of the Bethany Presbyterian Church in Philadelphia gave a series of sermons on the war, all of which later were printed as pamphlets. In one, he confessed that his object was to show that "the Kaiser was nothing less than the embodied representative of the Devil, the archenemy of God and man."[5]

Ray Abrams, in his *Preachers Present Arms* (1933), has argued that almost all American clerics vigorously supported the allied war effort. William R. Hutchison, however, believes that Abrams may have exaggerated. Over half of the liberal Protestant ministers Hutchison studied were "reluctant" supporters of the war, and many others were critical of it.[6] The minister of the Federated Church in Flagstaff, Arizona, for example, spoke out against allied bombing of civilian areas. A few clergymen, usually with German antecedents (such as Walter Rauschenbusch), viewed the war as a tragedy for both sides.

The question of the extent of ministerial involvement will never be satisfactorily resolved, for statements of outright opposition were rare because of concern for popular opinion. Pro-allied sermons were much more likely to have been printed. It is certain, however, that antagonisms between liberals and conservatives were momentarily forgotten as ministers of all shades of belief threw their efforts behind President Wilson. Statements on the war from such conservatives as Frank M. Goodchild, Cortland Meyers, Mark A. Matthews, George W. McPherson, and Isaac M. Haldeman could have been interchanged with those of such liberals as Shailer Mathews and Harry Emerson Fosdick.[7] On this issue, at least, there was genuine agreement.

The war also produced a revival of interest in biblical prophecy, for it seemed to vindicate many of the premillennialists' predictions of disaster. The idea that the war had inaugurated the "Last Days" received so much circulation that some people even began setting dates.[8] But the figure of Christ which the premillennialists now offered had changed considerably from the open-hearted savior pictured by Dwight L. Moody. Christ had now become the Avenging Angel who was to bring in His kingdom in a violent fashion. Arno C. Gaebelein claimed, "We can almost feel his breath," and Amzi C. Dixon noted in 1917, that "the Return of the Lord may be expected at any moment." Isaac M. Haldeman spoke of a Christ who "comes forth as one who no longer seeks either friendship or love. . . . His garments are dipped in blood, the blood of others. He descends that he may shed the blood of men."[9]

The war also brought about an increased number of premillennial conferences. The federal government was said to have become uneasy over the growth of such activities, and the titles of the conferences were changed from "Coming of the Lord" to "Prophetic Conferences" under its pressure. Premillennial views were said to be harmful to the doctrines of reform, peace, and democracy because they taught that no human activity was worthy of effort. If the end of the world were imminent, the argument went, why bother fighting the Germans?

Liberals were appalled at the spread of premillennial literature during wartime. Professor Shirley Jackson Case of the University of Chicago suggested in *The Millennial Hope* (1918) that the premillennialists were subversives.[10] In an interview with the *Chicago Daily News* in January, 1918, he said that money for the spread of this doctrine came largely from German sources. The Chicago Divinity School found itself besieged with requests to combat premillennialism.[11] Charles C. Morrison, editor of the liberal Protestant *Christian Century*, and Alfred Dieffenbach, editor of the Unitarian *Christian Register*, were especially critical of premillennialism. Dieffenbach called the idea of the imminent second coming "the most astounding mental aberration in the field of religious thinking" and claimed that it made Christianity materialistic.[12] The *Christian Century* ran a series by Herbert L. Willett in which he accused the premillennarians of deliberately trying to pervert the Bible and of gross and culpable ignorance. He felt that theirs was a theory of despair.[13] Shailer Mathews wrote "Will Christ Come Again?" to support Willett's position and declared premillennialists irresponsible.[14] Alva W. Taylor compared them with the Bolsheviks, claiming that both were cataclysmic thinkers who wanted the world remade in a day.[15]

Several conservative thinkers rose to defend the preaching of this doctrine. James M. Gray editorialized in the *Moody Bible Institute Monthly* that it was the opponents of the premillennial position who were dangerous to the war effort; their pacifism had allowed the army of the United States to decline and that of Germany to rise. All premillenarians were set on waging war, he said, and wanted no compromise that depended upon the faith of the Central Powers. Although he freely admitted that there were other truths in the Bible, he felt that existing circumstances had forced him to give the premillennial position primary attention.[16] Thomas C. Horton of BIOLA ranked Professor Shirley Case's charges of disloyalty with the Salem witchcraft accusations. Not only was the charge of German sources ridiculous, he said, but the real threat from Germany lay in another area—higher criticism.[17]

William B. Riley was quick to jump to the defense on another level. He argued that the liberals' claim that a billionaire was behind the wide distribution of premillennial literature was absurd; it had appeared simply in response to a public demand. He laughed at the idea that premillennialism had its source in Germany and should be investigated. No intelligent holder of their position he said, felt that John Wesley was the star seen to fall from heaven or that 666, the mark of the beast, applied to the kaiser. He countered the charge of subversion by citing the fact that four sons of conservative Canadian Reverend Philpotts were fighting in Europe. Riley saw the liberal charges as an attempt to divide the conservatives on the millennial issue. After the war he did his best to quell the rumors that the Northern Baptist Convention was about to split on the issue of the second coming.[18]

This chiliastic theme, however, eventually proved to be a divisive issue among conservatives. In 1921, Obadiah Holmes claimed that "the cult of 'fundamentalism,' with its verbal inspiration and infallibility, is chiliasm or premillennialism or adventism with a new name."[19] But the moderate conservatives vigorously denied this charge. Baptist Curtis Lee Laws insisted that Fundamentalism included pre-, post-, and a-millennialists, but his voice was drowned out by the radicals. George W. McPherson called postmillennialism "hersey." J. Frank Norris noted, "War is declared—the second coming is the issue."[20] On another occasion, Norris said: "But when a man tells me he believes in the literal, personal, bodily, visible, imminent return of the Lord to this earth as King, I know what he believes on every other question. . . . I know he is not a Modernist, and I know that he does not believe in the evolutionary hypothesis."[21] The search for one point on which to test the faithful settled on the Virgin Birth in the late 1920s, but for a period in the early 1920s, it included for many the eschatological question. Isaac M. Haldeman even insisted that this issue involved believing or disbelieving the Bible.[22]

For most of the war years, however, the spirit of cooperation prevailed, largely because American clerics of all beliefs hoped that the end of the conflict would usher in a new era of peace. Few voiced the pessimism of Georges Clemenceau, who stated that making a peace would be harder than winning the war.[23]

After the armistice of 1918, both liberals and conservatives were convinced that the nation was about to enter into a new and exciting period. William H. P. Faunce, president of Brown University, expressed this feeling:

> The great war has not yet brought us peace or happiness, but it has brought us amazing opportunity. Fused in the fires of the awful struggle, the whole world now lies plastic to the hand of faith. The foundations of the great deep are broken up, barriers are broken, boundaries are shattered and the whole world is a molten mass, and before it cools Christianity may stamp upon it the image and superscription of God. Twenty years from now it will be impossible; five years from now it will be too late. This one year will shape the thousand years that follow after.[24]

Hope that a new era was dawning was not limited to liberals. Conservative John R. Straton spoke of meeting the challenge of opportunity which the war had prepared and commented in *The Menace of Immorality in Church and State* (1920): "There never was a moment in history so solemn as the present moment, or one more pregnant with eternal destiny."[25] He rejoiced that the war was calling men back to a new sense of moral responsibility and religion. The sacrifices of the soldiers, he noted, made the idea of Christ's supernatural and vicarious sacrifice seem less strange. In a sermon he said, "Beyond any question we are at the dawning of a new day in the history of humanity. One era is closing and another is opening."[26] Four years later, he sadly noted that the Baptists had failed to take advantage of the greatest opportunity they had ever had.[27] James M. Gray, head of the Moody Bible Institute, felt much the same way. He spoke in September 1919 on the approaching end of an age, and another time he noted, "If our Lord tarries we are expecting a great revival of pure and undefiled religion after the war. . . . Yes we are looking for a great revival of religion when we bring the enemy to his knees. God hasten the day."[28]

But what form would a revival of religion take and what would a modern world be like? On this question liberals and conservatives had very different plans. Both shared great hope that the church would play a major role in the reconstruction, but they were talking about different kinds of churches, and both moved forward with their plans at approximately the same time.

Almost all liberals agreed with Rabbi Emanuel Sternheim, Brown President William H. P. Faunce, and University of Chicago theologian Gerald B. Smith that the new era would belong to the people. Democracy in the churches would be the order of the day.[29] Moreover, the new church would be united. John H. Holmes, pastor of the Unitarian Church of the Messiah in New York City noted: "In the fusing fires of battle, Presbyterian, Methodist, Episcopalian, Unitarian, and even Catholic, Protestant, and Jew have been melted, and now flow in a single flaming stream. Man after man has returned from the front to tell us that the denominational church is dead."[30] The task of religion in the new age, said Universalist minister John Smith Lowe, would be to abolish special privilege and to champion causes of world democracy and world brotherhood. Its task would be in this world. God would look after the next world without anyone's help, he said, but the Kingdom of God on earth could not even be approximated without human effort.[31]

Never had liberal hopes for reunion of Christendom been so high. The interdenominational societies of the nineteenth century (such as the American Bible Society, YMCA, and Evangelical Alliance) were seen as but precursors of the new alliance that was to emerge. Some even spoke of combining Protestantism with the Roman and Orthodox Catholics.[32]

Unfortunately, however, these attempts at interdenominational cooperation proved disastrous. Only the Canadians succeeded in uniting their major Protestant bodies in 1925. The chief fiasco was the ill-fated Interchurch

World Movement of North America, which flourished from 1919 to 1920. Born at a meeting in New York in December 1918, this movement was an attempt to unite all the benevolent and missionary agencies of American Protestantism into a single campaign for money, men, and spiritual power. One scholar has suggested that it was the final bloom of the Progressive and Social Gospel crusading spirit. It has even been called the religious counterpart of the League of Nations.[33]

Billed as a "religious reconstructional enterprise," the movement was an expression of the hope to sustain the wartime cooperation among the churches.[34] The wide publicity it received led to the rise of extravagant hopes. Great theologians were lacking, however, and the efforts of great bureaucrats were inadequate. Promises were made of over $140 million in contributions but only $3 million was raised, and the "friendly citizens" to whom financial appeals were directed never materialized. The churches were forced to contribute from their own budgets. Simultaneously with this financial difficulty came the great steel strike of 1919, and the Industrial Relations Department of the Interchurch Movement made a lengthy report on working conditions. They publicized the steel industry's twelve-hour day, seven-day week, and twenty-four-hour shift to a surprised national audience. Contemporaries, especially Rabbi Stephen S. Wise, felt certain that adverse reaction to this report killed the Interchurch Movement. Others, however, felt that it was already moribund when the report was published and that the report simply provided the coup de grace. Not until 1924 were the movement's numerous debts paid. One lesson to be learned, remarked the *Presbyterian of the South* sadly, was that the work of the Lord cannot be done as well outside the church as it can be done by the church itself.[35]

World War I, consequently, had an important effect on the development of the conservative conscience. It seemed to prove the truth of prophecy. It provided an enemy in "German thought," an aggressive rhetoric, and a feeling of what cooperation could accomplish. It also demonstrated that Christianity and violent action were not always incompatible. The only vital element lacking was direction, and William B. Riley was more than willing to supply leadership.

From about 1917 to 1922, the organizing genius of American Fundamentalism lay with William B. Riley. He had been eager to move in 1910 but had been unable to do so. In 1917, he entitled a chapter of his *Menace of Modernism* "Is a Confederacy of Conservatives the Call of the Hour?" In August of that year, he and Amzi C. Dixon attended Reuben A. Torrey's summer conference at Montrose, Pennsylvania. One rainy morning, they began a long discussion of the theological and church situations in the countries they knew best—England, Canada, and the United States—and decided to call a meeting of those present for the next afternoon in Torrey's home. At that meeting, they formed a new organization. W. H. Griffith-Thomas of Wycliff College in Toronto was chosen president, and William Evans was elected secretary. Eighteen months of inaction followed, however, until Riley decided to take matters into his own hands. Although he had great admiration for his comrades, Evans, Dixon, and Griffith-Thomas, he realized they lacked organizational ability.[36]

Riley decided to make his move at the New York Prophetic Conference held in Carnegie Hall, November 25–28, 1918, a meeting that was widely heralded as the greatest of its kind ever held in America. The call for the conference had been sent out by "100 New Yorkers" before the war had terminated and this timing, plus the calling of the 1914 conference before the war had broken out, was considered of special significance. Carnegie Hall overflowed nightly; the crowds listened to the music of Charles M. Alexander and to a wide variety of addresses. The format of the conference was traditional. The impassioned speeches were later printed as a book, *Christ and Glory*. W. H. Griffith-Thomas expressed grave doubt about the efficacy of a League of Nations. The world, he declared, should not so much be made safe for democracy as "made safe by the autocracy of Jesus Christ."[37]

Although Leander W. Munhall and Riley both credited the origin of the Fundamentalist movement not to any one person but to a demand emanating from the people, a good case can be made that the militant Minneapolis preacher did more to set the movement going than any other single individual.[38] Riley's organizational talents fitted perfectly with the demands of the time. He used the 1918 Prophetic Conference to set up the 1919 conference at Philadelphia. He was also the driving force behind this meeting, even though the actual arrangements were handled locally by J. D. Adams, whom Riley instructed about preparation of programs and composition of the executive committees. The same group of men who had underwritten the 1918 conference for $15,000 were again called upon and again they responded.

Most of the area newspapers gave wide coverage to the meeting. Six thousand conservatives from forty-two states and eight foreign countries met in Philadelphia for an eight-day session. The major addresses were published in *God Hath Spoken*, and the book was widely distributed. Riley was pleased at the turnout, especially the number of visitors from overseas, for he had planned this as a worldwide conference. "And I want it to shake this continent as it has never been shaken," he wrote, "and it is going to do it! The critics are already shaking with fear and the conservatives with delight."[39]

The Philadelphia conference completed the formation of the World's Christian Fundamentals Association (WCFA). After the conference concluded, Riley took a group of fourteen speakers and singers on a cross-country tour which he had spent almost a year arranging. The speakers included the cream of the Fundamentalist crop: Charles A. Blanchard, Jasper C.

Massee, W. Leon Tucker, William L. Pettingill, Luther Little, Mark A. Matthews, and Amzi C. Dixon. With the aid of local ministers, they moved in a three-pronged sweep across the continent from Philadelphia westward, holding three- to six-day conferences in major cities in their path.

Their long familiarity with church conferences made the Fundamentalists well aware of the value of the conference in the defense of the faith. The growth of the Bible schools, increased publications, and sympathetic ministers all aided their cause, but the organized conference provided the most effective mode of presenting their views to the public. Conferences gave them a sense of solidarity and often brought nationally famous speakers to local areas. This conference campaign of 1919 was probably one of the largest religious programs the nation had seen for two generations. Among the cities hit were Minneapolis, Des Moines, Denver, Great Falls, Calgary, Edmonton, Vancouver, Seattle, Portland, and Colorado Springs. The trip covered seven thousand miles and eighteen cities, and plans for regional conferences were set to follow. Whenever possible, a permanent organization was established before the campaign moved on.

Riley faced enormous problems in arranging this tour. It took him three weeks to set up the small Butler, Pennsylvania, conference, and no sooner was the one in Buffalo prepared than telegrams poured in demanding changes. "You think that you have a big job on your hands with this one conference," he complained to J. D. Adams, "and you have; but, man alive, think of me trying to get twenty-five of these, yea seventy-five, arranged and going. It is simply maddening."[40] Riley ingeniously planned each conference so that the principal speakers were not sitting around idle while the local ministers spoke. Each visitor gave his address and then moved on to the next conference. And, interestingly, hardly any of the speakers discussed the subject of evolution. "I believe the hour has come," noted E. A. Wollam in 1919, "when the evangelistic forces of this country, primarily the Bible Institutes, should not only rise up in defense of the faith, but should become a united and offensive power."[41]

The liberals were caught completely off guard. In only two cities were resolutions passed by liberal ministers protesting against such a Fundamentalist invasion. The response to Riley's series of conferences was so powerful that he was probably correct in saying that this movement was a major factor in bringing the conservatives to a consciousness of their strength.[42] He noted, for example: "The future will look back to the World Conference on Christian Fundamentals, held in Philadelphia, May 25 to June 1, 1919, as an event of more historical moment than the nailing up, at Wittenburg, of Martin Luther's ninety-five theses. The hour has struck for the rise of a new Protestantism."[43]

8

The Fundamentalist-Modernist Controversy, 1918–1930

A wave of optimism swept across the nation after the signing of the 1918 armistice. The war, one commentator noted, had formed "an abyss of fire and death between the past and the future."[1] Peace, said another, would usher in "a new age; not so much because the map of Europe will be changed but rather because the map of the human mind will be changed."[2] "This," said Presbyterian minister J. Wilbur Chapman in January 1919, "is the day of the churches' glorious opportunity."[3]

Failure of these grand hopes to come about is the key to understanding the Protestant reaction in the 1920s. The despair was almost as great as the hopes that had been raised. In addition to despair over Christianity's failure to capture the world in the 1920s, the churches were troubled by: the growing conservative conviction that liberalism was in the ascendancy in many denominations, a militant premillennialism that had entrenched itself in many Bible schools and was not yet viewed by other conservatives as appreciably different from their own position, new aggressive conservative leadership under William B. Riley, and the evolution issue as revived by William Jennings Bryan. Here were all the necessary ingredients for a major social upheaval. Disruption took the form of the Fundamentalist-Modernist controversy that racked the churches during the 1920s, with consequences that remain evident today.[4]

Bryan and evolution will be discussed in the next two chapters. This chapter will concentrate on the role of William B. Riley and the World's Christian Fundamentals Association; the reactions of the Northern Baptists and Presbyterians, the two denominations most directly affected; and the responses of the other major Protestant bodies.

The World's Christian Fundamentals Association was only one of the numerous interdenominational Fundamentalist groups formed in the post-war years.[5] Its eventual emergence as the major organization of its kind was largely due to the leadership of William B. Riley. Riley should be recognized as the most important Fundamentalist leader of the early 1920s, the organizer of the initial conservative response to the liberal threat.

The activity of William B. Riley during the early years of the decade, when the outcome of the Fundamentalist controversy was still in question, was astounding. He spent these years running a large, downtown Minneapolis church, speaking up to four times a day, administering his Northwestern College, organizing hundreds of conferences, and editing, at one time, three separate journals. His energy seemed limitless.

During the most active days of the conflict, however, Riley tended to leave Northwestern College affairs to his lieutenants while he concentrated on his role as founder, president, chairman of the Conference Committee, and later executive secretary of the WCFA. In many ways, the WCFA illustrated in miniature the problems that confronted the Fundamentalists in their attempts at interdenominational organization. Although it claimed the title "world's," it was hardly that, and it even came under criticism for having too many Baptists in positions of leadership.[6] Nor was it able to achieve its goal of creating a federation of all conservatives opposed to Modernism, as it had hoped. In spite of talk about union with the English Fundamentalists and the China Bible Union, no significant joint action was accomplished. In spite of the criticism that the WCFA was dominated by Baptists, the organization was not even able to garner support from all the conservative members of that denomination. Curtis L. Laws made it very clear in his *Watchman-Examiner* that the WCFA was the interdenominational Fundamentalist movement, whereas the Fundamentalist Fellowship represented the strictly Baptist movement.[7] Although an effort was made at first to include both pre- and postmillennialists, the WCFA soon coalesced around the former group. The strength, egos, and geographical location of the various Fundamentalist leaders also precluded close cooperation or federation. Each man was a giant in his own bailiwick, and no man other than Bryan was invited into another's area, except temporarily. Riley, for example, had little contact with John R. Straton, never met J. Gresham Machen, broke with J. Frank Norris in 1927 when Norris shot and killed a man, and bitterly attacked Edgar Y. Mullins in the pages of his *Beacon*. Because of its active role in the organization of the Tennessee, Kentucky, Arkansas, and Minnesota antievolution fights, the papers frequently considered the WCFA to be the directing force and center of the antievolution movement. Although the WCFA appears to have been the most powerful and, thanks to Riley, the most ably directed Fundamentalist organization, it would be a mistake to see it as the major directing force of Fundamentalism from which all others took their cue. It was active, but by no means the cogwheel of the movement.

The question of how the Fundamentalist movement was financed is complicated, and satisfactory evidence will probably never be compiled. The liberals were convinced that there were vast sums of money behind organized Fundamentalist activities. One Columbia professor postulated a fund of $60 million.[8] Riley insisted, however, that there was no such backing from men of wealth, and that, except for *The Fundamentals,* the movement had received no gift over $150. Instead, he claimed, all expenses were paid from membership fees, collections at the meetings, and voluntary contributions. Fundamentalism arose because of a public demand, he insisted, and was financed from the same source.[9] Riley had great ability in getting crowds to contribute, and in both Fundamentalism and antievolution he had issues that deeply moved many Americans. He felt convinced that the movement came simultaneously from both God and the people. There is good reason to believe, however, that at least some money came from the financial elite. Reuben Saillens, for example, was given $30,000 to start a Bible school in France. Riley's denial of any concerted attempt to attract the wealthy conflicts with the frequent appeal for fifty millionaires to donate to establish an orthodox premillennial seminary.[10] Although the fifty millionaires never appeared, such men as J. C. Penney and George F. Washburn always contributed freely, and the Stewart brothers of California provided a steady influx of money. It seems probable, therefore, that there was financial support from both above and below and more from above than Riley was willing to admit.

Throughout the decade, the WCFA held annual conferences, and these widely publicized gatherings offered a convenient public forum for speeches, resolutions, and statements of belief. The annual WCFA conferences were enthusiastically attended until 1930, when they declined abruptly because of the Depression. The organization, however, continued to hold smaller meetings well into the 1940s. The WCFA has been seen as the predecessor to the present National Association of Evangelicals.[11]

Equally as important to the Fundamentalist-Modernist controversy was the Fundamentalists' attempt to involve the various Protestant denominations in their activities. This they did immediately, for the leaders all began as strong denominational men, and here they came face to face with the situation described in the committee reports printed in *God Hath Spoken*. Over the years, the liberals had silently slipped into the positions of power and responsibility, especially in the two denominations most immediately affected, the Northern Baptists and Northern Presbyterians.

In the 1919 Northern Baptist Convention meeting at Denver, for example, the liberals engineered passage of a series of proposals that spread considerable fear among the conservatives. The convention voted to enter the Interchurch World Movement, to adopt a single unified budget, and to form a general board of promotion. All these were seen as moves toward centralization on a liberal basis. Centralization was especially feared by the Baptists, who were proud of their heritage of local control. In addition, the Northern Baptist Convention voted to consolidate most of the Baptist journals into one denominational magazine, the *Baptist,* which, it was hoped, would speak for all positions. Curtis Lee Laws was especially uneasy over this maneuver. He refused to give up his *Watchman-Examiner* and bitterly complained because the *Baptist* was given a subsidy, whereas his magazine received none. General suspicion over what views the *Baptist* would present were not entirely unfounded, for it maintained a wavering liberal position until it merged with the *Christian Century* in 1931. Thus, as a response, the regular 1920 convention in Buffalo was preceded by a conservative call for a preconvention meeting to discuss some of their grievances. At this meeting, the first major Fundamentalist movement within a main line denomination was launched. The conservatives were reacting against what they saw as a liberal takeover of the denominational machinery.

The Fundamentalist-Modernist conflict really began with the conservatives' action within the denominations. The stakes were high, for the ultimate question was which group and which theological position would control the churches. Religious affairs, especially when they are plagued by dispute, make interesting reading, and the nation's press was not long in publicizing the clash. An age that later would be labeled "post-Christian" was momentarily filled with heated discussions over the Westminster Confession, miracles, various creeds of belief, and the meaning of the biblical narratives. But the Bible is complex, and discussions over fine points were soon lost in the two issues around which most of the debate during the 1920s revolved: the imminent second coming of Christ and His Virgin Birth.

The Baptists were especially susceptible to controversy of this type because of the nature of their polity. The Northern Baptist Convention is simply a gathering of the individual Baptist churches to carry out their common interests. Consequently, it had not the power, as did the General Assembly of the Presbyterians, for example, to affirm any major position.[12] In addition, Baptists have always been proud of the fact that they have never been bound by any creed. Their past contains confessions of faith, but these have never been seen as binding in the sense of a creedal commitment. The creedal question, however, threw the 1922 Indianapolis convention into turmoil.[13] The previous year the Fundamentalists had adopted a statement of doctrine introduced by Frank M. Goodchild, but they had not introduced it at the convention. The journals predicted that a showdown on this issue might come at Indianapolis. The first two conservative preconvention meetings had been chiefly concerned with doctrine, but at Indianapolis they tried to put their beliefs into action. Jasper C. Massee of Tremont Temple in Boston emerged as floor leader of the Baptist Fundamentalist Fellowship, but the *Christian Century* hinted that someone else (perhaps Riley) was backing him. After interviewing some of the men involved, Robert Delnay felt that it was part of Riley's plan that the gentle Massee be the one to lead the initial fight.[14] The Fundamentalists' goal in Indianapolis was to get the New Hampshire Convention of Faith adopted by the convention, and their position received publicity from Bryan's trip to the city to speak to them.

The liberals halted this maneuver, however, when Cornelius Woelfkin introduced a counterresolution stating that the New Testament was sufficient for all Baptists. After a fierce debate, Woelfkin's resolution was finally passed. The liberals were greatly relieved, and the elected president, Mrs. W. A. Montgomery, noted that adopting an official confession of faith "would come perilously near to abandoning one of our fundamental principles."[15] After the convention, Laws, Goodchild, and Massee went to the Moody Bible Institute to give addresses. In his speech there, Laws noted, "We have lost a battle, but we have not lost the war."[16] In large part, however, the war had been lost. Had the Fundamentalists won control of the Baptist denomination, that victory would have had a major impact on main line Protestantism. Instead, they were soundly defeated, and within three years the moderate J. Whitcomb Brougher had inaugurated a widespread campaign to institute peace.

One reaction to this failure to secure a creedal commitment was the creation in 1923 of a separate conservative organization, the Baptist Bible Union (BBU) with Riley, T. T. Shields of Toronto, and J. Frank Norris of Fort Worth serving as its guiding lights. At Riley's insistence, Shields, whom the *Christian Century* labeled "the very incarnation of fanatical conviction," took over as president.[17] Riley's *Beacon* and Shields's *Gospel Witness* became the voices of their position. The historian of the Baptist Bible Union has claimed that, as originally established, it was primarily separatist in intent and that only the objections of Riley kept it from publishing a separatist pamphlet and immediately taking that position.[18] The goal of the BBU was to organize all the Baptists of North America into one unit—Norris leading the South, Riley, the North, and Shields, Canada—and thus destroy Modernism.[19] They saw themselves as the only true heirs of the Baptist democratic tradition. "Modernists are not Baptists, even though they are called by that name," said William M. Pettingill. "The name belongs to Bible believers and to no others."[20] Riley scoffed at the liberal use of the term "liberty of conscience," for he said that the liberties of the faith consisted in the liberty of believing what was written in the Bible and in Christ. "Every man has a right to independent thought," he said, "but he who thinks 'above that which is written,' apart from that which is revealed, is using his 'liberty for an occasion to the flesh,' and comes under the condemnation of the Scriptures."[21]

Shields insisted that the BBU and the Fundamentalists in the Northern Baptist Convention were one ideologically, but others were not so certain. Curtis L. Laws wrote a lengthy editorial in the *Watchman-Examiner* pointing out their differences. Laws was afraid that the new organization would destroy what the more moderate Fundamentalists were trying to do.[22] This division of forces caused considerable harm to their efforts. Eventually the BBU moved to establish separate foreign missionaries and, on their own, took over Des Moines University. By 1929, they were close to becoming a new denomination, and in 1932, they formed the heart of the group that split off to form the General Association of Regular Baptist Churches.

Because many foreign missionaries were supported by the denominations, the Fundamentalist controversy soon became international. China seems to have been the major area of concern, but Africa was also involved. The problems of getting an accurate view of the situation in the foreign missions field were many. The standard approach was for each denomination to send a person to visit the missions and mission schools and then write a report on his discoveries. The mission question, along with that of the soundness of schools, troubled the Baptists for many years.

John R. Straton's interest in the Baptist missions arose when Bertha Henshaw, who had served in China for some years but was then working for the American Baptist Foreign Missionary Society (ABFMS), became suspicious of the theological views of some of the current missionaries. A member of Straton's Calvary Church, she allied herself with his Fundamentalist league. For a while, she was both working for the ABFMS and preparing articles for Straton's *Fundamentalist*, a position she found decidedly uncomfortable. "If I speak of things, I feel like a traitor," she wrote, "if I keep still, I feel like a coward."[23]

In his magazine and his sermons, Straton suddenly began to demand an investigation of the foreign missionary situation. The Fundamentalist group that he led finally arranged a meeting with the Board of Managers of the ABFMS but they sustained an earlier ruling that Straton and his followers not be allowed access to the records. Straton claimed that they did not want to rummage through the files, but only to examine a few specific items. A stockholder should have access to a company's records, he declared.[24] The board, however, decided that many of the letters had been written in confidence and that to allow any such examination would be a violation of trust. The agitation Straton caused had considerable effect, and when the Northern Baptist Convention met in Milwaukee in 1924, Jasper C. Massee led the floor fight to get a commission to investigate their foreign missions. A group was organized and given $25,000 for this purpose.[25] Straton proposed that he and Riley do the investigating, but this was shouted down. The committee reported the next year that the sweeping criticism of the missionaries could not be verified and that the spreading of such rumors caused severe harm to their denominational efforts.[26] They urged peace on the issue. The plan they adopted was the so-called "inclusive policy," which recognized the existence of two points of view within the denomination. This decision was not satisfactory to many of the Fundamentalists. Bertha Henshaw exchanged sad letters with Riley about the ineffectiveness of Massee's leadership, and Straton exchanged harsh letters with the moderate Frank M. Goodchild, who suffered a heart attack because of the strain of his activities.

Straton and the others then began talking about a new foreign mission society, which eventually the more extreme Fundamentalists set up in the BBU. Eastern Baptist Seminary also was born in 1925 to counter Crozer, following the path of Northern, which had been established in 1913 to counter the influence of Chicago. For many, the only solution was to separate.

The last important fight in the Northern Baptist Convention came in 1926. Riley played an especially important role in that stormy gathering in Washington, D.C. The failure of the Fundamentalists to unseat the New York Park Avenue Church delegates the previous year at Seattle promised a fierce controversy, for the issue at stake was who should determine what constituted a true Baptist church. Harry Emerson Fosdick's Park Avenue Church administered baptism according to the joiner's wishes, but certain groups of Fundamentalists felt this was contrary to the traditional Baptist position. If the convention determined the practices of a local church, however, it would be taking upon itself the powers of a general assembly—which it had never done. By 1926, Jasper C. Massee had divested himself of the leadership of the Fundamentalist Fellowship, and Frank M. Goodchild and J. Whitcomb Brougher had replaced him as the moderate leaders. Brougher proposed a standing resolution that the Northern Baptist Convention recognize its constituency as consisting of those churches "in which the immersion of believers is recognized and practiced as the only Scriptural baptism; and the Convention hereby declares that only immersed members will be recognized as delegates to the Convention." Riley, however, felt that immersion and regeneration were irrevocably connected and proposed as an amendment that "the Northern Baptist Convention recognizes its constituency as consisting solely of those Baptist Churches in which the immersion of believers is recognized and practiced as a pre-requisite to membership."[27]

The fight on the floor was fierce. Holding the Bible in the air, Straton declared the Baptists would be aiding those who were out to destroy it if they failed to pass Riley's motion. He also criticized John D. Rockefeller's role in the denomination. Riley's motion was finally defeated 1,084 to 2,020, and Brougher's was then adopted. This was the last great Baptist floor fight for twenty years, for it was obvious by 1926 that the denomination was tiring of controversy. Although clearly a conservative, J. Whitcomb Brougher had spent the previous six months traveling across the nation urging one hundred thousand Baptists to "play ball." As a gesture of reconciliation, he was elected president of the convention. Jasper C. Massee proposed a six months' "armistice" on the controversey, which was well received except by a few extremists.[28] The 1927 convention was billed as the "harmony" meeting, but it did not receive much publicity because Charles Lindbergh's solo transatlantic flight occurred at the same time. The meetings in 1928 and 1929 were also quiet, and in 1930 William B. Riley and Harry Emerson

Fosdick appeared on the same platform. The controversy among the Baptists seemed to be over.

The Northern Presbyterians experienced only slightly less internal dissension than the Baptists. One contemporary declared the fight within the ranks to be "that of the Protestant Reformation over again."[29] The Baptists had no figure of national importance. William Jennings Bryan was the most widely known Presbyterian layman, however, and a good part of the denomination's troubles could be laid at his doorstep. Bryan had long been a frequent delegate to the Presbyterian General Assembly. He was there in 1919, and in 1920, although he was not scheduled to speak, in answer to demands from the crowd, he arose to deliver a few words. His major impact upon the Presbyterians, however, came in the 1923 convention when he ran for moderator of the General Assembly. Paolo Coletta's contention that Bryan was a shrewd politician is well borne out in his fight for moderator. Before he entered the race, he asked several prominent Presbyterians whose opinions he valued whether he should run. Not all of the replies were favorable, but he decided to have his name entered. The battle on the floor was long and heated, and although he led on the first two ballots, his opponent, Charles F. Wishart of Ohio, finally won on the third. Thus, the "most widely influential layman in the church," as the *Christian Century* called him, went down to defeat in what would be his last major bid for elected office.[30] This fight created the most strain the General Assembly had seen for years [31]

Had Bryan been elected moderator in 1923 the Northern Presbyterians might well have split into two factions, for he had been a divisive force in the denomination for over two years on the question of evolution. The prospect of the head of a major Protestant denomination traversing the land denouncing evolution would have caused untold controversy. In addition, 1923 was to be a year of organizational revision, and Bryan had never been closely involved with the inner workings of the church. Eventually, the issue of evolution swallowed up most of the doctrinal issues that had caused the appearance of the Auburn confession and the General Assembly's periodic reaffirmation of the points of the Westminster Confession. Theology did not come under consideration again until 1927–28, when J. Gresham Machen and his followers split from the church over the issue of Calvinism.[32]

The man at the center of both of these denominational controversies was Harry Emerson Fosdick. Fosdick was ordained to the Northern Baptist ministry in 1903, and he was a popular preacher from the beginning. One of his best books, *The Meaning of Prayer*, was published in 1915. He served as professor at Union Theological Seminary from 1915 to 1946 and as minister of the Riverside Church from 1926 to 1946. Before that, however, he served as a permanent Baptist "special minister" in New York City's Park Avenue Presbyterian Church. Thus, he was susceptible to attacks from both denominations.

A satisfactory definition of Protestant Modernism or liberalism (for the terms were used interchangeably) has so far eluded historians. "I am not going to undertake to give you a single definition of Modernism," said the president of Columbia Theological Seminary in South Carolina in an article entirely devoted to the subject, because "the modernist has a manifold personality. Modernism has many phases."[33] Sydney E. Ahlstrom, for example, in *A Religious History of the American People*, has a section entitled "The Varieties of Religious Liberalism."[34] Understanding of the term thus has revolved around the people concerned, and because of his great reputation as a preacher, Harry Emerson Fosdick came to be seen as the chief exemplar of the new theology. The *New Republic* claimed that he had made himself into "the prophet of modernism."[35]

When he visited the mission field in China in 1921, Fosdick found Fundamentalists engaged in an aggressive campaign against the liberals, even to the extent of trying to force their retirement. He saw similar troubles when he returned to the United States and was motivated to preach a sermon on May 22, 1922, called "The New Knowledge and the Christian Faith," which was also circulated under the title, "Shall the Fundamentalists Win?" Essentially pleading for tolerance, Fosdick also presented a good case for the liberal position on the major issues of the Virgin Birth, the second coming, and biblical interpretation.

The reaction to the distribution of this sermon was unprecedented. Conservatives in all denominations rushed to answer it. Presbyterian Clarence Macartney of Philadelphia published "Shall Unbelief Win?" Conservative *Bible Champion* editor William H. Bates replied with "Fundamentalism vs. Liberalism," Presbyterian Harry Bochne with "Can the Fundamentalists Lose?" Disciples minister Rupert C. Foster with "Shall the Fundamentalists Win?" and Baptist John R. Straton with "Shall the Funnymonkeyists Win?"

Fosdick's sermon became one of the most important pulpit statements of the decade. It caused a minor pamphlet war, and it thrust Fosdick onto center stage as the archetypal liberal. Conservative attacks on him knew no bounds. This view of Fosdick was unfortunate for all concerned, for, in spite of his prominence, he was not a representative figure for the new theology. As later studies have shown, his thinking was not typical. He was chiefly a preacher and a religious counselor, and the main burden of his message concerned the integrity of the human personality. Even more important, Fosdick was not aggressive, and, unlike many Fundamentalists, he never relished controversy. Eventually, the *Christian Century* urged the Fundamentalists to find another target, but the abuse he received did not cease until his death.[36]

Because of the premillennial issue, the presence of Harry Emerson Fosdick and William Jennings Bryan, and (perhaps) more aggressive conservative leadership, the Northern Baptists and the Northern Presbyterians were the denominations most disturbed by the Fundamentalist-Modernist controversy. But the other main line groups were also affected. The theological issues raised moved from denomination to denomination with conservatives and liberals each bending them to their own specifications.

Disciples of Christ members were never prominent in any of the interdenominational Fundamentalist organizations, nor was the denomination much concerned with the premillennial issue, but the controversy had considerable impact upon them. They had been divided into conservative and liberal wings for years, and the polarization of the issues exacerbated these divisions. Disciples' periodicals were filled with articles agonizing over the question of whether or not their conservatives were really Fundamentalists. The liberal periodicals declared they were not. Fundamentalism, they argued, was based on a creed, whereas the Disciples based their beliefs solely on the Bible.[37] At the end of the decade, however, the two distinct views were clearly evident in their churches.

Liberal denominations such as the Congregationalists and Unitarians watched the fray from one sideline. Congregationalists seemed little affected at the time, for they had long resolved the issues involved to their own satisfaction. In the 1920s, for example, the Tucson Congregationalists described themselves as "a liberal church." But aggressive conservatism made advances even there. Today, examples can be found of Fundamentalist Congregational churches (now called the United Church of Christ) in rural areas. Albert C. Dieffenbach, able editor of the Unitarian *Christian Register*, saw the rise of Modernism as a vindication of the Unitarian position. In issue after issue he urged the liberals to leave their churches and join his. He especially pressured Fosdick along these lines. Yet, surprisingly, few did so. Unitarians did not gain large numbers during the decade because most Modernists remained within their own denominations.

The Missouri Synod Lutherans cheered on the Fundamentalists from the conservative sidelines. They had no interest in premillennialism, but were sympathetic to conservative theology. The Missouri Synod leaned heavily on a literal interpretation of Scripture, and, of course, had little interest in materialistic evolution or the liberal view of Jesus. In the early 1970s, however, the synod split in two over issues almost identical to those raised in the 1920s: the historicity of Scripture, the use of higher criticism, and the rise of liberalism in their seminaries.

The Seventh-Day Adventists, Pentecostals, Holiness groups, Church of the Nazarene, Mormons, Salvation Army, and independent sects also sided with the Fundamentalists. They all shared a common conservative interpretation of Scripture. The Seventh-Day Adventists, moreover, attacked evolution with special vehemence. Some of them saw the struggle over the theory as the predicted battle with Anti-Christ. As will be shown in Chapter 9, Adventist George M. Price did yeoman work in supplying the Fundamentalists with antievolution arguments.

At first, the Fundamentalist organizations, such as the WCFA, disliked being lumped with such groups as the Pentecostals, Adventists, or Holiness churches. But eventually they realized they had more in common than they had first thought. Moreover, the popular mind rarely made fine distinctions, viewing all such groups as Fundamentalists.

In general, the Roman Catholics were bewildered by the controversy. They had effectively halted "Modernism" (the same name but a slightly different movement) in their churches by Pius X's 1907 encyclical, *Pascendi dominici gregis*. They were also little bothered by the evolution issue, for they made the distinction between the body (which might have come via materialistic evolution) and the soul (which came from God). One prelate even suggested that the controversy signaled the death knell of American Protestantism.[38]

Although Methodists, both North and South, prided themselves on being free from Fundamentalist agitation, whether they were is open to doubt. The quasi-official three-volume *History of American Methodism* credited their lack of involvement to three causes: Methodist theology, which stressed the personal experience of each individual as the only test of faith, could not be easily polarized; their central governing body met every four years and it was not in session in 1925; and no strong Methodist Fundamentalist leaders emerged.[39]

Historian William W. Sweet, who lived through the fracas, however, remembered it differently. He recalled that the Methodists were troubled. Their conservatives were centered in New Jersey, Philadelphia, and Baltimore, and in 1920 and 1924, they questioned the denomination's "course of study" program. They feared that reading liberal materials would cause young ministers to lose their faith. In 1925, they formed themselves into a Methodist League for Faith and Life, with a monthly periodical, *The Call to Colors*. The league's express purpose was "to reaffirm the vital and eternal truths of the Christian religion, such as the inspiration of the Scriptures, the deity of Jesus, his Virgin Birth, etc."[40] In 1923 the WCFA annual convention met in Fort Worth to hold a sensational "trial" of three Methodist schools: Texas Women's College, Southwestern University, and Southern Methodist University. Six students confessed that they had been taught evolution in these schools. Leander W. Munhall, irascible editor of the *Eastern Methodist*, frequently denounced liberal denominational leaders. In spite of claims to the contrary, Methodist periodicals for this time show much concern over the issues raised, especially the proper interpretation of Scripture.

The one issue that did not seem to bother Methodism was premillennialism. A few denominational churches and pastors held to this view, but it was not widespread.[41] Many regarded it as a Calvinist heresy and would have nothing to do with it. The Nashville *Christian Advocate* printed several articles denouncing premillennialism. BIOLA Dean Reuben A. Torrey once accused the Southern Methodists of trying to run premillennialism out of their church.[42]

Although the Episcopalians were bothered by neither evolution nor premillennialism and could hardly be classified as Fundamentalists, they were considerably affected by the theological issues raised by the controversy. For them the issue revolved around the interpretation of the historic church creeds: a "creedal traditionalism" versus a more liberal interpretation. Episcopalians had long been divided into conservative and liberal camps, and their denominational conflict formed over the necessity for belief in the Virgin Birth and bodily resurrection of Jesus. Liberals, such as Bishop William Lawrence of Massachusetts, argued that this might not be essential doctrine; conservatives, such as Bishop William T. Manning of New York, insisted that it was.

The quarrel was focused by Reverend Percy Stickney Grant's assertion that the church should allow for liberalism within its walls, a view for which his bishop, William Manning, rebuked him. Simultaneously, an obscure Texas rector named Heaton was cited for trial for his liberal views. In their Dallas meeting of 1923, the bishops of the church issued a pastoral letter affirming the Virgin Birth and bodily resurrection of Christ. Publication of this statement was expected to quiet the controversy, but it had the opposite effect. Dr. Leighton Parks attacked the pastoral letter and pleaded for intellectual integrity on the part of the clergy in their recitation of the Apostles' Creed. Parks challenged Manning to leave Heaton alone and bring both Lawrence and himself to trial as an object lesson. The faculty of the Episcopal Theological School at Cambridge sent out an official alumni bulletin suggesting more liberty by allowing recitation of the creeds to be permissive instead of obligatory. The 1924 Church Congress solemnly discussed the question of how the church should deal with Fundamentalism.

One of the most articulate defenders of the conservative position among the Episcopalians was New York's Bishop Manning. Much to his dismay, his defense of conservative Christianity caused him to be lumped with the antievolutionists, premillennialists, and biblical literalists.[43] In a widely publicized sermon in 1923, he argued that Episcopal conservatism and Fundamentalism were completely different. Fundamentalism rested on sixteenth-century confessions of faith that did not affect Episcopalians, he declared. "The question with us in this Church," he said, "is not Fundamentalism or Modernism but belief in Jesus Christ, the Son of God."[44] In his 1924 message to the diocese, he tried to reaffirm what he saw as basic Christian principles. Although few Episcopalians could legitimately be termed Fundamentalists, many of them were decidedly conservative Christians in their interpretation of theology. The Fundamentalist-Modernist controversy helped reawaken these old grievances.

The prominence the premillennial issue played in disrupting the northern denominations—Episcopalians and Disciples excepted—has led Ernest R. Sandeen to conclude that the "Fundamentalist movement of the 1920s was only the millenarian movement renamed."[45] Sandeen is only partially correct in this analysis, however, for the issues of conservative versus liberal interpretations of the Bible and the person of Jesus, which the Fundamentalists also raised, found response in all the denominations, especially in the South.

Except for the issue of the second coming, the South congealed quickly on the points raised. While the Northern churches were smoothing over their science-religion difficulties, in 1926 the powerful Southern Baptist Convention unanimously passed a resolution rejecting evolution and supporting Genesis. Bryan placed his faith primarily in the southern colleges, and in 1925 Southern Methodist Bishop Warren A. Candler declared that "the churches of the South must save the cause of evangelical Christianity in the United States or it will be lost."[46] The Fundamentalist controversy was instrumental in calling the South to a renewed consciousness of its distinctive religious position. The southern denominations are today one of the last remnants of Puritan America.

As the southern churches closed ranks, the incipient liberal trends of the previous decade came under fire. Even the moderate liberals such as Southern Baptist William L. Poteat, president of Wake Forest College, and Edgar Y. Mullins, president of the Southern Baptist Theological Seminary, Louisville, were denounced for their views on theistic evolution.[47] Southern Baptist periodicals rejoiced that their churches were relatively free from northern heresy. Historian James J. Thompson, Jr., has concluded that virtually all Southern Baptists during the 1920s disbelieved in the theory of evolution. Not all of them, however, wished to see its teaching prohibited by law.[48]

Southern Presbyterians equally rejoiced that their denomination was not much affected by Modernism. They were especially acerbic in their attacks on this point of view. In 1923, the president of their seminary in Columbia, South Carolina, declared Modernism "the greatest danger that menaces the world today."[49] Their prestigious *Presbyterian of the South* (Richmond) cheered the legislature of Tennessee for decreeing that evolution would not be taught in that state.[50] Although there were few liberals within the denomination proper, considerable division existed among their foreign missionaries.[51]

The Southern Methodists also had few liberals within their denomination, but those often were harassed. Local pressure forced the resignation of Dr. John Rice from the School of Theology at Southern Methodist University in Dallas, and at the May 1922 General Conference, a special commission urged responsible officials to take all necessary steps to drive out heretical doctrines. When a visiting speaker presented the Wellhausen theory of the Pentateuch at a Lake Junaluska conference in 1925, he was severely attacked by Bishop James Cannon.[52]

Because most of the southern churches held some type of conservative position, the South proved an especially congenial home for the last wave of Fundamentalist organizations in the 1920s, the most important of which was the Bible Crusaders. Born from a conversation between John R. Straton and wealthy real estate broker George F. Washburn, the Crusaders hoped to unify all the Fundamentalist forces of the country.[53] "If this movement only stops the invasion of modernists," Washburn was quoted as saying, "I would rather be known as the founder of it than President of the United States."[54]

In spite of the hopes with which they began, however, the Crusaders were never able to gain momentum. Their threats to "make and unmake" southern governors, senators, and state officials on the textbook question came to nothing. Their only success occurred when, through the efforts of T. T. Martin in the house and I. R. Deal and L. B. Morony in the senate, they were able to push an antievolution bill through the Mississippi legislature. The Crusaders did not become the clearing house for a federation of Fundamentalists as had been hoped. Their magazine, *Crusader's Champion*, ceased publication in October 1926, after having existed about a year. In 1929, Washburn reported that the collapse of the Florida land speculation in which he was engaged had forced him to consolidate his enterprises, discontinue his Crusaders work, and resign from all but the most essential business activity, and even so, he was barely able to save his Florida estate.[55]

The South's most controversial Fundamentalist leader, J. Frank Norris, also fell on hard times after 1925. Pastor of the First Baptist Church in Fort Worth since 1909, Norris stepped onto the national stage in the early 1920s. His continual attacks on Modernists, evolutionists (especially those on the faculty of Baylor University), Roman Catholics, city officials, and other Texas Baptists helped keep him in the public eye for many years.[56]

Although the Texas Baptist Convention refused to seat his delegates in 1922 and 1923 and permanently removed his church from their organization in 1924, Norris continually insisted that 90 percent of the Southern Baptists were in his camp.[57] Gradually, however, he separated himself from all local Baptist fellowship. Although his dreams of establishing a premillennial organization in every southern state never materialized, he did succeed in setting up his own Bible seminary.[58] The graduates from this school helped keep his militant conservatism alive.

On July 17, 1926, Norris shot and killed an unarmed Fort Worth lumberman, D. E. Chipps, after an argument in Norris's church study. Norris argued that he had feared his life was in danger, and a Texas jury accepted his plea of self-defense. The nation's press was outraged over this event, and it cost Norris most of his national stature. His popularity with his local congregation remained high, however, and he continued to serve it—as well as another (simultaneously) in Detroit—until his death in 1951.[59]

Thus, by the late 1920s, the Fundamentalist-Modernist controversy had diminished. The great crash of 1929 and the ensuing Depression administered what appeared to be the final blow. Yet during the 1920s, this social and religious movement proved of the utmost importance. It severely disrupted the Northern Baptists and Northern Presbyterians. It reaffirmed long-standing divisions within the Disciples, Episcopalians, and Northern and Southern Methodists. It caused the popular mind to consider Seventh-Day Adventists, Pentecostals, the Church of the Nazarene, and all other conservative groups as Fundamentalists, and it brought these groups to a realization of how many points they shared in common. It called the southern churches to a consciousness of their own distinctive conservative heritage. It confirmed the fact that the major divisions among the main line Protestant churches were really not denominational but based on whether one were liberal or conservative.[60] Finally, as will be shown in the next chapters, it awakened the old controversy over the theory of evolution.

9
Bryan and the
Controversy over Evolution

The Fundamentalist-Modernist controversy began as a dispute over theological doctrines and biblical interpretation. The shift in the focus of the controversy to the issue of evolution is one of its most crucial elements and has been overlooked by most historians. In 1921–22 the evolution issue rose to the forefront and promptly absorbed most of the conservatives' energy. Thereafter, their main effort was directed toward the passage of state laws to halt the teaching of evolution in tax-supported schools. The major monographs on the subject have slighted this shift in emphasis. Stewart Cole, in *History of Fundamentalism*, for example, treats the theological issue, but says little about the evolution question. Norman Furniss slights theology but devotes virtually his entire book, *The Fundamentalist Controversy, 1918–1931*, to evolution. Ernest R. Sandeen in *The Roots of Fundamentalism* is more concerned with the origins of the movement as a whole. S. K. Ratcliffe, writing in the British *Contemporary Review* in late 1925, noted that when he wrote an article in 1922 on America's religious difficulties, evolution was not an issue of Fundamentalism.[1] The shift in emphasis is documented in an article by William B. Riley in September 1927: "When the Fundamentals movement was originally formed, it was supposed that our particular foe was the so-called "higher criticism"; but, in the onward going affairs, we discovered that basal to the many forms of modern infidelity is the philosophy of evolution."[2] Within a short time, evolution came to be seen as central to all elements of religious conservatism. This focus can be credited largely to William Jennings Bryan.

The outbreak of World War I led conservatives to a renewed interest in evolution. The war was decried as a practical application of the idea of the "survival of the fittest." German "Kultur" was called the logical result of "Applied Evolution."[3] Conservatives had long been suspicious of "German theology," but this was conveniently subsumed in the rise of the evolution issue.[4] Yet only a few denominational papers made these connections before 1920.[5]

It is doubtful that the evolution issue would have spread to the general American public had it not been for William Jennings Bryan's interest in it. He alone popularized the framework within which the evolution controversy was fought out in the ensuing decade. It would not be an exaggeration to say that Bryan forced upon America his own view of the tragic consequences of World War I, but, of course, he had a ready audience. While World War I was raging, William B. Riley noted that when it was over, he would not be surprised to see the world "turn its tearstained and scarred face to William Jennings Bryan as the new Moses, raised up of God, to lead men out of this wilderness of awful warefare [sic] in which we have journeyed all too long."⁶ This prophecy was to be borne out in the next few years.

Just when Bryan first became interested in evolution is hard to document because his memory played tricks on him in his old age. His most famous address, "The Prince of Peace," contained only a mild aside against the theory; it was basically an appeal for service. In May of 1908, when he was gearing up for the November campaign and his last try for the highest office of the land, he gave a statement of faith to a reporter. "This is my theology," he said. "If a man looking at the life of Christ, beholding its freedom from sin, is inspired to approximate his own life to it—is sorry when he sins, not wishing to sin again—he is Christian. So is he who wants to do right, who is sorry when he does wrong, and who wishes to serve his party well, a patriot, regardless of his party."⁷ Similar thinking could be seen in his irenic comments on Charles Eliot's proposed "New Religion." Bryan showed little concern with liberal theology or evolution before World War I.

The war, then, apparently molded the way Bryan's future religious activity would turn. In spite of his eager service in the Spanish-American War, of which he was always proud, William Jennings Bryan was basically a man of peace. Many of the editorials at the time of his death in 1925 commented on the irony that he should be buried in Arlington National Cemetery. His most popular speech on the Chautauqua circuit was on peace, and the contribution to public service of which he was most proud was his negotiation of the so-called "cooling-off treaties" with various foreign nations. His official State Department portrait shows him holding one of these treaties. It was this "cooling off" principle which he saw embodied in the League of Nations. He had always been suspicious of militarism and war preparation, and he had severely attacked Theodore Roosevelt's aggressive activities along those lines.

As secretary of state, Bryan's anguish over Woodrow Wilson's notes to Germany was well known. When the president sent his second *Lusitania* note to the kaiser, Bryan resigned, sadly noting, "You have prepared for transmission to the German government a note in which I cannot join without violation of what I deem to be an obligation to my country."⁸ From 1915 to 1917, he spent much of his time in activities aimed toward bringing peace. He was invited to join Henry Ford's proposed Peace Ship and was anxious to meet other neutralist peace advocates.[9] He engaged in a written debate with William Howard Taft on the various aspects of the latter's League to Enforce Peace, but before this correspondence could be published, the country had become involved in the war.[10] As late as April 3, 1917, Bryan was so firmly opposed to U.S. entry into the war that, he said, were he a representative, he would have to resign if his constituents demanded entry.[11] When the United States entered the war, however, he dropped all such activities and in a startling gesture offered his services to Woodrow Wilson as a private. In March 1917, he wrote to his brother Charles that their popular journal the *Commoner* should print no criticism of the government should war break out. In later editorials he spoke out against resisting the draft. He freely gave of his time to urge participation in Liberty Loan drives, but private correspondence indicates that his heart was not in these activities.[12]

In 1915, Baptist minister Amzi C. Dixon suggested to Bryan that German militarism was not so much based on the writings of Friedrich Nietzsche as on the following of Darwinism to its logical conclusion. Shortly thereafter, Bryan came across Benjamin Kidd's *The Science of Power,* which argued a related thesis, and recommended the book to his friends. Speaking at the Lake Mohonk Conference in 1916, he suggested that a false philosophy of force and fear had brought Europe into war. Each country believed that it could terrorize the others into maintaining peace, and the result was chaos. During this period, Bryan composed an address, "The War in Europe and Its Lessons for Us," which he delivered throughout the United States in 1916. In it, he expanded on this theme:

> I have tried to find the cause of this war, and, if my analysis of the situation is correct, the cause is to be found in a false philosophy—in the doctrine that "might makes right." And that you may see more clearly the importance of reaching a conclusion and proclaiming it, I call your attention to the fact that there is but one code of morals known among men and that is the code that regulates individual life. If this code of morals is not to be applied to nations, there is no moral code which can be invoked for the regulation of international affairs.[13]

Bryan recalled his feelings to a Chicago audience in April 1923: "So I began to feel a little more earnestly about the effect of Darwinism. I had found that Darwin was undermining the Christian faith, and then I found he had become the basis of the world's most brutal war, and then I found that Benjamin Kidd pointed out that he is the basis of the discord in industry."[14] He continued to give occasional antievolution addresses throughout the war, but, because he was somewhat under a cloud then, they were reported only in the denominational papers. He did convince a few editors, however, that if the Darwinian theory were true, then Christianity was false.[15]

Many admirers wrote supporting Bryan's position on evolution, and some suggested that he campaign against the theory. One minister said Bryan could spend his latter days in no greater service.[16] By 1920, he had become suspicious of the writings of Harry Emerson Fosdick. On January 22, 1919, after having heard Bryan speak, Walter W. Moore, president of Union Theological Seminary in Richmond, Virginia, wrote to ask him if he would deliver the James P. Sprunt Lectures on religion at Union. Bryan replied that he would be eager to do so and agreed to speak in October 1921, following a lecture by J. Gresham Machen.[17] Bryan's lectures were published in 1922 as *In His Image* and sold over a hundred thousand copies. Billed as "Bryan's Answer to Darwin," it was one of the most influential religious books of the time. A reviewer of *In His Image* said of Bryan: "He is the spokesman for a numerically large segment of the people who are for the most part inarticulate. In fact, he is almost the only exponent of their ideas who has the public ear. They are a part of the body politic by no means negligible or to be regarded solely with derision as 'lunatic fringe.' "[18]

As long as he spoke largely to church circles, his ideas met with general approbation, but in the fall of 1920, he made his first major foray into the public arena with this issue. In November of that year he visited the University of Michigan, headed by his old friend, Marion L. Burton, and gave a Sunday address to an estimated 4,500 persons in which he soundly attacked Darwinism as a false and vicious mode of thinking. No sooner had he left than he began to receive letters commenting on the controversy he had stirred up. One that particularly rankled him came from Reverend Arthur W. Stalker of the First Methodist Church in Ann Arbor. Reverend Stalker criticized him for the false alternatives he had posed and claimed that until his speech, the issue of evolution had been a dead one for most of the Michigan students. He intimated that Bryan would lose his influence with the people if he continued speaking along these lines. Hurt and annoyed, Bryan fired an angry letter back and then sat down to expand and elaborate his antievolution argument. He had five thousand copies of this new speech printed and sent them out for distribution. A large number were sent to Michigan, and he was pleased to discover when he returned to the campus that both a scientist and a philosopher had taken time to denounce him publicly. All the ministers in Florida, excluding only Catholic priests, were sent complimentary copies of the address at his request.[19]

The wide dissemination of this speech sparked Lloyd C. Douglas's article, "Mr. Bryan's New Crusade," in the *Christian Century*. The *Century* ran intermittent articles on Bryan's new interest, and their "The Passing of Mr. Bryan" in October 1921 drew a couple of angry letters in defense of his efforts. "We feel he is just coming into his own," wrote W. L. Packard of Omaha, "as a moral and spiritual leader and defender of the 'faith once delivered to the saints.' "[20] In the fall of 1921, Bryan caused a small controversy when he spoke on the campus of Will R. Moody's Middlebury

College in Vermont. But evolution did not receive much publicity until early in 1922, when he again went to a large midwestern state university, the University of Wisconsin at Madison. The Big Ten schools were especially vulnerable to pressures involving sensitive issues because of their public financial support, their large enrollment, and the fact that they usually were cultural bastions in essentially nonurban environments. Edward A. Birge, the president of the university and a scientist, who was seated on the platform when Bryan gave his address to a crowd of two thousand, was furious when Bryan had completed his remarks. After the talk, heated words were exchanged, and in the next day's papers Birge accused Bryan of trying to "induce young people to unite their religious faith to discredited scientific doctrines." Bryan in turn replied in the *Commoner* that perhaps the people of Wisconsin might like to select a new head of their university, one who would not ridicule the faith of the students' parents. He intimated that Birge might be an atheist. He also propounded what would be a standard element in the antievolution fight—that the taxpayers had a right to determine what should be taught in the university and should not tolerate any teaching that would negate the Christian religion.[21] Bryan's controversy with Birge lasted more than a year and a half.[22]

The press, already aware of the controversy in the various churches, seized upon Bryan as representative of the entire Fundamentalist movement. The *New York Times* asked him to present his objections to Darwinism, and he did so in the February 26, 1922, Sunday edition in the article "God and Evolution." Harry Emerson Fosdick's vigorous reply, "Mr. Bryan and Evolution," was carried by the *Times* a month later and reprinted by the *Christian Century*. Responses also came from scientists Henry F. Osborn and E. G. Conklin, the former saying, "Early in the year of 1922, I was suddenly aroused from my resposeful researches in paleontology by an article in the *New York Times* . . . by William Jennings Bryan . . . and it struck me immediately that Bryan's article was far more able and convincing than any previous utterance of his or any other fundamentalist, and that there should not be a moment's delay in replying to it."[23] In 1923, the *Forum* asked Bryan to write an article on Fundamentalism, which he gladly did.[24] The *Literary Digest* called the anti-evolution agitation in Minnesota a Bryan-made controversy, and in an article in *Century*, Glenn Frank boldly stated: "Mr. Bryan is Fundamentalism. If we can understand him, we can understand Fundamentalism."[25]

In the spring of 1921, William B. Riley organized a series of twenty-two antievolution meetings in Kentucky, and Bryan gave them a needed boost by speaking to the state legislature on the subject. The first antievolution bill introduced in any state legislature was defeated in the Kentucky house by one vote. Bryan was blamed for the bill, but disclaimed any responsibility for it.[26]

Letters began to pour in to Bryan from both sides as the people awakened to the fact that a new crusade was beginning. William P. Merrill of Brick Presbyterian Church in New York City urged that he spend his time in presenting the Gospel and not attacking what was surely a fad. J. D. Coon of Sioux Falls, South Dakota, also opposed single-minded attention to evolution: "W. B. Riley of Minneapolis, for whom you preached on evolution last fall, attacks evolution the same as you do. But I don't worry over him for a moment. He is a preacher and has no influence in politics and nobody knows that he is talking evolution outside of his congregation. You, however, have your world influence in politics and prohibition at stake and you are sacrificing your influence for prohibition by stirring up the old theological discussion on evolution."[27] The comments from the other side, however, found more favor with Bryan. He received many letters urging him to make opposition to evolution his life's work. "You are the first to fundamentally assume the offensive against evolution," wrote one admirer, "and you have triumphantly demolished it forever as a rational system."[28] Bryan had set his mind on the issue, and once he decided something was morally right, he never turned back. By publicizing evolution, he, more than anyone else, was responsible for shaping the emerging Fundamentalist movement. "It is because ministers holding your views fail to defend the Bible account of creation," he wrote to Reverend Stalker "that I feel *called*—as distinctly as you are called to the ministry—to try to save young people from Darwin's false and demoralizing guesses."[29]

Whatever ill feeling Bryan might have incurred because of quitting Wilson's cabinet was quickly dispersed by his volunteering to serve as a private, his wartime efforts, and his moderate advocacy of the League of Nations. When women's suffrage and prohibition, two reforms he had long championed, were finally adopted, he received his share of the glory. His regular speeches on the Chautauqua circuit brought him into the public eye, and his activities in the evolution controversy kept him there until his death. "While my power in politics has waned," he wrote Reverend John A. Marquis in 1923, "I think it has increased in religious matters and I have invitations from preachers in all the churches. An evidence of the change is found in the fact that my correspondence in religious subjects is very much larger than my correspondence in political subjects."[30]

His popular and profitable "Bryan Bible Talks" (biblical and moralistic sermons designed as a newspaper series) were an excellent forum from which to spread his views. In spite of repeated suggestions from the head of the Republic Syndicate that he treat fewer controversial issues, Bryan continued on his own way. In *Christ and His Companions*, for example, a collection based on the Talks, he took care to point out that Christ did not come about through evolution. When he discussed the Christmas story, he stressed the Virgin Birth. When he treated the tale of Christ at Cana, he claimed the wine was actually grape juice and used the story to attack the liquor interests. When discussing Christ and Lazarus, he pointed out that if this miracle were rejected, then it would be logical to reject all miracles.[31] Yet, despite these examples, his Talks were basically a vague and general affirmation of moral principles. Even at his harshest, Bryan could not launch into the invective of his followers.

Bryan was also unique in that he was able to maintain contacts with both religious liberals and conservatives until his death, as shown by the variety of his correspondence. In 1919, he called the Federal Council of Churches "the greatest religious organization in our nation," and he served on its commission on temperance. He spoke on applied Christianity that same year at the Ministerial Union of Baltimore.[32] He also was elected to the general committee of the Interchurch World Movement of North America. In 1924, in an address to a meeting of the Federal Council of Churches in Atlanta, he urged that the churches work to establish peace. His liberal friends included W. R. Moody, Washington Gladden, and Charles Stelzle, all strong advocates of the Social Gospel. He often used the *Commoner* to further the cause of the Social Gospel. Liberals who wrote him in an honest manner usually received an honest reply in return. In one letter he admitted that he could understand why some men thought he was doing as much harm to Christianity as he thought they were doing. In another he said that the Lord would take care of His own, whoever that turned out to be.[33] He did, however, markedly increase his correspondence and contacts with men of the conservative and especially the premillennial position. T. T. Martin and Arno C. Gaebelein introduced themselves in letters, and his correspondents came to include Amzi C. Dixon, W. H. Griffith-Thomas, J. Frank Norris, Jasper C. Massee, William B. Riley, and John R. Straton. Conservative magazines such as the *Moody Bible Institute Monthly* and the *King's Business* increased their coverage of his activities.

Bryan's national prominence and his general disposition, however, caused many people and organizations to try to use him for their own benefit. The organized Fundamentalist groups such as the WCFA were especially guilty, and their success might well be credited to Bryan's failure to realize how much their respective programs and methods differed.

As soon as they discovered that Bryan was an ally, the organized Fundamentalists increasingly demanded his aid. Thomas C. Horton of BIOLA and John W. Porter, Baptist pastor in Louisville, bombarded him with suggestions that he lead a national organization devoted to their cause.[34] He toyed with the idea and even designed an emblem. His son, William J. Bryan, Jr., also talked with Horton about the possibility, but no action was taken. William B. Riley brought Bryan to speak twice in Minneapolis and urged him, unsuccessfully, to let him arrange a series of additional addresses. Riley was more than willing to push Bryan to the forefront of his WCFA. In 1922, the WCFA voted to ask him to head a committee to organize the laymen of the country but, because of his other work and the illness of his wife, he refused.[35] The next year, without his knowledge, they voted him president of the entire organization, but he refused to accept.[36] Many of their magazines pestered him for articles and, when he did write for them, they wanted to use his name on the masthead as an associate editor.[37] The most blatant attempt to use his efforts came from the National Federated Evangelistic Committee. When Bryan expressed general approval of their work, the general secretary, James H. Larson, named him president of the organization, typing Bryan's name over that of the former president on the official stationery. Bryan's friend, William E. Biederwolf, assured him that he would not have to take an active part, but Bryan was surprised to discover that the organization's new stationery prominently displayed his name and that Larson had, with much publicity, scheduled an extensive tour for him across the continent. Finally, he sent Larson an angry letter withdrawing entirely from the organization. "While I feel interest in your work," he wrote, "it is not mine, and I will not allow you to decide for me what God wants me to do. . . . I have my work to do and I must do it in my way. Your way and my way are entirely different and opposite." Further pleas from Larson were ignored.[38]

Another overt attempt to use Bryan came from Riley and J. Frank Norris concerning the 1923 WCFA convention in Fort Worth. The governor of Texas was thinking of introducing an antievolution bill into the legislature, and Norris believed Bryan's presence would have a great impact. "The Southwest is now the battleground," he wrote. "Your influence is simply immeasurable here." Norris predicted that two Bryan addresses would change the minds of ten million people and made arrangements for special trains to bring in the faithful from the surrounding area. "Mr. Bryan," he wrote, "we have given evolution a body blow here and you can give it a knockout for the final count." Bryan toyed with the idea of journeying to Texas for this event because he also had an invitation from the Texas legislature, but he did not believe it would be worth his effort unless the governor decided to have his forces submit the bill on the house floor. This was not done, and Bryan did not make the trip. He was mortified when Norris offered him $1,000 if he would change his mind. "I am doing the best I can," he angrily replied, "and those who are not satisfied with the amount of work I am doing are, I hope, in a position to do more."[39] He refused to believe the letters he received that accused Norris of also trying to use him in his fight with the Texas Baptists. Because Norris was sound on the question of evolution, he said, he would consider him sound on the other questions also.[40] The variegated conservative organizations had their own ideas on how Bryan should spend his life, and, considering the pressures that were placed on him, it is surprising he resisted as well as he did.

In many cases, Bryan was willing to be used, but one wonders if he realized how vastly different his program was from those of most of the organized Fundamentalists. It is doubtful if many had ever voted for him—at the time of his death, the officials of Moody Bible Institute admitted that they never had.[41] There were other differences, too. Bryan had no theological training, and much of the controversy went over his head. For example, he did not believe in the premillennial return of Christ, a position many (but not all) conservatives regarded as central to Christianity. Bryan once commented that too many people did not believe in the first coming of Christ to worry about those who did not believe in the second.[42] Although the major conservative movement in the Presbyterian church was postmillennial, the most active and best organized Fundamentalist elements were premillennial. The ministers whose names Riley had given to J. D. Adams in connection with the initial set of conferences were all premillennialists. Bryan was not a dispensationalist, fearful of merging the church and the world, and probably did not know the meaning of the term. In his voluminous writings the word appears once, in another context. He was not pessimistic concerning the role of man in bringing about changes in society. He did not view the periodic cataclysmic entrance of the Lord into history as an important item of belief. The burden of Riley's message was the removal of the church from a sinful world, and this hope was shared with other Fundamentalists. Bryan did not have this aim. He wanted to bring more elements of society under the Christian spirit. He wanted, in some sense, to merge Christianity and the world. Although he would have denied it vigorously, this was almost a liberal position. The issue over which the Presbyterian conservative J. Gresham Machen left Princeton was Calvinism, but Bryan was not a Calvinist. Thus, he did not hold the same doctrinal position as the conservatives among either Baptists or Presbyterians.

There were also decided differences in the means favored by Bryan and the other Fundamentalists. Bryan did not approve of strong penalties for violation of an antievolution law. His faith in legality was strong enough that he thought the simple passage of a law by a fairly elected legislature would be sufficient. Many of the others demanded harsh penalties, even prison terms. Although as much scorn was heaped upon Bryan as on any other antievolutionist, he was not anti-Semitic or anti-Catholic and he did not engage in any sinister machinations. In fact, the breadth and depth of Bryan's personality held the movement together. When he died in 1925, its varied elements went their own way. Glenn Frank's comment that Bryan was Fundamentalism could not have been further from the mark. He was unique, and the Fundamentalists were trying to use him for all his worth.

Bryan's antievolution speeches increased in numbers in the years before the 1925 Scopes trial. He spoke before the House of Representatives in West Virginia in a futile attempt to get a bill passed. He was successful in urging the legislature of Florida to pass a resolution against evolution that provided no penalty. In addition to addressing the legislatures of West Virginia, Kentucky, and Florida, Bryan moved his antievolution campaign into the colleges. He picked an area of "the enemy's country," Dartmouth, Brown, and Harvard, to deliver his message. He spoke at Dartmouth in December of 1923, and although large crowds came to hear his talk, a survey of the undergraduates taken later showed he had made few converts.[43] In December 1924, he spoke at Sayles Hall at Brown University, where he met with some resistance, and five months later he returned to the Harvard campus after an absence of twenty years. One Harvard professor commented that Bryan was worth hearing on any subject, regardless of his knowledge of it.[44]

In May of 1925, he attended the seventh annual WCFA convention in Memphis, giving two addresses to an audience estimated at between eight and ten thousand. He pointed out that Bishop Candler of the Southern Methodist church had called his attention to James H. Leuba's book, *Belief in God and Immortality,* which reported that most scientists and college students had become religious skeptics. If such people should decide what should be taught in the schools, he argued, it would establish "the most hated oligarchy in the history of the world."[45]

These talks by Bryan served to keep the issue of evolution in the newspapers and before the people. He felt a larger majority was on his side than ever before with this issue, as well as the most intolerant opponents he had ever faced.[46] The agitation he helped provoke eventually came to a head in the famous trial of John Thomas Scopes in Dayton, Tennessee.

10
Bryan and
the Scopes Trial

The Fundamentalist switch to antievolution activity was bound to bring on a confrontation, for the issues that troubled them had now been moved into the more tangible realm of politics. The state of Tennessee provided the occasion when John W. Butler introduced a bill to prevent the teaching of evolution in the public schools. It passed the legislature, and on March 21, 1925, Governor Austin Peay signed it into law.[1] "Right or wrong," said Peay, "there is a deep and widespread belief that something is shaking the fundamentals of the country, both in religion and morals. It is the opinion of many that an abandonment of the old fashioned faith and belief in the Bible is our trouble in large degree. It is my own belief."[2] Unlike the University of Kentucky two years earlier, the University of Tennessee did not engage in any large-scale effort to prevent the bill's passage. Bryan came to Nashville to speak on its behalf, and, lacking any organized opposition, the antievolution group was able to push it through.[3]

One day shortly thereafter, George Rappelyea, manager of some mining properties near Dayton, suggested the possibility of John Thomas Scopes being brought to trial on this issue. Those present in Robinson's drugstore, where this discussion occurred, all agreed the law was foolish, and Scopes, who had once substituted for his school principal in his biology class, agreed to be arrested for teaching evolution. He later confessed that at the time he was not sure whether he really had taught it. The American Civil Liberties Union (ACLU) had been keeping a close watch on the law, and Roger N. Baldwin, then its director, had placed advertisements in the newspapers offering to defend any teacher who was prosecuted under it. The ACLU advertisement in the *Chattanooga News* had caught Rappelyea's eye.[4]

When the WCFA met in Memphis in early May, Riley led the executive committee, and later the convention proper, in passing the following resolution: "We name as our attorney for this trial William Jennings Bryan and pledge him whatever support is needful to secure equity and justice and to conserve the righteous law of the Commonwealth of Tennessee."[5] On May

13, Bryan let it be known that he would represent the WCFA in the case and that he would serve without charge. He agreed to serve with some hesitation, however, for he was conscious that he had not been in a courtroom for twenty-eight years. Bryan was the perfect choice for this case, for he had training in law, a long-standing interest in religion, and a national reputation. No other figure seemed better suited to defend the Fundamentalist cause.

The trial embodied many of the issues in the Fundamentalist movement. It was a graphic illustration of the polarization of religion in the 1920s, for the entrance of Bryan provoked Clarence Darrow, who, ironically, had campaigned for Bryan in his 1896 presidential bid, also to volunteer his services. Darrow had been Scopes's boyhood hero, and when he traveled to New York for instructions from the ACLU, he asked that the lawyer's offer be accepted.[6] The entrance of Bryan and Darrow abruptly changed the complexion of the case. Although the legal question was the issue at hand, few people were able to see the trial in terms other than "the meeting of the great forces of skepticism and faith."[7] Darrow always insisted he was not an atheist, but he was well known as a strong advocate of the rationalist position. Although the ACLU wanted to keep dramatic personal elements out of the case as much as they could, this became less and less possible as the time of the trial approached.[8]

The trial also gave a clear picture of the Fundamentalists' conception of democracy. They insisted that no matter what position the experts held, ultimate decisions must always rest with the people. "The trial will be a success in proportion as it enables the public to understand the two sides and the reasons on both sides," Bryan wrote to a friend in 1925. "Every question has to be settled at last by the public and the sooner the subject is understood, the sooner it can be settled. It is much better to have both sides represented by the strongest men so that the decision can turn upon the principles rather than upon individualities."[9]

The trial also gave great opportunity for ballyhoo and extravagance, and the publicity that surrounded it drew vast attention from the mass media. In spite of the ACLU's insistence that serious matters were involved, Dayton, from the beginning of the trial, took on an atmosphere that was a combination of circus and boosterism. Over one hundred reporters poured into the little village to rub shoulders with militant rationalists and people with "obvious mental irregularities of a religious tendency."[10] White-haired T. T. Martin, billed as the Blue Mountain (Mississippi) Evangelist, author of *Hell and the High Schools: Christ or Evolution—Which*, was very much in evidence. J. R. Darwin, who ran the local hardware store, had a large sign, "Darwin is Right . . . inside," in front of his building. Looking back years later, Scopes noted that Dayton that July contained "one of the rarest collection of screwballs" he had ever seen.[11]

One of the reporters who did much to keep this atmosphere alive was H. L. Mencken, editor of the *American Mercury*. He argued in the *Nation* before the trial began that whatever the correct position on the theory of evolution, the people of Tennessee had a right to prohibit or to teach anything they pleased. A democracy had every right to make itself look as foolish as it could. Paleontologist George Gaylord Simpson, then a graduate student at Yale, rejected such reasoning outright. Scientific questions, he later argued, could never be decided by judge and jury. The only people to decide such issues must be those who know something about the subject. Moreover, even the scientists should never "vote" on such questions; majority rule was out of place here. Instead, all decisions had to be made on the basis of evidence.[12]

Mencken had his own opinion, however, and during his stay at Dayton, he sent out a stream of editorials to the *Baltimore Evening Sun*. Although not as bitter as they might have been, these were very much in the iconoclastic Mencken style. In one he claimed that the Pastors' Association of Dayton was so orthodox that beside them Straton would seem as an Ingersoll.[13] He had always hated Bryan and what he stood for and probably was in Dayton to ridicule him as much as possible.[14] He accused Bryan of trying to become the "Pope" of the "peasants," after three times failing to become their president.[15] His essay on Bryan, "In Memoriam: WJB," in his *Prejudices* series is vitriolic, and he is one of the few commentators who ever accused Bryan of being insincere.[16] It was rumored, however, that Bryan saved Mencken from being lynched, for he convinced the self-appointed committee designated for this purpose simply to ask him to leave the state, which Mencken hurriedly did. He was not present for the final day of the trial, and he wrote very little about it afterward. When asked later about the case, he commented, "Well, we killed the son-of-a-bitch."[17]

That the trial was a drama there is no doubt; the question is whether it was a tragedy, a comedy, or a farce.[18] Clarence Darrow, Arthur Hays, and Dudley Field Malone, the mainstays of the defense, treated it with deadly seriousness. So did Bryan and his followers. Scopes himself, however, felt that no one could have held an absolutely serious attitude toward the trial without losing his sanity,[19] and perhaps Scopes's perspective is the best one from which to view the proceedings. The trial was a product of the general atmosphere of the 1920s—a decade that produced weighty moral causes side by side with magnificent trivialities. The Scopes trial shared equally in both.

Each side was close-mouthed as to strategy, but both expected that expert witnesses would be called to testify. Consequently, Bryan did his best to gather men of like mind around him. He wanted J. Frank Norris, Jasper C. Massee, and William B. Riley to be present at Dayton, but they were all planning to be on the West Coast during the trial because, ironically, the Northern Baptist Convention was being held at the same time. A crucial fight was expected at the meeting in Seattle, and all Baptist Fundamentalists were urged to be there. Obviously, they had no idea of the excitement that the Scopes trial would cause.

John R. Straton was not planning to attend the convention, however, and Bryan urged him to come to Tennessee to testify that evolution disputed the Mosaic account of the creation story. On July 13, Straton got a telegram from Bryan reminding him to start by train immediately for Dayton. Bryan said he would have wires awaiting Straton at Pittsburgh and Cincinnati. "[S]o much is at stake," Bryan wrote, "we cannot afford to take chances."[20]

The ACLU also spent much energy in gathering expert witnesses, one of the most important of whom was Kirtley F. Mather, then a young professor of geology at Harvard. Mather had realized that Darrow would have little difficulty in demolishing Bryan's views of evolution and Christianity, but he feared that the liberal Christian position would lack publicity. He communicated his feelings to Roger Baldwin, who urged him to go. "I went there particularly," Mather later recalled, "to get it into the record that there is a valid version of Christianity which is completely respectable in the light of modern science."[21] At the trial, however, Judge John Raulston refused to allow expert testimony, and none of those who came for either side were allowed to testify. Dudley Field Malone, however, convinced Raulston that the expert witnesses should write out what they would have said so the appeals court could decide whether Raulston had been correct in his decision. This they all did, and the extensive newspaper coverage gave the "statements of noted scientists" much publicity.[22]

Bryan wished at first to get both Jewish and Roman Catholic support for his position, and he suggested that his old friends, Samuel Untermeyer and Thomas Walsh, might be good men to have on their side. He did not seem to realize that the Catholics had avoided the evolution controversy or to be aware of the general tenor of feeling within the Jewish community. Only reluctantly did he agree to the objection of his partner, Sue Hicks, to including any Jews or Catholics.[23] He believed that the authority of the Bible was at stake, and he naively thought that all branches of the Judeo-Christian tradition would be equally interested in defending it.

Bryan was in his element at Dayton that July, and virtually the entire town turned out to greet him when he arrived.[24] He received admiring glances as he walked up and down the main streets. He added to the circus atmosphere by having brought along a sound truck to advertise the benefits of Florida land. Bryan was his old generous self in this milieu. He was free with his time and made several speeches throughout the county. When he was introduced to Scopes, he greeted him warmly, "John, we are on opposite sides this time. I hope we will not let that interfere in any way with our relationship."[25] He even fraternized with Darrow on occasion. The Bryan of Dayton was not the malicious, bitter old man he is often portrayed.

The jury chosen for the trial consisted of men with limited educational backgrounds, one of whom was completely illiterate. The judge insisted on opening the court with a prayer and was no match for the keenness of the imported defense attorneys. There was no tension, such as murder trials contain, however, for no one doubted the outcome of the *State of Tennessee v. John Thomas Scopes*. Indeed, Scopes was virtually forgotten. He showed little interest in his trial at the time and seemed to have even less afterward. The maximum fine was only $100, and the *Baltimore Evening Sun* had promised to pay that, as the ACLU had promised to pay the court costs. Bryan would have preferred a law with no penalty and said he was glad that no harm would come to Scopes because of the trial.[26]

The trial lasted for several weeks and was marked by some moments of real drama. Scopes felt that the turning point came the Thursday before it closed when Bryan clashed in the crowded courtroom with Dudley Field Malone. Malone was his old friend, for he had been Bryan's undersecretary in the Department of State in the Woodrow Wilson administration. Bryan spoke for an hour about the duel to the death between science and religion and had the crowd in the palm of his hand. Then Malone rose and in twenty-five minutes totally crushed Bryan's hold on the audience. He spoke intensely, beginning with an essay on Thomas Jefferson's ideas of religious toleration which Bryan himself had written twenty years earlier. Malone pointed out the distinction between God, the church, the Bible, Christianity, and Bryan. "There is going to be no duel," he said. "There is never a duel with the truth. The truth always wins—and we are not afraid of it. The truth does not need the law. The truth does not need Mr. Bryan. The truth is imperishable, eternal, immortal."[27] Tremendous applause greeted his oration, and when the courtroom cleared to leave only Malone, Bryan, and Scopes, Bryan wearily said to Malone, "Dudley, that was the greatest speech I have ever heard." "Thank you, Mr. Bryan," said Malone, "I am sorry that it was I who had to make it."[28] Scopes has suggested that Malone's speech was the most dramatic event in his life. Bryan was eager to recoup his lost prestige on the stand the following Monday.

That weekend, the defense began laying plans for its final thrust. On Sunday, Malone, Hays, and Darrow sat Mather down to pretend he was William Jennings Bryan. They grilled him as they hoped to do Bryan the next day, and Mather gave the replies he thought Bryan would give; he even suggested a few more questions the lawyers might ask. He later estimated his batting average at about .300.[29]

The most famous scene in the trial proceedings came that final Monday when Darrow called Bryan to the witness stand and cross-examined him mercilessly about his religious beliefs. There, before the world, he exposed the simplicity and inconsistencies of Bryan's biblical knowledge. When the cross-examination was over, the crowd rushed to congratulate Darrow. The fact that this testimony was later expunged from the record made little difference. Bryan probably did not realize how badly he had been handled until a special local committee approached him to ask why he had let them down.[30] Then his demeanor suffered a bit, and he felt forced to issue a statement defending his education and his college degrees. He resented being designated an "ignoramus," which, he claimed, he had never been called except by an evolutionist.[31]

Although he may have been humiliated on the platform, Bryan remained very active in the five days yet remaining to him. He spent the time working on an antievolution address that he thought would be one of his best. The day before his death, he traveled over two hundred miles, and on Sunday, July 26, when he attended church, the minister called on him for a prayer. Mather believed that Bryan's desire to recoup his lost prestige was what eventually led to his demise. After church, Bryan had a large country meal, called Chattanooga to inquire about his speech, and went to take his usual nap. When his wife felt he had slept long enough, she sent the chauffeur to awaken him. He was unable to do so. The Great Commoner had passed away.[32]

The furor from the Scopes trial had hardly begun when the news of Bryan's sudden death plunged most of the nation into mourning. The hooting of the skeptics stopped as abruptly as it had started. A Broadway play making fun of him closed immediately, and twenty thousand issues of a national magazine were halted halfway across the continent so that a two-page section ridiculing him could be removed.[33] The editorials ranged from the extensive coverage of the *New York Times* to the comments of the humblest weekly and from the banal to the perceptive. "Here in Great Britain we had almost no clue to him," remarked Baptist G. O. Griffith. "He remained an enigma, for his mentality eluded us."[34] Lord Asquith conceded that only America could have produced such a man.[35] It was speculated that he had probably seen and spoken to more Americans than any other person until that time and that his name was spoken more often than any other man's of his generation. The *Omaha World Herald* noted:

> The pastel colors of life, its shadows, its indecisions and doubts and uncertainties, were neither of him nor for him; they disturbed him not. What he believed he knew. There was in life for him truth and error. They were easily distinguishable. There was no twilight zone in between. Where he stood was truth's side and with all his power he battled for the Lord. Other men fought between whiles. Bryan fought all the while. Others rested on their arms when the day was done. Bryan hewed on through the night. Others might pause to refresh body and soul. Bryan knew no need of it.[36]

William Allen White called him the best political diagnostician and the worst political practitioner the country had ever seen: never had he been wrong on a single diagnosis or right on a single solution.[37] He had never questioned whether his positions on the "paramount" issues of free silver, anti-imperialism, prohibition, and evolution were effective but only if they were morally right.[38] But in an era of political corruption and a dearth of political heroes, the *Little Rock Democrat* asked if Bryan might not well have been the greatest man of his day.[39]

Whispers abounded, however, as he was laid to rest in Arlington National Cemetery that it was best for his reputation that he passed away when he did. Few felt that the cause of antievolution, to which he appeared to be devoting his life, was worth the same degree of effort as had been his others. Dudley F. Malone, in a talk to a group of Unitarians, claimed that at his death Bryan was leading the most sinister movement of his time.[40] Strong evidence can be marshaled to suggest that, in spite of his protestations that he had no plans after the Scopes trial, Bryan was indeed laying plans for what might well have been a new national crusade.

The Scopes trial is often seen as the high point of the Fundamentalist controversy, but this view is open to doubt. Because of the reputations of the men involved, it received the most publicity, but instead of being the apex, it was really just the beginning of the concerted antievolution agitation. The trial proved that an antievolution law could be passed and upheld, and pressure on many of the legislatures increased after 1925 until the peak year, 1927, when such laws had been introduced in thirteen states. Most failed to pass, and Rhode Island relegated theirs to the Committee on Fish and Game, but Mississippi and Arkansas put antievolution laws on their books. California allowed the teaching of evolution only as "theory." The governor of Texas, Miriam "Ma" Ferguson, personally saw that evolution was eliminated from the school textbooks. Even more effective, and impossible to uncover, were the actions by the various local school boards. They could decide to choose one text over another on any basis they wanted. Although there was no repetition of the Scopes case, perhaps because no other state wanted to appear as backward as Tennessee, it is difficult to see the Dayton trial as a milestone of any sort. It was hardly a battle for liberal religion, as the *Christian Register* saw it, nor was it successful in the battle for freedom in the classroom.[41] Furthermore, antievolution agitation is not dead yet. In 1964, a Baptist minister in Phoenix, Arizona, campaigned for an amendment to the state constitution to forbid the teaching of evolution, and every issue of *Plain Truth*, a slick southern California publication, contains an attack on the theory. In the 1970s, under considerable pressure from Seventh-Day Adventists, the California board that oversees high school textbooks decreed that equal space must be given to the biblical version of divine creation. Renewed antievolution agitation in California in the early 1980s brought the evolution issue again to the nation's attention. All this has occurred without the assistance of any major figure, and one wonders what would have happened had Bryan been around to lend the magic of his name to the controversy for another ten years.

Bryan was under much pressure to begin such a crusade. He appreciated the chance that the WCFA had given him to defend his position. J. Frank Norris wrote him, "I repeat what I said to you in Memphis, you are now in the greatest work of your life and giving 10,000 times more service to the cause of righteousness than a dozen presidents."[42] Wealthy backers were not lacking either, for George F. Washburn wired him during the trial that he would offer $10,000 to establish a Fundamentalist university at Dayton. William Upshaw, congressman from Georgia, let it be known that he would be glad to introduce a federal bill into Congress to prohibit the teaching of evolution.[43] William B. Riley and T. T. Martin were eager to begin state-by-state agitation, as their later activities proved. The question of whether Bryan could have controlled these pressures upon him is a moot one. In his *Memoirs,* his wife noted that he always felt he could, but the correctness of this view is debatable.

The most conclusive piece of evidence concerning his post-trial plans, however, can be found in a letter he wrote to his son, William, after learning that he would join the Dayton party:

> In the first place, this trial will become one of the greatest trials in history and I want your name associated with it. In the second place, the issue will be raised in every state and I want you to be in a position to take up my work and carry it on in this matter. I can't return to the practice of law but you can take my place in the various states. The fact that you are my son, added to your connection with the case, will give you a standing no one else can have. Every attack from our opponents draws the orthodox Christians more closely to me, and you will share in the benefits. Don't fail to come; it would be a very grave mistake for you to miss this opportunity.[44]

All evidence seems to suggest, therefore, that another "paramount" issue was in the offing and that, once again, William Jennings Bryan was ready to take to the hustings on behalf of a cause. His last speech attacking evolution was well stated, and though his sudden death caused it to be widely printed, the effect was negligible compared with what might have been had he delivered it several hundred times across the nation.

Frank Kent, writing in the *New Republic,* noted that had a bolt of lightning struck down Clarence Darrow during the trial, few of the onlookers would have been surprised.[45] But it was Bryan, not Darrow, who was taken, and to the Fundamentalist mind, this was not done without purpose. When Reverend Paul Rood addressed a crowd of twenty-five hundred in California, he suggested that God's plan was to take Bryan at the time when the whole world's attention was riveted upon his message.[46] Consequently, Rood formed the Bryan Bible League to push a program of antievolution. The league published a journal and distributed campaign literature and buttons, but was very short-lived.

After 1925, conservatives promised that Scopes trials would be multiplied, but a more immediate question was who would take Bryan's place. Several names were suggested: Mark A. Matthews, Clarence E. Macartney, G. Campbell-Morgan, and George F. Washburn. The names most often suggested, however, were those of Straton and Riley. "Everywhere I have been, I have been urged to take up Mr. Bryan's work," Straton was quoted as saying. "It was unique and should be carried on. I would be willing to attempt it."[47] Riley, who was conscious of the organizational role he himself had played, said that was acceptable to him. Curtis Lee Laws, however, noted that he could find no one authorized to select Straton to become the leader of the Fundamentalists. "Mr. Bryan was never the leader of fundamentalism except that his prominence caused the papers to count him the leader. Fundamentalism has never had a leader. Any man can assume the leadership of a small or a large portion of the fundamentalists when they are willing to be led. It has been our experience and observation that the leadership of the fundamentalists is a pretty hard job."[48] Riley noted that after 1922 Bryan had been by far the outstanding member of the movement and said: "Our judgment is that it will take a number of us, and at our best, to fill the place vacated by the fall of this magnificent thinker and leader."[49]

No one could take over the Fundamentalist movement from William Jennings Bryan because William Jennings Bryan had taken over the Fundamentalist movement. His sudden increased interest in evolution, his lack of theological training, his concern for all aspects of Christianity, especially the Social Gospel, and the magic of his name had thrust him into the center of the controversy. Moreover, Bryan was an inclusive force whereas the other Fundamentalists were primarily exclusive. His tolerance, perspective, and genial warmth would be found in none of his successors. In spite of their activities, no one who followed him could approach the publicity Bryan received just by being Bryan. "The newspapers ought to put up the money to build a memorial for Wm. Jennings," wrote a friend to Mark Sullivan, "because he was to the world of news what Babe Ruth is to baseball—the real drawing card, for anyone who is halfway fair has to admit that Bryan was news to his friends and enemies and the reading public 365 days in the year."[50] His mantle, as Moody's thirty years earlier, could find no shoulders strong enough to carry it. Bryan was unique in the Fundamentalist movement. He could never be replaced.

11
The Many Meanings
of "Evolution"

Thanks largely to William Jennings Bryan, a question was reopened in the 1920s that had been closed for almost two generations. Bryan's words and actions thrust the relationship between evolution and religion onto the front pages, not only of the smaller church periodicals but also of the nation's major dailies. Once raised, the question remained prominent for several years. It is obvious in retrospect that the meaning of "evolution" in the 1920s went far beyond the developmental theories of Darwin or Spencer. The word became a symbol for everything that was wrong with the nation in that decade. The symbolic use of evolution provided conservatives with an easy means to criticize society.

From the conservative point of view, something *had* gone wrong with American life after World War I. The war produced few of the glittering results promised by President Wilson. Although media reports may have been exaggerated, the nation's youth seemed to be behaving in strange, new ways.[1] The spread of higher criticism of the Scriptures had brought about a new understanding of the Bible, and theological liberals seemed everywhere to be in the ascendancy. Scientific naturalism was rife in the universities and broke into the popular realm with Joseph Wood Krutch's *The Modern Temper* (1929) and Walter Lippmann's *Preface to Morals* (1929).[2] Anthropologists such as Franz Boas and Margaret Mead seemed to argue that human nature was infinitely plastic, that all ethical systems were the product of circumstances, and that no universal morality existed.[3] All of these themes eventually became subsumed under the rubric of "evolution."

Evolution served as an explanation or a solution to these problems largely because the term was so loosely used that everyone could maintain an individual understanding of it. The multiple meanings given the word may have been confusing, but they enabled conservatives to marshal support from a wide variety of people. In the 1920s, evolution proved to be a very democratic idea. Everyone could have an opinion on it.

Perhaps the most common position was that evolution meant simply naturalism or materialism. This position received much publicity during the decade because the most aggressive defenders of evolution—not, it should be noted, those who knew the most about it—fought the battle under this banner: Maynard Shipley's Science League of America and the American Freethinkers.

A vast amount of publicity surrounded the confrontation between Freethinkers and Fundamentalists because they staged perhaps one hundred platform debates on evolution during the latter part of the 1920s. No area of the country was excluded; each side traveled about, hiring halls and drumming up crowds. William B. Riley alone debated nineteen times, and several of his West Coast exchanges were carried live by radio. Crowds filled Madison Square Garden to hear John R. Straton debate with Unitarian minister Charles F. Potter. Straton later held five heated exchanges in California with Maynard Shipley. Numerous lesser figures also took to the debate platform, and several magazines carried on lengthy written quarrels.[4]

The Fundamentalists claimed that there were only two possible theories as to the origin of the Universe and man. As John R. Straton once put it, "One is creation by the living God; the other is evolution by dead force."[5] Evolution, they claimed, was not scientifically proven, but only an idle speculation. No one need accept the "consensus of scientific opinion" on a subject of such importance to both individual and nation. To teach evolution was to teach atheism, and the results of such teaching could easily be seen in the holocaust of the war and the declining morality of the times. To contemplate a Universe without divine purpose was to enter into despair. Riley said that the two sides of the issue were perfectly illustrated by the beliefs of the two debaters: atheism was the religion of the evolutionist and Fundamentalism was the religion of the Christian. In closing their debates, the Fundamentalist candidates usually urged the audience to support the local antievolution law.[6]

The Freethinkers often began with the assumption that materialistic evolution was already scientifically proven and that their job was simply to get people to accept this fact. All scientists and philosophers of note, they said, believed in the theory. The growth and development of children and the fossil record in the rocks all proved it beyond a doubt. The Genesis account of Creation was obviously a myth. As Charles Smith said, "Atheists hold with Charles Darwin that man descends from the monkey."[7] Evolution was scientific, the Freethinkers said, and therefore it obviously was true and should be taught in the public schools. Joseph McCabe, who spoke of "Science the Redeemer," claimed: "It is in science that the vitality of our age finds its supreme expression, and by our science we must be judged."[8]

Emotions ran high in these encounters, and occasionally local groups intervened with disruptive consequences. In North Carolina in 1927, for example, T. T. Martin of the WCFA and Howell England of the American

Association for the Advancement of Atheism (AAAA) were able to complete only two of their scheduled series because of angry local reaction. The Ku Klux Klan opposed England as an atheist, and the local ministers opposed Martin as an outsider.[9] The next year, in Arkansas, the scheduled debates between William B. Riley, head of the WCFA, and Charles Smith, head of the AAAA, were halted abruptly when Smith, who had declared that he wanted to convert Arkansas to atheism, was thrown into jail on a minor charge.

The debaters often agreed that an audience vote would determine the winner, and this practice encouraged candidates to play to the crowd. Although the audiences generally favored the Fundamentalists, the loser inevitably accused the winner of packing the crowd. It is highly likely, therefore, that the ratio of Freethinkers to Fundamentalists was the same at the end of these debates as it was at the beginning.

Side by side with the naturalistic position, however, came the theistic interpretation of evolution. Evolution need not necessarily mean atheism, said a chorus of reconcilers, both scientists and theologians. Such articulate speakers as physicist Robert A. Millikan, astronomer Henry Norris Russell, geologist Kirtley Mather, theologian Edgar Y. Mullins, and college president William L. Poteat argued for theistic evolution. Kirtley Mather declared that evolution was a method only and that the book of Genesis contained at least two Creation stories, neither one of which mentioned how God created the world. Genesis spoke of the power (the Lord Jehovah), the raw material (the dust of the earth), and the results (the world as it is). Nowhere did it mention the means by which the results came about.[10] The popularizers of the 1880s and 1890s, Henry Ward Beecher, Lyman Abbott, and John Fiske, would have felt comfortable with these arguments.

Trying to unravel who meant what when they used the term evolution has been the despair of historians. Nor was this problem lost on contemporaries. "For some," complained the editor of the *Alabama Baptist,* "evolution meant a materialism which denied God in the creation of things. For others, it meant the process by which God created, controlled, and directed all things." From this, he observed, it ran through "about 57 other varieties and, as most often used in common parlance, it had nothing to do with creation but referred only to the growth and development of anything." "We most firmly believe," he concluded, "that it is the different meanings attached to the word that have brought about the great confusion in the minds of many people."[11]

This analysis was certainly true. People read just about anything they wished into the idea of evolution. Some opposed it because they saw it as atheism; others, because they viewed it as moral relativity.[12] William J. Bryan opposed evolution, in large part (as the recent studies by Willard H. Smith and Lawrence W. Levine have shown), because by destroying regeneration he felt it would also destroy social reform. In his last speech against evolution, he noted that "by paralyzing the hope of reform, it discourages those who labor for the improvement of man's position."[13] The burden of Bryan's inspirational talks, which sent literally hundreds of young men into religious occupations, was service. You must measure your life not by what you can have done for you, he told countless young midwesterners on the Chautauqua circuit, but by what you yourself can do. It was the job of man to overflow with righteous life, and one way to do this was to be a reformer. Bryan felt that in their hearts all men were in some sense reformers. But he also thought that evolution limited social improvements to a slow, gradual process that man could not affect. The doctrines of the survival of the fittest and of gradual improvement he felt would paralyze individual Christian action and the application of Christian principles to all aspects of society.[14]

Many conservatives followed Bryan in fearing that all evolution, even when labeled "theistic," was materialistic and that this theory did much harm to the person of Jesus.[15] They believed that evolution did more than just remove God to what might be a neodeist position; it also eliminated their understanding of Christ. This was the heart and soul of many ministers' concept of evangelism. If evolution described the way the world operated, then they felt the conversion experience—giving the self wholly to Christ— was no longer possible. Bryan called his conversion at fourteen the most important day of his life, and the decisions Riley and Straton made as young men determined the careers to which they devoted their lives. Christ in a naturalistic, evolutionary Universe was no longer the Savior who could come into man's heart and redeem the fallen. He was, at best, a philosopher, a teacher of a viable, but perhaps outdated, moral code. Straton criticized evolution for locking God up in time as a resident force, for making Him a principle that came to self-consciousness in man alone. Evolution, he felt, substituted a blind force for a living God and was an explicit denial of Christ. It made Him as other men.[16] "The world does not need a purely human Christ," Bryan wrote to Graham Patterson in 1925. "It has had philosophers enough."[17] Riley's message was similar.

Of all keys to the source of the Fundamentalist agitation, the position of Christ was central. William G. Shepherd commented in 1925 that the crucial distinction between a Fundamentalist and a liberal was whether or not the man had been converted. Of the fourteen ministers Shepherd interviewed, eight had been converted and six had not. All of the eight were Fundamentalists. The Fundamentalist "invites us to a mystic experience," he wrote. "The liberal invites us to a mental experience."[18] "The Christ you preach is not the Christ I preach and in whom I put my trust for this life and for that which is to come," wrote Clarence E. Macartney to Harry Emerson Fosdick.[19] The Christs to which each side appealed were indeed different. A large part of the Fundamentalist agitation resulted from fear that they would no longer be able to preach the Christ they knew.

By opposing materialistic evolution, many conservatives put forth strong defenses of supernaturalism against pure naturalism. In fact, able conservative spokesmen such as Edgar Y. Mullins generally took this tack in their arguments.[20] They maintained that life and the Universe could not have originated spontaneously.[21] "[T]he philosophy of naturalism whose cornerstone is mechanism is what we as Christian scholars need to fight," remarked Fraser Hood.[22] The most perceptive conservatives agreed. This defense of the idea of divine purpose may well have been the major conservative contribution to the ideological arguments of the decade. But when they began to marshal their attacks on science, they soon moved out of their depths.

Like most men of their moral nineteenth-century background, conservative opponents of evolution were very unclear about scientific terminology. Riley, for example, defined science as "knowledge gained and verified by exact observation and correct thinking." He spoke contemptuously of "theories" and contrasted them with the "facts" of love, hope, and faith. Bryan, in his *New York Times* article, equated "hypothesis" with "guess." Not one of them understood the difference between the idea of a positivistic fact and a theory for which evidence is gathered, arranged into a pattern, and perhaps discarded as more research develops. It was a standard part of their argument that the church had nothing to fear from truth and from facts, but only from guesses that were groundless. Because a theory was not based on fact, it could be judged by the results it caused. "We know that *nothing can be intellectually true that is morally false,*" said Straton. "But where there is *no proof,*" said Bryan, "we have a right to consider the *effect* of the acceptance of an unsupported hypothesis."[23] These ideas were widely held.[24]

Few of the religious opponents of evolution had any scientific training, of course, and what science they had absorbed in their lifetimes was minimal. Their arguments came from several sources, but none of them had had any scientific training either. Alfred W. McCann's *God—or Gorilla* (1922) was widely quoted even though he was Roman Catholic. Alfred Fairhurst sent a series of questionnaires to scientists in America and from them compiled *Atheism in Our Universities* (1923), which also tried to marshal scientific proof to show that the theory of evolution was in error. The most famous Fundamentalist scientist, however, was Seventh-Day Adventist George McCready Price, and his views received wide dissemination in the 1920s. Although he had no formal training, he held posts as professor of geology at the College of Medical Evangelists, Loma Linda, California, professor of English literature at Fernando Academy, and professor of chemistry and physics at Lodi Academy in California. In 1922, he became professor of geology at Union College in Nebraska. Price wrote several articles and books, including *Fundamentals of Geology* (1913), *Q.E.D., or New Light on the Doctrine of Creation* (1917), and *The New Geology* (1923). He believed that a great world catastrophe—a flood—had established the earth's strata in the position in which it now lay and that no fossils were older than those of man. He concluded that "there must have been just such a literal creation as [*sic*] the beginning as the Bible describes."[25] Price confessed in 1924 that when he first came to his conclusions in 1909, he decided not to present them in orthodox scientific journals but to publish them through the popular and religious journals. He said that although he realized such publication would mean ostracism by the regular scientists, he did not mind.[26] Thus, the Seventh-Day Adventist position on evolution was widely spread by others.

Perhaps more nonsense was written on the subject of evolution than on any other during the decade. "My ancestors may have hung by their necks," John Straton said, "but they never hung by their tails." At the packed Charles Smith–William Riley debate over evolution at Tulane University, Smith arranged to have a stuffed monkey lowered from the ceiling behind Riley's chair. Riley, in turn, replied to his opponent's argument that there were gill slits in the human fetus with, "That sounds fishy." On another occasion, he declared: "I selected the best educated and most beautiful woman I knew and married her. What more can an antievolutionist do for the survival of the fittest?"[27] Riley, who continued to attack evolution long after it had ceased to be an issue except in the most isolated areas of the country, once called Darwin the father of skepticism, agnosticism, Modernism, higher criticism, Unitarianism, and Hitlerism. He said that evolution was antibiblical, antisocial, antimoral, antinational, and antiglobal. The *Bible Champion*, the organ of the Bible League of North America, entitled one of their articles "Evolution-Devilution."[28] Even poet Robert Frost took on an angry group of Dartmouth students over their views of evolution. They were so sure of themselves, Frost complained to a friend, that they had not taken the trouble to think out their position. "Did they think it was ever going to be any easier to be good?" Frost asked. "I wouldn't call it an evolution unless there was hope of screwing virtue to the sticking point so it would cost less effort and vigilance than now to maintain."[29] "We believe," groaned the *Presbyterian of the South*, that "no subject has ever been talked and written about by so many people who knew very little of what they were discussing."[30]

Evolution eventually overshadowed all the other issues raised by the conservative evangelical revolt against liberal Christianity. Many conservatives despaired at this, for they felt that the real issues were being lost along the way. "We are in great danger of being obsessed by anti-evolutionism," complained L. R. Scarborough in the *Alabama Baptist*, "we must remember that we have other enemies of the truth besides evolution."[31] In 1925, Curtis Lee Laws, editor of the *Watchman-Examiner*, sourly remarked that it was a vast mistake that the Scopes trial and evolution ever became an issue of Fundamentalism.[32] Yet this confused understanding of evolution provided Fundamentalism with its power. Everyone could, and did, hold a position on it. By 1925, evolution had become the ultimate symbol for what was wrong with the nation.

In the last analysis, however, the fight in the 1920s over the issue of evolution brought with it something that had been missing from the Gilded Age conflict and that, in the long run, may have more importance than any other aspect of the controversy—the role of experts in a democracy. Opposition to an "educational elite" was a major part of Fundamentalism, and this makes the controversy as much a social movement as a religious one. Those who restrict their analyses to religion are bound to slight this social element. In fact, Fundamentalism might be seen as the last revolt of "the average man," the person who believed that nothing was beyond his grasp. Of course, the average man could understand and evaluate the question of evolution for himself, said conservatives. If he could not, then who could? "People who are not scientists are sometimes criticized for discussing the subject of evolution, but this is not justifiable," wrote Fundamentalist C. V. Dunn. "All [one] needs is common sense and a fair degree of power to reason on facts."[33]

Dunn's comment spoke volumes, for it was clear by World War I that the general trend of American society was toward ever greater distinctions, especially those favoring the educated specialist.[34] America was approaching that period, predicted by Henry Adams, when only a few highly trained, intelligent people would be able to understand each other.[35]

In many disciplines of knowledge ordinary people were being left behind. In science, for example, the expert slowly gained ground on the educated layman in the early twentieth century. Most of the scientific publications in the post–Civil War period were oriented toward technology, but gradually these gave way to highly technical professional articles. By the 1870s, a significant number of American scientists had begun to articulate the idea of "science for science's sake." By the next decade, they were decidedly elitist and chafed at any democratic control over their work.[36] Simultaneously, the work of isolated geniuses such as Thomas Edison and Alexander Graham Bell was replaced around the turn of the century by the professional consciousness of the emerging scientific community. Edison is almost as important in the history of American science for establishing his Research Laboratory at Menlo Park—where scientists could gather together—as for his thousand inventions.

Between 1870 and 1920, over two hundred professional societies either were formed or assumed major status. Professionalization brought the emergence of experts in economics, history, education, theology, architecture, medicine, law, social work, and all the sciences, and it also often brought arrogance. The president of the American physicists' society in 1899 reminded his audience that they formed the new aristocracy, not of wealth or pedigree, but of intellect and ideals.[37] Richard C. Cabot, M.D., believed that expertise would be the salvation of American life, the solution to the problem of distinctions within a democracy: "Superiority there is and ought to be, but superiority in one respect—the obvious superiority of the expert. We can look up to the expert with ready acknowledgement of his superiority. We are not his equal here, but there is not a particle of sense of shame on the one side or of condescension on the other."[38]

The rise of expertise was an important facet of this generation's social outlook. It had far-reaching results. "The passage of the scientific amateur is due largely to the fact that science has become too difficult for him," noted the *Nation* in 1906. "In its recent generalizations, physics may be followed only by an expert in the higher, not to say the transcendental mathematics. . . . In short, one may say not that the average cultivated man has given up science, but that science has deserted him."[39]

The popularization of Albert Einstein's theory of relativity after 1919 continued this process for the postwar generation. Yet for a people who had always believed that science was only "organized common sense," such criticism proved difficult to swallow. Even the scholars were alleged not to comprehend what Einstein had written. Said Yale economics professor Irving Fisher in despair: "Astronomers and physicists must fight it out and the rest of us must wait." Edward L. Rice, zoologist at Ohio Wesleyan University, insisted on the interpretative role of the modern scientist. Because the "non-scientific" person had no time to study the theory of evolution for himself, Rice argued that he must accept it "largely on the authority of those who have studied the subject, just as he accepts on authority the medicine prescribed by his physician."[40]

Scientists in the 1920s were no longer simple, humble truthseekers; an arrogant scientific complacency was also part of the spirit of the decade.[41] Suddenly science seemed to be the sole prerogative of the expert. He alone could tell what was true and what was not. Fundamentalists, who felt that truth was easily accessible to all, were dismayed.

Many felt the rise of higher criticism had virtually the same effect on the Bible. One theologian urged laymen to look to the experts in this realm, too, because the right of private judgment had resulted in the anarchy of sects.[42] Although the argument was made that higher criticism was so technical ordinary Christians could never understand it, many conservatives disagreed, believing that ordinary people could and should make their own theological decisions.[43] Higher criticism, however, usually was considered to belong to the experts. Never before had so much been known about the Bible, observed the *Methodist Review* in 1922. The only trouble was that so few people had this knowledge. "A religion that didn't appeal to any but college graduates," William Jennings Bryan said, "would be over the head or under the feet of 99 percent of our people. The God I worship is the God of the ignorant as well as the God of the learned man."[44]

Ordinary citizens might be content to leave some fields to the experts, but others remained in the public realm, including social mores, public education, and the interpretation of the Bible, subjects on which ordinary people insisted they had a right to express an opinion. Bryan's antievolution comments were laced with leveling statements. He denounced the use of "experts" in the Scopes trial as an attempt to mislead the people of Tennessee.[45] He accused scientists of trying "to set up an oligarchy in free America, the most tyrannical that has been attempted in history."[46] In 1925, Straton offered to debate Dudley F. Malone on the question, "Resolved, that the American people should henceforth be ruled by an aristocracy of scholastics," but Malone wanted no part of it. Riley believed that "democracy is at an end" if a few men could set themselves up as educational aristocrats to determine what should and should not be taught.

The Fundamentalists' complete confidence in ordinary people, however, carried within it a distrust of those who proved to be exceptional, a scorn for advanced learning and often for scholarship in general. In a letter to John Dewey on the publication of Will Durant's *Story of Philosophy*, David Swenson hit the heart of the issue:

> Real philosophy and real science cannot in that sense be popularized, and it seems to me that the attempt to do so only plays into the hands of the journalists, sophists and charlatans. For it is my opinion that the evil of the age is the silly and nonsensical notion that everybody can understand everything, and especially that he can understand it without working, provided only some journalist or popularizer will make it plain. It is this lack of respect for competence, and for the discipline and the work without which there is no competence, which is today the chief intellectual ingredient in the fundamentalist movement, whereby it proves itself to be at bottom quite "modernist," in spite of its attacks on Modernism.[47]

The teaching of evolution in the public schools presented a new and different challenge to democracy as the conservatives understood it. A new elite seemed to be dictating a "truth" that was incomprehensible or repugnant to many citizens. Moreover, this new professional and scientific elite seemed different from the old aristocracy of character, entrance into which, it was widely assumed, was barred only by lack of effort. An intellectual and professional elite was not open to all, for mental ability, unlike pluck and luck, was intimately connected with genetics. Thus it presented a direct threat to the conservatives' understanding of American democracy.

Evolution, then, served as the ultimate issue of the 1920s. It engulfed and refocused many of the arguments raised by the conservative Protestants.

Passing antievolution legislation seemed a concrete means of attacking a set of problems that otherwise remained bewilderingly vague. It is clear in retrospect, however, that concentration on that issue produced a great misdirection of energy. Evolution has not proved to be an important point in conservative Christianity. Yet, ironically, without the broad appeal of this issue, Christian conservatives would not have attracted the large following evolution gave them. What evolution took with one hand, it gave away with the other.

Conclusion

From 1880 to 1930, American Protestantism was a vital part of the American nation. During that time, the churches exerted a major impact on most areas of American life. When industrialism, immigration, and technology transformed a primarily rural nation into an industrial giant, the churches responded with a force of overwhelming proportions. During the Progressive Era, both liberal and conservative Christians provided a broadly based evangelical rhetoric from which all reformers drew strength. Woodrow Wilson's appeal to the nation in 1917 seemed a logical extension of this evangelical position. After the war, the evangelical rhetoric was distorted as the churches fought with one another over issues of theology and evolution.

Changes in American life during this period had an equally major impact on the Protestant churches. The gates of Ellis Island channeled millions of non-Protestant immigrants into the mainstream of national activities. The expansion and specialization of thought in all fields, especially in science and the higher criticism of the Scriptures, caused an intellectual crisis of the first magnitude. Whether the churches or the nation have changed more is a question that will probably never be resolved.

Also over these years, two distinct groups began to develop in main line American Protestantism. Within half a century, the traditional denominational distinctions came to have less meaning; the newer ones—which asked whether one were a "liberal" or a "conservative" in biblical matters—came to have much more.

These tensions took several years to form, but immediately after World War I, they surfaced in the Fundamentalist-Modernist controversy. The Northern Presbyterians and Northern Baptists almost split in two, while the other major Protestant groups—Episcopalians, Disciples, and Methodists—all dealt with related, if not identical, issues within their own denominational frameworks. The southern churches moved quickly to join the conservative side, offering loud thanks that they were not as divided as their northern brethren. The uneasiness with which the Yale Divinity

School faculty listens to evangelist Billy Graham today indicates that the division shows little sign of disappearing.[1]

The theory of evolution emerged alongside these divisions, but the soothing words of the late nineteenth-century "reconcilers" enabled many Protestants to accept it without difficulty. Consequently, it did not become a matter of serious public debate until World War I, and its emergence was largely due to William Jennings Bryan. Almost single-handedly, Bryan revived the issue of evolution and brought it to the attention of the American public. With the 1925 trial of John Thomas Scopes in Dayton, Tennessee, it assumed national proportions.

After the 1920s, however, the evolution issue faded somewhat into the background. The other points of conservative-liberal disagreement have shown more staying power and are as alive today as they were in the early years of the century. Did Jesus come into the world via a Virgin Birth? Was He primarily human or divine? How did He understand His mission? What is the meaning of the Incarnation? Did He perform miracles, or can all the biblical events be described scientifically? How necessary is an experience of Grace? What is meant by salvation? Does the Old Testament prefigure the major events in the New? Should the crucial passages of Scripture be taken in a figurative or a literal sense? How much of one's faith and life should be given over to the experts? Liberal and conservative responses to these questions are given by honest men and women on both sides. The answers, moreover, can never really be proved. They rest, as they should, on faith.

Although the northern churches have had a liberal leaning since the late 1920s and the southern churches a conservative one, it could not be said that either side really won the battle. The *Christian Century* called it a "tolerationist" victory, and in most mainstream denominations today Fundamentalists and Modernists sit side by side on Sunday morning.[2] The issues were never resolved; they simply retreated, and from time to time they continue to disturb the uneasy truce that exists among the Protestant churches of America.

The Fundamentalist controversy raised important theological and social issues. When these were popularized and, inevitably, distorted, they produced a fatal crack in the prevailing Protestant ethos. From the united front of the Progressive Era, which was characterized by a unified attack against injustice, the Protestants of the 1920s turned against each other, splitting into separate factions. Alfred North Whitehead observed of Protestantism in 1933: "Its dogmas no longer dominate; its divisions no longer interest; its institutions no longer direct the patterns of life."[3]

This split marked the passing of the Protestant hegemony in the United States. After 1920, few clerical leaders would have major influence in the decision-making centers of the nation. Thousands of individual ministers would continue to labor at their callings, but theology itself—the brief heyday of Reinhold Niebuhr and Paul Tillich excepted—ceased to have widespread influence outside narrow academic circles. As the theologians lost touch with the masses of people they were supposed to be serving, the gap between the scholar and the churchgoer widened considerably.[4] As Henry Steele Commager remarked of an earlier period, this meant that organized religion could prosper but theology was going slowly bankrupt.[5]

Thus, in the fifty years from 1880 to 1930, the religious dimension of American life experienced a dynamic revolution. In the 1880s, the nation's culture was largely dominated by organized Protestantism (certain ethnic areas obviously excluded). By 1930 no one could make that claim. In the interim, Protestantism had been pushed from the center of national life to the periphery, where it began to occupy the same sorts of regional enclaves that had separated immigrant groups from the mainstream a generation earlier.

In those fifty years, a new culture emerged within the American nation. In this new culture, Protestantism was only one segment of a multifaceted society in a nation that was reaching out for a new mode of life. The American people were becoming pluralistic in their religion, secular in their world outlook, and, some would say, amoral in their attitude toward their fellow citizens. What direction this new culture would take was anyone's guess, but it clearly would be vastly different from what had gone before.

Notes

Preface

1. This phrase comes from Sidney E. Mead, who suggested it as an alternative title for this book.
2. Will Herberg, *Protestant-Catholic-Jew* (New York, 1955).
3. Robert T. Handy, *A Christian America: Protestant Hopes and Historical Realities* (New York, 1971), 215.

Chapter 1

1. "The Argument from Design as Affected by the Theory of Evolution," in Protestant Episcopal Church, *Papers and Speeches of the Church Congress* (New York, 1894), 172.
2. Loren Eiseley, *Darwin's Century: Evolution and the Men Who Discovered It* (New York, 1961), 2; Cynthia Eagle Russett, *Darwin in America: The Intellectual Response, 1865–1912* (San Francisco, 1976), vii; J. S. Wilkie, "Buffon, Lamarck, and Darwin: The Originality of Darwin's Theory of Evolution," in Peter R. Ball, ed., *Darwin's Biological Work: Some Aspects Reconsidered* (Cambridge, 1959), 262–343.
3. Several good introductions are Stow Persons, ed., *Evolutionary Thought in America* (New Haven, 1950); Mody C. Boatright, ed., *The Impact of Darwinian Thought on American Life and Culture* (Austin, 1959); George Daniels, ed., *Darwin Comes to America* (Waltham, Mass., 1968); John C. Greene, *The Death of Adam: Evolution and Its Impact on Western Thought* (Ames, 1959); Bert James Loewenberg, "The Controversy over Evolution in New England, 1859–1873," *New England Quarterly* 8 (1935):232–57; Bert James Loewenberg, "Darwinism Comes to America, 1859–1900," *Mississippi Valley Historical Review* 28 (1941):339–68.
4. Lynn White, Jr., *Dynamo and Virgin Reconsidered* (Cambridge, 1968), 49; Pierre Teilhard de Chardin, *The Phenomenon of Man* (New York, 1959), 216–28; Pierre Teilhard de Chardin, *The Future of Man* (New York, 1964), 261–62.
5. Minot J. Savage, *The Irrepressible Conflict between Two World-Theories* (Boston, 1892), 27.

6. Two fine studies, both published too recently to be extensively used here, are James R. Moore, *The Post-Darwinian Controversies: A Study of the Protestant Struggle to Come to Terms with Darwin in Great Britain and America, 1870–1900* (Cambridge, 1979), and George M. Marsden, *Fundamentalism and American Culture: The Shaping of Twentieth Century Evangelicalism, 1870–1925* (New York, 1980).

7. Stow Persons, "Evolution and Theology in America," in Persons, ed., *Evolutionary Thought in America,* is an excellent study of this phenomenon.

8. Two good accounts illustrating the harmony of science and religion during antebellum times are E. Brooks Holifield, *The Gentlemen Theologians: American Theology in Southern Culture, 1795–1860* (Durham, 1978), and Theodore Dwight Bozeman, *Protestants in an Age of Science: The Baconian Ideal and Antebellum American Religious Thought* (Chapel Hill, 1977).

9. Darwin as quoted in Greene, *Death of Adam,* 303.

10. A. Hunter Dupree, *Asa Gray* (Cambridge, 1959), 296–99, 301.

11. "Argument from Design," 192.

12. Irvin G. Wyllie, "Social Darwinism and the Businessman," *Proceedings of the American Philosophical Society* 103 (1959):629–35.

13. John S. Haller, Jr., *Outcasts from Evolution: Scientific Attitudes of Racial Inferiority, 1859–1900* (Urbana, 1971), is the best study of this issue.

14. Maurice Mandelbaum, "Darwin's Religious Views," *Journal of the History of Ideas* 19 (1958):363–78; Francis Darwin, ed., *The Life and Letters of Charles Darwin,* 2 vols. (New York, 1891), 1:272–81.

15. Sidney Ratner, "Evolution and the Rise of the Scientific Spirit in America," *Philosophy of Science* 3 (1936):108.

16. Edward Lurie, *Louis Agassiz: A Life in Science* (Chicago, 1960), and Dupree, *Asa Gray,* are the standard biographies of the two protagonists. See also Ernest Mayr, "Agassiz, Darwin, and Evolution," *Harvard Library Bulletin* 13 (1959):165–93.

17. Herbert W. Schneider, "The Influence of Darwin and Spencer on American Philosophical Theology," *Journal of the History of Ideas* 6 (1945):3–18.

18. R. J. Wilson, ed., *Darwinism and the American Intellectual* (Homewood, Ill., 1967); Russett, *Darwin in America;* cf. D. H. Meyer, "American Intellectuals and the Victorian Crisis of Faith," in Daniel Walker Howe, ed., *Victorian America* (Philadelphia, 1976), 60–77.

19. Quoted in Russett, *Darwin in America,* 38.

20. James Woodrow, *Evolution* (Columbia, 1884), 8; *Complaint of James Woodrow versus the Synod of Georgia* (Columbia, 1888), esp. 9–10. Ernest T. Thompson treats the controversy in his excellent *Presbyterians in the South,* 3 vols. (Richmond, 1973), 2:457–90. Clement Eaton used the episode to make a point in his "Professor James Woodrow and the Freedom of Teaching in the South," *Journal of Southern History* 28 (1962):1–11.

21. Quoted in Eaton, "Woodrow," 4.

22. John L. Girardeau, *The Substance of Two Speeches on the Teaching of Evolution in Columbia Theological Seminary Delivered in the Synod of South Carolina at Greenville, S.C., October 1884* (Columbia, 1885); *Complaint of James*

Woodrow, 12; James L. Martin, *Dr. Girardeau's Anti-evolution* (Columbia, 1889); James L. Martin, *Anti-evolution, Girardeau vs. Woodrow* (Columbia, ca. 1888); *A Defense of True Presbyterianism against Two Deliverances of the Augusta Assembly* (Charleston [?], 1886), 3; *Professor Woodrow's Speech before the Synod of South Carolina, October 27 and 28, 1884* (Columbia, 1885), 33–35; William Adams, *Evolution Errors* (Augusta, Ga., 1886), 7; James Woodrow, *A Further Examination of Certain Recent Assaults on Physical Science* (Columbia, 1884), 34.

23. *Complaint of James Woodrow*, 40–41.

24. George D. Armstrong, *A Defense of the "Deliverance" on Evolution* (Norfolk, Va., 1886), quoting the president of Yale from the *New York Tribune*, May 26, 1886, 7.

25. Quoted in *A Defense of True Presbyterianism*, 12.

26. Armstrong, *Defense*, 18; Thompson, *Presbyterians in the South*, 2:481.

27. *New York Times*, November 2, 4, 1884, April 8, December 12, 1885, December 10, 1886.

28. Phillips Brooks, *Lectures on Preaching* (New York, 1873), 231.

29. Henry Ward Beecher, *Evolution and Religion*, 2 vols. (New York, 1885).

30. Lurie, *Louis Agassiz*, 298.

31. Dupree, *Asa Gray*, esp. chapter 18, "A Theist in the Age of Darwin." The scientific world was also split over the theories of Lamarck.

32. Milton Berman, *John Fiske: The Evolution of a Popularizer* (Cambridge, 1961), is the best study of Fiske.

33. Charles M. Haar, "E. L. Youmans: A Chapter in the Diffusion of Science in America," *Journal of the History of Ideas* 9 (1948):193–213; William E. Leverette, Jr., "E. L. Youmans' Crusade for Scientific Autonomy and Respectability," *American Quarterly* 17 (1965):12–32.

34. "Mr. Herbert Spencer," *American Review of Reviews* 12 (1895):699–707. The quotation is on 699.

35. Quoted in Henry M. Simmons, "Henry Drummond and His Books," *New World* 6 (1877):475.

36. Quoted in Joseph A. Baromé, "The Evolution Controversy," in Donald Sheehan, ed., *Essays in American Historiography* (New York, 1960), 185.

37. Savage, *Irrepressible Conflict*, 11, 18, 33.

38. W. H. Mallock, "Science and Religion at the Dawn of the Twentieth Century," *Fortnightly* 76 (1901):395; Newell Dwight Hillis, *The Influence of Christ in Modern Life: Being a Study of the New Problems of the Church in American Society* (New York, 1900), 206–7.

39. Hillis, *Influence of Christ*, 211.

40. Richard E. MacLaurin, "Science and Religion: The End of the Battle," *Outlook* 99 (1911):71–74; Benjamin E. Smith, "The Darwin Centenary," *Century* 78 (1909):306; Andrew Sherwood, "Lincoln and Darwin," *World's Work* 17 (1909):11128–32; Herbert L. Willett, "The Deeper Issues of Present Religious Thinking," *Campbell Institute Bulletin* 10 (May 1914):4–8.

41. "The Passing of Evolution," *Christian Standard* 42 (1906):1111–12; "About Evolution," ibid. 27 (1891):602; "What Is Evolution," ibid. 28 (1892):254; "Evolution," ibid. 37 (1901):1170; "Is Evolution Atheistic," ibid. 37 (1901):1638.

42. The best study of this phase of Bryan's career is Paolo E. Coletta, *William Jennings Bryan: Political Evangelist, 1860–1908* (Lincoln, 1964).

43. T. DeWitt Talmage, *Live Coals* (Chicago, 1886), 271.

44. Sermons, T. DeWitt Talmage Manuscripts, Box 6, Library of Congress, Washington, D.C.

45. Quoted in Greene, *Death of Adam*, 308.

46. "Buddha and Christ," *Evangelist* 14 (1880):306–7; James F. Clarke, "Affinities of Buddhism and Christianity," *North American Review* 136 (1883):467–77; Edwin Lord Weeks, "Hindu and Moslem," *Harper's* 91 (1895):651–70.

47. *Current Literature* 32 (1902):292; Sydney E. Ahlstrom, *The American Protestant Encounter with World Religions* (Beloit, 1962), is a perceptive study.

48. Lewis G. Janes, "The Comparative Study of Religion: Its Pitfalls and Its Promise," *Sewanee Review* 7 (January 1897):1–20.

49. T. DeWitt Talmage, *The Earth Girdled: The World as Seen To-day* (Philadelphia, 1896), 340–49; Francis E. Clarke, "Christianity as Seen by a Voyage around the World," in John Henry Barrows, ed., *The World's Parliament of Religions* (Chicago, 1893), 2:1238; Joseph Cook, "Modern Novel Opportunities in Comparative Religion," *Boston Monday Lectures* (Boston and New York, 1887), 154.

50. Edmund D. Soper, "Comparative Religion and the Preacher," *Methodist Review* 101 (1918):375; William F. Warren, "Comparative Religion, So-Called," *Methodist Review* 96 (1914):9–13.

51. John R. Mott, *History of the Student Volunteer Movement for Foreign Missions* (Chicago, 1892), 10, pamphlet; *The Twenty-fifth Anniversary of the Student Volunteer Movement* (Philadelphia, 1911), 17, pamphlet, both in Presbyterian Historical Society, Philadelphia.

52. Robert E. Speer, "The Achievements of Yesterday," in Jesse R. Wilson ed., *Students and the Christian World Mission* (New York, 1936), 175–76.

53. *Chicago Times*, September 10, 1893.

54. Quoted in *Public Opinion* 16 (1893):56.

55. Washington Gladden, "The World's Parliament of Religions," Sermon 536, September 10, 1893, Washington Gladden Manuscripts, Ohio Historical Society, Columbus, Ohio.

56. Francis Herbert Stead, "The Story of the World's Parliament of Religions," *American Review of Reviews* 9 (1894):299; Washington Gladden, "The Brotherhood of Christian Unity," Sermon 538, October 1, 1893, Gladden Manuscripts.

57. David F. Burg, *Chicago's White City of 1893* (Lexington, 1976), 266–68; Egal Feldman, "American Ecumenism: Chicago's World's Parliament of Religions of 1893," *Journal of Church and State* 9 (1967):180–91.

58. Henry B. Hartzler, *Moody in Chicago* (New York, 1894); *Chicago Times*, September 14, 1891, September 13, 21, 26, 28, 1893; Stead, "Story," 307.

59. *Christian Evangelist* 30 (1893):674.

60. Charles Little, "The Chicago Parliament of Religions," *Methodist Review* 75 (1894):213.

61. "The Parliament of Religions," *Methodist Quarterly Review* 16 (1894):198.

62. Morgan Dix, *A Parliament of Religions*, pamphlet, Historical Archives of the Protestant Episcopal Church, Austin, Texas; *Public Opinion* 16 (1893):57.

Chapter 2

1. Henry Otis Dwight, *The Bible among the Nations: A Brief Review of One Hundred Years of the American Bible Society* (New York, 1916), pamphlet, Presbyterian Historical Society, Philadelphia.

2. Ibid., 14.

3. Perry Miller, "The Garden of Eden and the Deacon's Meadow," *American Heritage* 7 (December 1955):54–61.

4. Alfred A. Wright, *Anticipated Improvements in the New New Testament* (Lynn, Mass., 1881), 7, pamphlet, Andover-Newton Theological Seminary, Newton Centre, Mass.

5. Henry Van Dyke, "The Influence of the Bible in Literature," *Century* 80 (1910):893.

6. Beryl Smalley, *The Study of the Bible in the Middle Ages* (Oxford, 1941), 5.

7. Ibid., 27, 234.

8. George L. Haskins, *Law and Authority in Early Massachusetts: A Study in Tradition and Design* (New York, 1960), treats this issue.

9. Stephen Allen, *The Bible and National Prosperity* (Waterville, Maine, 1851), 8.

10. William A. Stone, *The Tale of a Plain Man* (n.p., 1917), 42, 43; Herbert L. Willett, "The Corridor of Years," 147, manuscript, Disciples of Christ Historical Society, Nashville, Tenn.

11. William Newton Clarke, *Sixty Years with the Bible: A Record of Experience* (New York, 1909), 27.

12. Washington Gladden, "The New Bible," *Arena* 9 (1894):296–97; Washington Gladden, *Recollections* (Boston, 1909), passim.

13. R. Heber Newton, *The Right and Wrong Uses of the Bible* (New York, 1883), 16.

14. Willard C. Selleck, *The New Appreciation of the Bible: A Story of the Spiritual Outcome of Biblical Criticism* (Chicago, 1907), 49.

15. Lyman Abbott, "The New Bible," *Outlook* 98 (1911):56.

16. Frederick C. Prussner, "The Covenant of David and the Problem of Unity in Old Testament Theology," in J. Coert Rylaarsdam, ed., *Transitions in Biblical Scholarship* (Chicago, 1968), 17; Henry S. Nash, *The History of the Higher Criticism of the New Testament* (New York, 1901), 12–14.

17. M. B. Lambdin, "The Higher Criticism: Its Rationalistic Type," *Union Seminary Magazine* 19 (1907–8):114.

18. The only works in this area are Jerry Wayne Brown, *The Rise of Biblical Criticism in America, 1800–1870: The New England Scholars* (Middletown, 1969); Ira V. Brown, "The Higher Criticism Comes to America, 1880–1900," *Journal of the Presbyterian Historical Society* 38 (1960):193–212; Walter F. Peterson, "American Protestantism and the Higher Criticism, 1870–1910," *Transactions of the Wisconsin Academy of Sciences, Arts and Letters* 50 (1962):321–29.

19. Brown, *Rise of Biblical Criticism*, esp. chapter 10.

20. A. O. J. Cockshut, ed., *Religious Controversies of the Nineteenth Century: Selected Documents* (Lincoln, 1966), 8–12.

21. *New York Times*, June 23, July 7, 1878, July 27, 1880.

22. Ibid., March 2, 1878, July 27, 1880.

23. Brown, "Higher Criticism Comes to America," 198–201.

24. Robert W. Funk, "The Watershed of the American Biblical Tradition: The Chicago School, First Phase, 1892–1924," 5, manuscript, Disciples of Christ Historical Society; Powel Mills Dawley, *The Story of the General Theological Seminary* (New York, 1969), 272–73; John Barnard, *From Evangelism to Progressivism at Oberlin College, 1866–1917* (Columbus, 1969), 77.

25. Edward L. Curtis, "The Present State of Old Testament Criticism," *Century* 45 (1893):727; Alvah Hovey, *An Epitome of Textual Criticism of the New Testament* (Boston, 1905?), pamphlet, Andover-Newton Theological Seminary.

26. Philip Schaff, "The Old Version and the New Testament," *North American Review* 132 (1881):427–36.

27. *New York Times,* May 18, 1879.

28. Gladden, *Recollections,* 259; Wright, *Anticipated Improvements;* William Binnie, *The Proposed Reconstruction of the Old Testament History,* 2d ed. (Edinburgh, 1880), 31.

29. *New York Times,* May 18, 1879.

30. "The Making of the Bible," *American Review of Reviews* 15 (1897):206; Alfred Perry, *The Pre-eminence of the Bible as a Book* (Hartford, 1899), 13, pamphlet, Historical Foundation of the Presbyterian and Reformed Churches, Montreat, N.C.

31. *New York Times,* November 21, 1897. Cf. F. F. Bruce, *History of the Bible in English,* 3d ed. (New York, 1978).

32. *New York Times,* June 6, 1881.

33. There is a good synopsis in Thorp, "The Religious Novel as Best Seller," in James Ward Smith and A. Leland Jamison, eds., *Religious Perspectives in American Culture* 2 vols. (Princeton, 1961), 2:222–24.

34. Margaret Deland, *John Ward, Preacher* (New York, 1888), 168, 256, 261. The quotation is from 308.

35. William Lyon Phelps, "Mrs. Humphrey Ward," in *Essays on Modern Novelists* (Chautauqua, 1909), 192.

36. Willett, "Corridor of Years," 147ff.

37. Clyde de L. Ryals, Introduction to Mrs. Humphrey Ward, *Robert Elsmere* (Lincoln, 1969), vii.

38. Herbert Ross Brown, *The Sentimental Novel in America, 1789–1860* (Durham, 1940), 347.

39. Ward, *Robert Elsmere,* 404.

40. *New York Times,* March 17, 1889.

41. Ibid., November 16, 1890; "A Sign of the Times: '*Lux Mundi*' as the Book for May," *Review of Reviews* 1 (1890):434, 435, 442–45; W. C. Doane, "The Bishop's Address," *Diocese of Albany Convention Journal* (1890), 19–29.

42. Pastoral Letter in the *Journal of the [1895] General Convention* (New York, 1896), 411–23; *New York Times,* March 18, 30, 1891.

43. *New York Times,* May 18, 1890.

44. Ibid., October 24, 1889.

45. Ibid., April 5, 1894.

46. Ibid., February 17, 1897.

47. Ibid., June 28, 1892.

48. William DeWitt Hyde, "Reform in Theological Education," *Atlantic Monthly* 85 (1900):16; Albert C. Knudson, "The Evolution of Modern Bible Study," *Methodist Review* 93 (1911):910.

49. Gladden, *Recollections*, 261. The best biography is Jacob H. Dorn, *Washington Gladden: Prophet of the Social Gospel* (Columbus, 1966).

50. Gladden, *Recollections*, 319–22; Washington Gladden, *How Much Is Left of the Old Doctrines?* (Boston, 1899), 15. Washington Gladden, *Who Wrote the Bible? A Book for the People* (Boston, 1891), 134.

51. Nash, *History of the Higher Criticism*, and Henry C. Vedder, *Our New Testament: How Did We Get It?* (New York, 1908), were its two closest popular rivals.

52. *Congregationalist*, May 21, 1891; *Chicago Standard*, n.d.; see also *New York Christian Intelligencer*, n.d.; *San Francisco Bulletin*, n.d.; *New York Examiner*, n.d.; *Portland* (Maine) *Christian Mirror* n.d., all in Gladden Papers, Ohio Historical Society, Columbus, Ohio.

53. Gladden, *Who Wrote the Bible?* 20.

54. Ibid., 134, 196; *New York Examiner*, n.d., Gladden Papers.

55. Gladden, *Who Wrote the Bible?* 43.

56. Ira V. Brown, *Lyman Abbott, Christian Evolutionist: A Study in Religious Liberalism* (Westport, Conn., 1949), vii, viii.

57. Willett, "Corridor of Years," 40, 149.

58. *Christian Century* 61 (1944):454.

59. Biographical facts are from ibid. and his autobiography, "Corridor of Years."

60. Undated clipping (about 1905) in Willett Scrapbook, Disciples of Christ Historical Society.

61. Clipping file, many undated, but September–October 1908, Los Angeles, Chicago, and Detroit papers, *New York World*, August 1, 1908, ibid.

62. *Fort Dodge* (Iowa) *Evening Messenger*, June 10, 1901; undated clipping; *Los Angeles Examiner*, August 12, 22, 1908; Willett, *My Religion* (n.d., ca. 1935), pamphlet, ibid.

63. William R. Hutchison, "Disapproval of Chicago: The Symbolic Trial of David Swing," *Journal of American History* 59 (1972), 30–47; George H. Shriver, ed., *American Religious Heretics: Formal and Informal Trials* (Nashville, 1966), 56–88; untitled typescript, Albert H. Newman Papers, Historical Commission of the Southern Baptist Convention, Nashville; *New York Times*, June 9, 1877.

64. *New York Sun*, September 20, 1896, cited by Dores R. Sharpe, *Walter Rauschenbusch* (New York, 1942), 104.

65. *New York Times*, October 14, 1878, October 27, March 23, 1879, April 20, May 1, 1880; Sydney E. Ahlstrom, *A Religious History of the American People* (New Haven, 1972), 814–15.

66. *New York Times*, December 27, 1882.

67. *Public Opinion* 14 (1893):332–33; *New York Times*, May 21, 1891. The best studies are Channing R. Jeschke, "The Briggs Case: The Focus of a Study in Nineteenth Century Presbyterian History" (Ph.D. dissertation, University of Chicago, 1967), and Carl E. Hatch, "The First Heresy Trial of Charles Augustus Briggs:

American Higher Criticism in the 1890s" (Ph.D. dissertation, University of Buffalo, 1964); Shriver, ed., *American Religious Heretics*, 89–147. A good contemporary account is Charles R. Gillett, "The Briggs Heresy Trial," *New World* 2 (1893):141–69.

68. *New York Times*, May 27, June 2, 3, 1893.

69. *Christian Century* 30 (1913):389ff.

70. *New York Times*, June 10, 1893.

71. Ibid.; *Observer* as quoted in *Public Opinion* 15 (1893):255.

72. *New York Times*, June 1, 1893.

73. Ibid., May 23, 1893.

74. Ibid., June 28, 1891.

75. All cited by *Public Opinion* 15 (1893):255.

76. Savannah, Georgia, *News* as reported in *Public Opinion* 14 (1893):333.

77. *New York Times*, May 3, 1895, May 2, 8, 16, September 21, 1899.

78. *New York Times*, March 29, 1896.

Chapter 3

1. Stephen Neill, *The Interpretation of the New Testament, 1861–1961* (New York, 1966), 26.

2. "Dates of the New Testament Books," *Methodist Quarterly Review* 51 (1902):127; H. Holtzman, "Baur's New Testament Criticism in the Light of the Present," *New World* 3 (1894):203; Francis A. Christie, "Harnack's Chronology of the New Testament," *New World* 6 (1897):452–67; Ernest DeWitt Burton, "The Present Problem of New Testament Study," *American Journal of Theology* 9 (1905):201–37; Alfred W. Benn, "The Higher Criticism and the Supernatural," *New World* 9 (1895):442.

3. Edward H. Hall, "The New Orthodoxy," *New World* 1 (1892):127–28.

4. Interview with members of the Crapsey family, December 26, 1975, Albuquerque, New Mexico.

5. Algernon S. Crapsey, *The Last of the Heretics* (New York, 1924), 252–53, 179–80; the quotation is from 268. George H. Shriver, ed., *American Religious Heretics: Formal and Informal Trials* (Nashville, 1966), 188–224, provides the best account of the case.

6. *Scroll* 4 (December 1906):61.

7. Quoted by Harold Bolce, "Christianity in the Crucible," *Cosmopolitan* 47 (1909):315, 317.

8. "Is It Safe To Study the New Testament?" *Outlook* 83 (1906):643; "The Right Use of the Bible," *Outlook* 77 (1904):208–11.

9. E. L. Curtis in *Bibliotheca Sacra*, January 1899, as quoted in *Public Opinion* 26 (1899):49.

10. "Assassins of the Bible," *Outlook* 111 (1915):402.

11. Washington Gladden, *Who Wrote the Bible? A Book for the People* (Boston, 1891), 46.

12. Lyman Abbott, *The Bible as Literature* (1896), pamphlet, Presbyterian Historical Society, Philadelphia.

13. T. S. Hamlin, "Modern Bible Study—Its Aim, Methods, and Results," *Outlook* 27 (1903):283.

14. Henry C. King, *Reconstruction in Theology* (New York, 1901, 1909 ed.), 113.

15. Joseph Henry Thayer, *The Change of Attitude towards the Bible* (Boston, 1891), 60, pamphlet, Andover-Newton Theological Seminary, Newton Centre, Mass.

16. Crawford H. Toy, *Modern Biblical Criticism* (Boston, n.d.) 9, pamphlet, ibid.

17. *Outlook* 49 (1894):485.

18. Herbert L. Willett, "My Confession of Faith," *Christian Century* 21 (1908), first page of Scrapbook, Willett Papers, Disciples of Christ Historical Society, Nashville, Tenn.

19. William S. Rainsford, *The Story of a Varied Life: An Autobiography* (Garden City, 1922), 148.

20. Cited in A. C. Zenos, "The Present Status of Biblical Criticism," *American Journal of Theology* 8 (1904):85.

21. Crawford in Protestant Episcopal Church, *Papers and Speeches of the Church Congress* (New York, 1897), 104.

22. William R. Hutchison, *The Modernist Impulse in American Protestantism* (Cambridge, 1976), is a brilliant work on American liberalism as is his "Cultural Strain and Protestant Liberalism," *American Historical Review* 76 (1971):386–411. For a good analysis, see Henry W. Bowden, *Church History in the Age of Science: Historiographical Patterns in the United States, 1876–1918* (Chapel Hill, 1971), 136–69.

23. Charles Hodge, *Systematic Theology*, 3 vols. (New York, 1873), 1:152, as quoted in Ira V. Brown, "The Higher Criticism Comes to America," *Journal of the Presbyterian Historical Society* 38 (1960):194.

24. Obituary of Green in *Christian Evangelist*, March 29, 1902; copy in Willett Papers.

25. Quoted in Louis Wallis, "Professor Orr and Higher Criticism," *American Journal of Theology* 12 (1908):241; Charles M. Sharpe, "Professor Orr and Higher Criticism," *Scroll* 4 (February 1907):85–89.

26. Reverend D. MacDill, *The Authority of the Scriptures* (Bellfontaine, Ohio, 1891), 89, pamphlet, Historical Foundation of the Presbyterian and Reformed Churches, Montreat, N.C.; W. W. Elwang, "Isaiah versus the Divisive Critics," *Union Seminary Magazine* 1 (1893), 186; Ford C. Ottman, *Modern Scholarship and Apostasy* (New York, ca. 1907), 4, pamphlet, Historical Foundation of the Presbyterian and Reformed Churches.

27. *The Truth* (New York) as quoted in *Public Opinion* 18 (1895):254; cf. D. K. Paton, *The Higher Criticism: The Greatest Apostasy of the Age* (London, 1898), 6–8.

28. *Methodist Review*, as quoted in *Public Opinion* 12 (1891):136.

29. Egbert W. Smith, "Some Impressions of Radical Old Testament Criticism," *Union Seminary Magazine* 19 (1908):171.

30. Quoted in Gladden, *Who Wrote the Bible?* 98; cf. John Peters, "Archaeology and the Higher Criticism," *New World* 7 (1899):28.

31. *New York Observer* as quoted in *Public Opinion* 16 (1894):582.

32. Howard Osgood, *Christ and the Old Testament* (Rochester, 1902), pamphlet, Andover Newton Theological Seminary.

33. Bishop's Address, Diocese of Albany, in *Convention Journal* (1890), 21.

34. Clifton Harby Levy, "Professor Haupt and the 'Polychrome' Bible," *American Review of Reviews* 14 (1896):669–86.

35. *Christian Times,* September 12, 1893.

36. John Peters, "Archaeology and the Higher Criticism," *New World* 8 (1899):28.

37. From the 1880s until his death in 1902, Talmage attacked virtually everything he felt detracted from traditional Christianity. He deserves a full-length biographical study.

38. T. DeWitt Talmage, *Live Coals* (Chicago, 1886), 291; "Splendors of Orthodoxy," in *500 Selected Sermons,* 20 vols. (Grand Rapids, 1956) 3:281ff.

39. Clippings from *Christian Commonwealth,* July 7, 1892, Box 27; Small Scrapbook, T. DeWitt Talmage Manuscripts, Library of Congress, Washington, D.C.

40. Alfred W. Benn, "The Higher Criticism and the Supernatural," *New World* 9 (1895):429.

41. Manuscript sermon (1900), Carver Family Manuscripts, Historical Commission of the Southern Baptist Convention, Nashville.

42. *New York Times,* April 5, 1894.

43. Ibid., February 1, 1897.

44. Quoted in Albion W. Small, "The Bonds of Nationality," *American Journal of Sociology* 20 (1915):681.

45. *Christian Standard* 38 (1902):247; 38 (1902):313; 44 (1908):1548; 45 (1909):102–5; 50 (1915):1118.

46. Pastoral Letter, *Journal of the General Convention* (New York, 1902), 367.

47. James Mudge, "Seventy-five Years of the 'Methodist Review,' " *Methodist Review* 75 (1894):531–32.

48. R. M. Heriges, "The Passing of the *Methodist Quarterly Review,*" *Methodist Quarterly Review* 79 (1930):644–45.

49. Charles M. Stuart, "Charles Cardwell McCabe," *Methodist Review* 90 (1908):13–15.

50. *New York Times,* May 8, 1899.

51. Robert F. Horton, *The Bible and the Child* (New York, 1896), 35.

52. William Kirkus, "The Terminology of the New Theology," *New World* 6 (1897):433.

53. Charles A. Briggs, "Sunday-School and Modern Biblical Criticism," *North American Review* 158 (1894):64–76.

54. *New York Times,* April 18, 1899.

55. M. B. Lambdin, "The Higher Criticism: Its Rationalistic Type," *Union Seminary Magazine* 19 (1907–8):118.

56. Paton, *Higher Criticism,* 25.

57. William S. Turner, *Story of my Life* (Cincinnati, 1904), 319.

58. W. H. Griffith-Thomas, "Some Tests of Old Testament Criticism," *King's Business* 9 (1918):12.

59. Louis Ruffet, *Our Attitudes as Pastors toward Modern Biblical Criticism* (New York, 1905), pamphlet, Presbyterian Historical Society, Philadelphia; *New York Times,* December 21, 1898.

60. William Hyde, "Reform in Theological Education," *Atlantic Monthly* 85 (1900):16.

61. Arthur T. Pierson, "Inspiration, Prophecy, and Higher Criticism," (originally written 1900), *King's Business* 15 (1924):336–37.

62. Cited in Norman H. Maring, "Baptists and Changing Views of the Bible, 1865–1918," *Foundations* 1 (July 1958):53.

63. Albert C. Knudson, "The Evolution of Modern Biblical Study," *Methodist Review* 93 (1911):910.

Chapter 4

1. Lyman Abbott, "The Message of the Nineteenth Century to the Men of the Twentieth," *Outlook* 102 (1912):351–54.

2. George E. Mowry, "The California Progressive and His Rationale: A Study in Middle Class Politics," *Mississippi Valley Historical Review* 36 (1949):241–50; Samuel P. Hays, "The Politics of Reform in Municipal Government in the Progressive Era," *Pacific Northwest Quarterly* 55 (1964):159–69; J. Joseph Huthmacher, "Urban Liberalism and the Age of Reform," *Mississippi Valley Historical Review* 69 (1962):231–41; John D. Buenker, *Urban Liberalism and Progressive Reform* (New York, 1973).

3. Gabriel Kolko, *The Triumph of Conservatism* (New York, 1963); James Weinstein, "Big Business and the Origins of Workmen's Compensation," *Labor History* 7 (1967):156–74.

4. Nancy J. Weiss, "The Negro and the New Freedom: Fighting Wilsonian Segregation," *Political Science Quarterly* 84 (1969):61–79; Dewey W. Grantham, Jr., "The Progressive Movement and the Negro," *South Atlantic Quarterly* 54 (1955):461–77. Gilbert Osofsky, "Progressivism and the Negro, 1900–1915," *American Quarterly* 16 (1964):153–68, views their accomplishments more favorably.

5. Samuel P. Hays, *Conservation and the Gospel of Efficiency: The Progressive Conservation Movement, 1890–1920* (Cambridge, 1959); Roy Lubove, *The Professional Altruist: The Emergence of Social Work as a Career, 1880–1930* (Cambridge, 1965); Samuel Haber, *Efficiency and Uplift: Scientific Management in the Progressive Era, 1890–1920* (Chicago, 1964).

6. Roy Lubove, "The Twentieth Century City: The Progressive as Municipal Reformer," *Mid-America* 41 (1959):206. Haber called it a "secular Great Awakening" (*Efficiency and Uplift*, ix); see also Arthur Mann, "British Social Thought and American Reforms of the Progressive Era," *Mississippi Valley Historical Review* 42 (1956):678.

7. Alexander J. McKelway, "Justice, Kindness, Religion," sermon given at the National Conference of Charities and Correction, 1913, Alexander J. McKelway Manuscripts, Box 1, Library of Congress.

8. Robert Kerr to McKelway, July 14, 1913, ibid.

9. Frederick Howe, *The Confessions of a Reformer* (Chicago, 1925, 1967), 16–17; Lubove, "Twentieth Century City," 202ff.; cf. Herbert Janick, "The Mind of the Connecticut Progressive," *Mid-America* 52 (1970):89–90.

10. A good discussion of the Kingdom idea can be found in Robert T. Handy, *A Christian America: Protestant Hopes and Historical Realities* (New York, 1971), 98ff.; Walter L. Lingle, "The Teachings of Jesus and Modern Social Problems," *Union Seminary Review* 27 (1916):esp. 193–97; Dores R. Sharpe, *Walter Rauschenbusch* (New York, 1942), 226–30.

11. Abbott, "Message of the Nineteenth Century," 354.

12. H. Richard Niebuhr, *The Kingdom of God in America* (New York, 1937), and Sherwood Eddy, *The Kingdom of God and the American Dream: The Religious and Secular Ideals of American History* (New York, 1941), are the two standard accounts.

13. I have examined this idea more fully in "The Progressive Clergy and the Kingdom of God," *Mid-America* 55 (1973):3–20.

14. David Starr Jordan, *The Call of the Twentieth Century: An Address to Young Men* (Boston, 1903), 6.

15. Edward Alsworth Ross, *Sin and Society: An Analysis of Latter-Day Iniquity* (New York, 1973; originally published in 1907), 3. "Men now feel that society is an organism, no member of which can say, 'I have no need of Thee,' " said Samuel Plantz (*The Church and the Social Problem: A Study in Applied Christianity* [Cincinnati, 1906], 151). See also Jeremiah W. Jenks, *The Political and Social Significance of the Life and Teachings of Jesus* (New York, 1912), 5.

16. A. J. McKelway, "The Conservation of Manhood, Womanhood, and Childhood in Industry," address at Delaware State Conference on Social Welfare Work, December 7, 1911, McKelway Manuscripts, Box 3, Library of Congress.

17. Henry F. Ward, *Social Service for Many People*, (n.p., 1914), 1.

18. Henry F. May, *Protestant Churches and Industrial America* (New York, 1949); Charles H. Hopkins, *The Rise of the Social Gospel in American Protestantism, 1865–1915* (New Haven, 1940). Ronald C. White, Jr., and C. Howard Hopkins, eds., *The Social Gospel: Religion and Reform in Changing America* (Philadelphia, 1976), offers a good collection of materials.

19. Charles Foster Kent, *The Social Teachings of the Prophets and Jesus* (New York, 1920; originally published 1917), v; Frank L. Loveland, "The Mutual Obligations of Church and State in Building Human Character," in Paul Little, ed., *The Pacific Northwest Puplit*, 59–75 (New York, 1915).

20. "The Supreme Need of the Modern Church," *Outlook* 82 (1906):879–80.

21. Ray Stannard Baker, "The Spiritual Unrest: A Vision of the New Christianity," *American Magazine* 69 (1909):178.

22. Ross, *Sin and Society*, 10.

23. Walter Rauschenbusch, *For God and the People: Prayers of the Social Awakening* (Boston, 1910), 17.

24. Ibid., 19.

25. Ibid., 23.

26. Alexander G. Cummins, "The Relationship of Social Service to Christianity," Protestant Episcopal Church, *Papers and Speeches of the Church Congress* (New York, 1913), 42; Chester C. McCown, *Genesis of the Social Gospel* (New York, 1927), vii; Robert R. Roberts, "The Social Gospel and the Trust Busters," *Church History* 25 (1956):256; James Dombroski, *The Early Days of Christian Socialism in America* (New York, 1936); Robert T. Handy, ed., *The Social Gospel in America, 1870–1920: Gladden, Ely, Rauschenbusch* (New York, 1966).

27. John A. Hutchinson, *We Are Not Divided: A Critical and Historical Study of the Federal Council of the Churches of Christ in America* (New York, 1941), is the best study.

28. Herbert J. Doherty, Jr., "Alexander J. McKelway: Preacher to Progressive," *Journal of Southern History* 24 (1958):177–90; Presbyterian *Standard*, May 1, 1918, Alexander J. McKelway Manuscripts, Library of Congress; Hugh C. Bailey, *Edgar Gardner Murphy: Gentle Progressive* (Coral Gables, 1968).

29. John T. Stewart, *The Deacon Wore Spats: Profiles from America's Changing Religious Scene* (New York, 1965), 35; W. P. Lovejoy, "Is a Christian Socialism Possible?" *Methodist Quarterly Review* 54 (1905):738–53.

30. Cummins, "Relationship of Social Service to Christianity," 46–50.

31. Everett P. Wheeler, "The Church of Today as a Factor in Human Progress," Protestant Episcopal Church, *Papers and Speeches of the Church Congress* (New York, 1910), 80; Susan T. Knapp, "The Relation of Social Service to Christianity," *Papers and Speeches of the Church Congress* (New York, 1913), 27.

32. Bertha Henry Smith, "Every-day Church Work," *Munsey's Magazine* 32 (1905):481.

33. "Progress of the Institutional Church,"*American Review of Reviews* 15 (1897):207.

34. William R. Hutchison, "The Americanness of the Social Gospel: An Inquiry in Comparative History," *Church History* 44 (1975):367–81.

35. Quoted by Howard N. Rabinowitz, *Race Relations in the Urban South, 1865–1890* (New York, 1978), 198.

36. Rabinowitz, *Race Relations*, 210, 213–14; Isabel D. Allen, "Negro Enterprise: An Institutional Church," *Outlook* 78 (1904):181, 182.

37. "Bishop's Address," *Journal of the Fifteenth General Conference of the Methodist Episcopal Church, South* (1906), 25.

38. *American Review of Reviews* 15 (1897):207–8.

39. William S. Rainsford, *The Story of a Varied Life: An Autobiography* (Garden City, 1922), 211.

40. Ibid., 165.

41. George Iver, "How a Great Free Lecture System Works," *World's Work* 5 (1903):3327–34; Charles Sprague Smith, "Ethical Work of the People's Institute," *Outlook* 79 (1905):1001–3.

42. Isaac F. Marcosson, "A Practical School of Democracy," *World's Work* 10 (1905):6414–17.

43. Charles Stelzle, *A Son of the Bowery: The Life Story of an East Side American* (New York, 1926), 52.

44. Charles Stelzle, "The Workingman and the Church: A Composite Letter," *Outlook* 68 (1901):717–21; see also ibid., 333–34.

45. C. M. Meyer, "An Apostle to Labor," *World's Work* 19 (1909):12217–21.

46. Charles Stelzle, "The Workingman and the Church," *Outlook* 89 (1908):798–99.

47. William T. Ellis, "A Union Preacher,"*Outlook* 91 (1910):838.

48. Charles Stelzle, *The Church and Labor* (Boston, 1910), 58, 66; Stelzle, *Christianity's Storm Centre: A Study of the Modern City* (New York, 1907), 34–50; Stelzle, *The Workingman and Social Problems* (New York, 1903), 50, 100, 102.

49. *Outlook* 92 (1909):79.

50. Charles Stelzle, "Jebusites versus Chicagoites," *Outlook* 92 (1909):76–77.

51. Charles Stelzle, *American Social and Religious Conditions* (New York, 1912), 198.

52. Stelzle, *Workingman and Social Problems*, 103.

53. Charles Stelzle, *Messages to Workingmen* (New York, 1906), 49.

54. Warren A. Wilson to G. Ernest Merriam, December 22, 1908, in folder, "Correspondence and Financial Reports, Labor Temple, 1908–1919," Presbyterian Historical Society, Philadelphia.

55. Edmund Chafee, "Labor Temple after Thirteen Years," *Continent* (1924),

395–96, in clipping file, ibid.; A. J. Muste, "The Church Cares," *Pageant* (October 1938):10–12, ibid.

56. Charles Stelzle, "The Beginnings of Labor Temple," *Continent,* October 25, 1923, pp. 1291–92, in clipping file, ibid.

57. Charles Stelzle, "Proposals with Regard to the Labor Temple," typescript, February 21, 1911, ibid.

58. Stelzle, *Son of the Bowery,* 130.

59. Charles Stelzle, "Why I Liked Roosevelt," undated clipping, Folder, "Labor Temple," Presbyterian Historical Society; Theodore Roosevelt, "The Church and the People," *Outlook* 100 (1912):161–63.

60. Quoted in Stelzle, *Son of the Bowery,* Foreword.

Chapter 5

1. John W. Ripley, "The Strange Story of Charles M. Sheldon's *In His Steps,*" *Kansas Historical Quarterly* 34 (1978):241–65.

2. Eric Goldman, "Books That Have Changed America," *Saturday Review* 36 (July 4, 1954):7–9ff.

3. George R. Stuart, *Sermons* (Philadelphia, 1904), 10.

4. Ibid., 19.

5. Samuel Paynter Wilson, *Chicago by Gaslight* (Chicago, 1909), 57, 105–6.

6. Mason Long, *Save the Girls* (Fort Wayne, 1888), 37, 133.

7. Compare the more critical treatment given to Riley and Straton by C. Allyn Russell in *Voices of American Fundamentalism: Seven Biographical Studies* (Philadelphia, 1976). He discusses Matthews in "Mark Allison Matthews: Seattle Fundamentalist and Civic Reformer," *Journal of Presbyterian History* 57 (1979):446–66.

8. "Seattle's Devil," "The Muzzled Pulpit," "The Protestant Church: The Great Arbitrator," and "As Christ Sees the Alienated Affections of Society People," sermonettes, 1906–8, Mark A. Matthews Manuscript Collection, University of Washington Library, Seattle.

9. "The Gospel's Message for This City and the Coast," sermonette, 1909, ibid.

10. "The Quack Doctor and Fake Medical School Are Menacing the Morals and Health of Seattle Citizens," "The One Thing More Essential," "The Seattle Problem," and "What I Would Do If I Were Mayor of Seattle," sermonettes, 1908, 1910, 1926, ibid.

11. Matthews to Hi Gill, January 24, 1912, scrapbook, undated clippings, ibid.

12. *Seattle Star,* 1940, copy, ibid.

13. Ezra P. Giboney and Agnes M. Potter, *The Life of Mark A. Matthews* (Grand Rapids, 1948), 26.

14. John R. Straton, *The Salvation of Society and Other Addresses* (Baltimore, 1908), 13.

15. Ibid.; "Justice versus Charity," sermon printed in *Baltimore News,* January 20, 1914.

16. *Baltimore Evening Herald,* January 8, 1914.

17. John R. Straton, *The Scarlet Stain on the City* (Norfolk, ca. 1916), 54. Cf Hillyer H. Straton, "John Roach Straton: Prophet of Social Righteousness," *Foundations* 5 (January 1962):17–38.

18. John R. Straton, *The Gardens of Life* (New York, 1921), 76.

19. *The Redemption of the Downtown* (1900), pamphlet, William Bell Riley Manuscripts, Northwestern College, Roseville, Minn.

20. Scrapbook in unmarked box, ibid.

21. Charles S. Mundell, "Some Side-Lights on J. Frank Norris," in Marcet Haldeman-Julius, *A Report of the J. Frank Norris Trial* (Girard, Kans., 1927), 78–79; Timothy P. Weber, *Living in the Shadow of the Second Coming: American Premillennialism, 1875–1925* (New York, 1979), 101. *Denver News,* November 13, 1922; Dawson Scrapbooks, Colorado Heritage Center, Denver, Colorado.

22. *Rocky Mountain News,* December 8, 1965; biographical data is from the Uzzell vertical file, Western Room, Denver Public Library.

23. Norris Magnuson, *Salvation in the Slums: Evangelical Social Work, 1865–1920* (Metuchen, N.J., 1977).

24. Kenneth K. Bailey, *Southern White Protestantism in the Twentieth Century* (New York, 1964); Rufus B. Spain, *At Ease in Zion: Social History of the Southern Baptists, 1865–1900* (Nashville, 1967); Wayne Flynt, "Dissent in Zion: Alabama Baptists and Social Issues, 1900–1914," *Journal of Southern History* 25 (1969):523–42.

25. Robert C. McMath, Jr , *Populist Vanguard: A History of the Southern Farmers' Alliance* (Chapel Hill, 1975), 62.

26. Frederick A. Bode, *Protestantism and the New South: North Carolina Baptists and Methodists in Political Crisis, 1894–1903* (Charlottesville, 1975), 11–13.

27. McMath, *Populist Vanguard,* 133–37, Thompson is quoted, 135; also quoted in Bode, *Protestantism and the New South,* 40.

28. Bode, *Protestantism and the New South,* 141–59. But this does not necessarily mean that southern clerics would oppose the newly emerging Progressive social programs; the child labor issue always received strong clerical support.

29. Flynt, "Dissent in Zion," 523–42; William E. Ellis, "Edgar Young Mullins: Southern Baptist Theologian, Administrator, and Denominational Leader" (Ph.D. dissertation, University of Kentucky, 1974), 99–100, 144.

30. Kenneth K. Bailey, "Southern White Protestantism at the Turn of the Century," *American Historical Review* 68 (1963):630n; John Lee Eighmy, "Religious Liberalism in the South during the Progressive Era," *Church History* 38 (1969):359–72; cf. Arthur S. Link, "The Progressive Movement in the South, 1870–1914," *North Carolina Historical Review* 23 (1946):172–95; Anne F. Scott, "A Progressive Wind from the South," *Journal of Southern History* 29 (1963):53–70; Hugh C. Bailey, *Liberalism in the New South: Southern Social Reformers and the Progressive Movement* (Coral Gables, 1969).

31. Jane Zimmerman, "The Penal Reform Movement in the South during the Progressive Era, 1890–1917," *Journal of Southern History* 17 (1951):482, 492; Flynt, "Dissent in Zion," 528–29.

32. James Gray McAllister and Grace Owings Guerrant, *Edward O. Guerrant: Apostle to the Southern Highlanders* (Richmond, 1950), 114–18, 134–87, 190.

33. Robert F. Campbell, *Some Aspects of the Race Problem in the South* (1899); *Harmful Child Labor in the United States* (1907); *The Use and Abuse of Animals* (1907); *Mission Work among the Mountain Whites* (1899), pamphlets, Historical Foundation of the Presbyterian and Reformed Churches, Montreat, N.C.

34. Charles Nabers, ed., *The Southern Presbyterian Pulpit* (New York, 1928), passim.

35. Henry A. Atkinson, "Cooperative Efforts of the Church and Organized Labor in Behalf of Social Health and Justice," in James E. McCulloch, ed., *The South Mobilizing for Social Service* (Nashville, 1913), 572–78.

36. Samuel Z. Batten, "The Church and Social Service," in James E. McCulloch, ed., *The Call of the New South* (Nashville, 1912), 283.

37. Report of the Committee on the Church and Social Service by its Chairman in McCulloch, ed., *The South Mobilizing for Social Service*, 489.

38. "The Protestant Church and Social Service," ibid., 609; "The Preparation of the Church for Social Service," in James E. McCulloch, ed., *Battling for Social Betterment* (Nashville, 1914), 107.

39. McCulloch, ed., *Battling*, 104.

40. James H. Timberlake, *Prohibition and the Progressive Movement, 1900–1920* (Cambridge, 1963), is an excellent study; Joseph R. Gusfield, *Symbolic Crusade: Status Politics and the American Temperance Movement* (Urbana, 1963), is thought-provoking.

41. "Opponents Change Attitude," Sermons, Box 3, Riley Manuscripts.

42. William B. Riley, *Messages for the Metropolis* (Chicago, 1906), preface.

43. Stuart, *Sermons*, 12–13.

44. William G. McLoughlin, *Billy Sunday Was His Real Name* (Chicago, 1955), is the best biography. William G. McLoughlin, *Modern Revivalism: Charles Grandison Finney to Billy Graham* (New York, 1959), covers wider ground.

45. W. C. Poole, "Ministers as Reformers," *Methodist Review* 101 (1918).

46. "The Man and Hoe in America," *Christian Standard* 35 (1899):1005.

47. Walter L. Lingle, "The Teachings of Jesus and Modern Social Problems," *Union Seminary Review* 27 (1916):191–205.

48. Lyman Abbott, "The Progressive Movement," *Outlook* 102 (1912):57–58.

49. Sidney Strong Manuscripts, Box 54, University of Washington Library, Seattle.

50. James H. Tufts, "The Adjustment of the Church to the Psychological Conditions of the Present," *American Journal of Theology* 12 (1908):184.

51. Samuel Z. Batten, "The Church as the Maker of Conscience," *American Journal of Sociology* 7 (1902):625.

52. Graham Taylor, "The Social Function of the Church," *American Journal of Sociology* 5 (1899):305–21.

53. Batten, "Church as Maker of Conscience," 611–28.

54. The best studies of this issue are Paul A. Carter, *The Decline and Revival of the Social Gospel: Social and Political Liberalism in American Protestant Churches, 1920–1940* (Ithaca, 1956); Donald B. Meyer, *The Protestant Search for Political Realism, 1919–1941* (Berkeley, 1960); Robert Moats Miller, *American Protestantism and Social Issues, 1919–1939* (Chapel Hill, 1958).

Chapter 6

1. A good synopsis is W. M. Horton, "The Development of Theological Thought," in Stephen Neill, ed., *Twentieth Century Christianity* (rev. ed., Garden City, 1963), 253–83.

2. Earl M. Wilbur, *The First Century of the Liberal Movement in American Religion* (Boston, 1916), 6, pamphlet, Andover Newton Theological Seminary, Newton Centre, Mass.

3. William R. Hutchison, *The Modernist Impulse in American Protestantism* (Cambridge, 1976), esp. chapter 1.

4. John A. Faulkner, "One Hundred Years of Episcopal Methodism," *Christian Advocate* (New York), September 9, 1926, 1124.

5. Norman H. Maring, "Baptists and Changing Views of the Bible, 1865–1918," *Foundations* 1 (July 1958):72–75, (October 1958):30–59.

6. Henry C. Sheldon wrote on the Methodists, Albert H. Newman on the Baptists, William Adams Brown on the Presbyterians, Williston Walker on the Congregationalists; the writer on Episcopalians preferred to remain anonymous. *See* William Adams Brown, "Changes in Theological Thought during the Last Generation," *Methodist Quarterly Review* 60 (1911):38–47.

7. William H. P. Faunce, "Religious Advance of Fifty Years," *American Journal of Theology* 20 (1916):341.

8. Albion W. Small, "Bonds of Nationality," *American Journal of Sociology* 20 (1915):874.

9. Ray Stannard Baker, *The Spiritual Unrest* (New York, 1910), 51, 79, 81–82; the quotation is on 111.

10. Charles W. Eliot, "The Religion of the Future," *Harvard Theological Review* 2 (1909):394; "Mr. Eliot's Religion of the Future," *World's Work* 18 (1909):11974–75; "The Religion of the Future," *Outlook* 92 (1909):828.

11. Eliot, "Religion of the Future," 397–99.

12. Quoted in "Mr. Eliot's Religion of the Future," 11974–75.

13. Winston Churchill, "The Modern Quest for a Religion," *Century* 87 (1913):170, 171; Robert W. Schneider, *Novelist to a Generation: The Life and Thought of Winston Churchill* (Bowling Green, 1976), is the best biography.

14. Samuel McComb, *Christianity and the Modern Mind* (New York, 1910), ix–xi; Willard Chamberlain Selleck, *The New Appreciation of the Bible: A study of the Spiritual Outcome of Biblical Criticism* (Chicago, 1907), vii–xi.

15. Ernest R. Sandeen, *The Roots of Fundamentalism: British and American Millennarianism, 1800–1930* (Chicago, 1970); Timothy P. Weber, *Living in the Shadow of the Second Coming: American Premillennialism, 1875–1925* (New York, 1979).

16. Sandeen, *Roots of Fundamentalism*, xiii–xix.

17. Ibid., 103–31.

18. Lefferts A. Loetscher, *The Broadening Church: A Study of Theological Issues in the Presbyterian Church since 1869* (Philadelphia, 1957), 67–68.

19. Sandeen, *Roots of Fundamentalism*, 42–58; Weber, *Living in the Shadow of the Second Coming*, 13.

20. Weber, *Living in the Shadow of the Second Coming*, 16.

21. Arnold D. Ehlert, ed., *A Bibliographic History of Dispensationalism* (Grand Rapids, 1965), 48ff.; Clarence B. Bass, *Backgrounds to Dispensationalism: Its Historical Genesis and Ecclesiastical Implications* (Grand Rapids, 1960), 149; Harris F. Rall, *Modern Premillennialism and the Christian Hope* (New York, 1920), 1–15.

22. George Ladd, *The Blessed Hope* (Grand Rapids, 1956), 150–63.

23. A. J. Gordon, "The Second Coming of Our Lord," *Watchman-Examiner*, February 5, 1920, 147; Clyde Norman Kraus, *Dispensationalism in America: Its Rise and Development* (Richmond, 1958), 18ff.

24. Willson H. Coates, Hayden V. White, J. Salwyn Schapiro, *The Emergence of Liberal Humanism* (New York, 1966), 136–37.

25. *Moody Bible Institute Monthly* 22 (1922):1104–5; ibid., 31 (1930):51; William M. Runyan, ed., *Dr. Gray at Moody Bible Institute* (New York, 1935), passim.

26. *Prophetic Studies of the International Prophetic Conference* (Chicago, 1886), preface. "Prophetic Conferences," *King's Business* 5 (1914):239; ibid. (1914):324–25.

27. Robert T. Handy, "The Protestant Quest for a Christian America, 1830–1930," *Church History* 22 (1953):20; Rall, *Modern Premillennialism*; Kraus, *Dispensationalism*, 83.

28. Nathaniel West, "History of the Pre-millennial Doctrine," in Nathaniel West, ed., *Premillennial Essays of the Prophetic Conference Held in the Church of the Holy Trinity, New York City, 1878* (Chicago, 1878), 386.

29. William B. Riley, "The Significant Signs of the Times," A Symposium on The Lord's Coming in Relation to Israel, in *The Coming and Kingdom of Christ* (Chicago, 1914), 103, 205.

30. W. P. Mackay, "Return of Christ and Foreign Missions," in West, ed., *Premillennial Esaays*, 459.

31. Cortland Myers, "War on Theology," in *Light on Prophecy* (Philadelphia, 1918), 178, 181.

32. J. M. Stifler, "The Second Coming and Christian Doctrine," in *Addresses on the Second Coming of the Lord* (Pittsburgh, 1895), 160–61.

33. *Prophetic Studies*, 25, 32.

34. Charles G. Trumbull, "How I Became a Pre-Millennialist," in *Coming and Kingdom of Christ*, 65–70.

35. Howard W. Pope, "Address," in *Coming and Kingdom of Christ*, 73–77.

36. James M. Gray, "The Relation of the Hope to Holiness," in *Second Coming of the Lord*, 183.

37. Roland T. Nelson, "Fundamentalism and the Northern Baptist Convention" (Ph.D. dissertation, Divinity School of the University of Chicago, 1964), 46–53.

38. The World's Christian Fundamentals Association had a premillennial point in their creed (VII) as well as elaboration of the story of the Fall. The Presbyterians said little about the bodily return of Christ. Caroll E. Harrington is mistaken when he claims that the booklets *The Fundamentals* were no more than an elaboration of the Niagara five-point creed ("The Fundamentalist Movement in America, 1870–1920" [Ph.D. dissertation, University of California, 1959], 35).

39. Quoted in Gene A. Getz, *MBI: The Story of Moody Bible Institute* (Chicago, 1969), 24.

40. Ibid., 36.

41. Ibid., 49. James F. Findlay, Jr., *Dwight L. Moody: American Evangelist, 1837–1899* (Chicago, 1969), is the best biography.

42. Safara Austin Witmer, *The Bible College Story: Education with Dimension* (Manhasset, N.Y., 1962), 36–45; Harold W. Boon, "The Development of the Bible College or Institute in the United States and Canada since 1880 and Its Relationship to the Field of Theological Education in America" (Ph.D. dissertation, New York University, 1950).

43. James M. Gray to Arthur P. Fitt, May 22, 1907, in James M. Gray Papers, Moody Bible Institute, Chicago; L. C. Rudolph "Fundamentalism," in Arnold B. Rhodes, ed., *The Church Faces the Isms* (New York, 1958), 47ff.

44. Stewart to K. F. Norris, January 2, 1894, Lyman Stewart Manuscripts, Bible Institute of Los Angeles.

45. Mrs. Howard Mills to Lyman Stewart, December 4, 1906, ibid.

46. Stewart to Baer, July 27, August 4, 1906, February 8, 1907, September 21, 22, 30, 1910; L. E. Holden to Stewart, April 22, 1907, ibid.

47. Stewart to Mary B. Henderson, August 18, 1909, ibid.

48. Stewart to Baer, August 4, 1906, ibid.; *Los Angeles Times*, February 28, 1932. *King's Business* 49 (1958) carried a study by James O. Henry, "Black Oil and Souls To Win," which is a biography of Stewart and relates to his connection with BIOLA.

49. Rollin Lynde Hartt, "The War in the Churches," *World's Work* 46 (1923):472.

50. One unidentified commentator called Dixon "the sanest of the early fundamentalist group" (letter in Box 10, Folder 4, Amzi C. Dixon papers, Historical Commission of the Southern Baptist Convention, Nashville, Tenn.).

51. Lyman Stewart to Milton Stewart, October 26, 1909, Stewart Manuscripts.

52. Ibid., September 24, 1909.

53. Foreword to *The Fundamentals: A Testimony to the Truth*, 12 vols. (Chicago, 1910–15).

54. This information is in *The Fundamentals*, passim. See also George M. Marsden, "Fundamentalism as an American Phenomenon: A Comparison with English Evangelicalism," *Church History* 46 (1977):215–32.

55. The books have been reissued, with certain of the excesses deleted: Charles L. Feinberg, ed., *The Fundamentals for Today*, 2 vols. (Grand Rapids, 1958).

56. Robert Anderson, "Christ and Criticism," *Fundamentals*, 2:60–84; Canon Dyson Hague, "History of the Higher Criticism," ibid., 1:18.

57. W. H. Griffith-Thomas, "Old Testament Criticism and New Testament Christianity," ibid., 8:14.

58. Letters from F. G. Floyd, December 3, 1910, and James W. Leonard, December 2, 1910, Stewart Manuscripts.

59. *King's Business* 4 (1913):235; Clarence A. Beckwith, "Authority in Present-Day Religious Teaching," *American Journal of Theology* 16 (1912):503–4.

60. *King's Business* 3 (1912):247.

61. Torrey to Stewart, April 1, 1915, Stewart Manuscripts.

62. John H. Burrows to Stewart, n.d., ibid.

63. Lyman Stewart to Fred, May 22, 1916; Lyman Stewart to Milton Stewart, June 5, 1915; Lyman Stewart to Mrs. S. L. Mills, January 3, 1909, ibid.

64. Weber, *Living in the Shadow of the Second Coming*, 137–41. Cf. David Rausch, *Zionism within Early American Fundamentalism, 1878–1914: A Convergence of Two Traditions* (New York, 1979).

65. Statement by J. W. Chapman, September 14, 1907, in files, Bible Institute of Los Angeles; William E. Blackstone, *Jesus Is Coming* (New York, 1908), preface; Sandeen, *Roots of Fundamentalism*, 191n.

66. Stewart to Thomas E. Stephens, December 22, 1917; Stewart to William E. Blackstone, July 7, 1917, Stewart Manuscripts; Memorial on Blackstone by David L. Cooper for *Prophecy Monthly* (January 1936), copy, ibid.

67. *Minneapolis Tribune*, August 3, 1908.

68. Riley to S. T. Ford, January 25, 31, 1910; Riley to Dr. John H. Earl, March 7, 1910, William Bell Riley Manuscripts, Northwestern College, Roseville, Minn.

69. Riley to Reverend John M. Dean, January 31, 1910; Riley to Reverend John Earl, January 17, 1910; Riley to S. T. Ford, January 17, 1910, ibid.

70. Riley to S. T. Ford, January 18, 1910; Riley to Johnston Myers, January 18, 1910, ibid.

Chapter 7

1. Gladden is quoted in Henry F. May, *The End of American Innocence: A Story of the First Years of Our Own Time, 1912–1917* (New York, 1959), 13.

2. John M. Mecklin, "The War and the Dilemma of the Christian Ethic," *American Journal of Theology* 23 (1913):23; *The Presbyterian Church and the War* (1917), pamphlet, Historical Foundation of the Presbyterian and Reformed Churches, Montreat, N.C.

3. E. W. Thornton, "Made in Germany," *Christian Standard* 53 (1918):761.

4. Charles Stelzle, *Why Prohibition!* (New York, 1918), 23; *King's Business* 9 (1918):643.

5. George F. Pentecost, *Why We Fight* (1918), 17, pamphlet, Historical Foundation of the Presbyterian and Reformed Churches.

6. William R. Hutchison, *The Modernist Impulse in American Protestantism* (Cambridge, Mass., 1976), 237n; Ray H. Abrams, *Preachers Present Arms: A Study of the War-time Attitues and Activities of the Churches and the Clergy in the United States, 1914–1918* (New York, 1933).

7. Abrams, *Preachers Present Arms*, 29, 35, 54, 80, 114, 129.

8. Timothy P. Weber, *Living in the Shadow of the Second Coming: American Premillennialsm, 1875–1925* (New York, 1979), 105–20.

9. *Christian Century* 36 (1921):15; *Christian Register* 101 (1922):195; undated clipping in box marked "Dr. Riley's old scrapbooks," William Bell Riley Manuscripts, Northwestern College, Roseville, Minn.

10. Shirley Jackson Case, *The Millennial Hope: A Phase of War-Time Thinking* (Chicago, 1918), esp. vi, vii.

11. "Unprincipled Methods of Post-Millennialists," *King's Business* 9 (1918):276.

12. *Christian Register* 100 (1921):26.

13. Herbert L. Willett, "Activities and Menace of Millennialism," *Christian Century* 35 (1918):6–7; Willett, "Millennarian Misuse of Scripture," ibid. 35 (1918):7–8.

14. "Dr. Shailer Mathews and the Premillenniarians," *King's Business* 9 (1918):3–5.

15. Alva W. Taylor, "Millenarians and Bolsheviks," *Christian Century* 36 (1919):16–17; cf. ibid. (1919):10.

16. *Moody Bible Institute Monthly* 19 (1918):83; ibid. (1919):302.

17. "Unprincipled Methods of Post-Millennialists," 276–77.

18. *Standard*, March 9, 1918, 7; *Christian Fundamentals in School and Church*, October-November-December 1921, 4; William B. Riley, "The Gospel for War-times" (1918), Sermon, Riley Manuscripts.

19. Obadiah Holmes, "The Threat of Millennialism," *Christian Century* 38 (1921):11.

20. G. W. McPherson, *The Modern Conflict over the Bible in Synthesis and Comparison* (Yonkers, 1919), 135, quoted in William H Day and Sherwood Eddy, *The Modernist-Fundamentalist Controversy* (New York, 1924), 6. Reverend W. H. Bates of Greeley, Colorado, noted the absence of the premillennial position in the Westminster Confession of faith and resolved the question by commenting, "To be sure, the divines had not got that far. They stopped their studies too soon" *Moody Bible Institute Monthly* 21 [1921]:215.

21. Quoted in William Henry Smith, *Modernism, Fundamentalism, and Catholicism* (Milwaukee, 1926), 42.

22. Isaac M. Haldeman, *Professor Shailer Mathews' Burlesque on the Second Coming of Our Lord Jesus Christ* (New York, 1918), 28.

23. George Perry Morris, "Review of 1919," *Universalist Leader* 23 (1920):8.

24. "The Church and Social Reconstruction," *Christian Century* 30 (1910):0.

25. John R. Straton, *The Menace of Immorality in Church and State: Messages of Wrath and Judgment* (New York, 1920), 102.

26. "The Trumpet that Gives a Wavering Sound, or The Need of Certainties in Religion," October 16, 1918, folder "Baptists"; "The Political, Economic, and Religious Lesson of the Great War," folder "War," John R. Straton Manuscripts, American Baptist Historical Society, Rochester, N.Y.

27. "Shall the Funnymonkeyists Win?" preached September 24, 1922, and published in *Religious Searchlight* 1 (October 1922).

28. *Moody Bible Institute Monthly* 20 (1919):14; ibid. 19 (1918):164; ibid. 19 (1919):534.

29. *The Church and Social Reconstruction* (1919); William H. P. Faunce, "The Church and Reconstruction," *Universalist Leader* 23 (1920):141–43; Gerald Birney Smith, "Christianity and the Spirit of Democracy," *American Journal of Theology* 21 (1917):339–40.

30. Quoted in Wilson G. Cole, "The Church and the Returning Soldiers," *Methodist Review* 102 (1919):257–58.

31. John Smith Lowe, "The Task of Religion in the New Age," *Universalist Leader* 21 (1918):1002–3.

32. Charles MacFarland, "The Progress of Federation among the Churches," *American Journal of Theology* 20 (1917):392–410; George Cross, "Federation of the Christian Churches in America—An Interpretation," ibid. 23 (1919):134.

33. Eldon G. Ernst, *Moment of Truth for Protestant America: Interchurch Campaigns following World War One* (Missoula, 1974).

34. Peter G. Mode, "Aims and Methods of Contemporary Church-Union Movements in America," *American Journal of Theology* 24 (1920):248–51.

35. *Presbyterian of the South* 98 (April 23, 1924).

36. William B. Riley, *The Menace of Modernism* (New York, 1917), 167; William B. Riley, "Fundamentalism versus Liberalism," Sermons, Box 2, Riley Manuscripts.

37. *New York Times,* November 23, 29, 1918.

38. Riley Scrapbooks; "Fundamentalism or the Faith's Defense," Sermons, Box 2, Riley Manuscripts.

39. Riley to J. D. Adams (first page missing, n.d.), ibid.

40. Riley to J. D. Adams, April 28, 1919, ibid.

41. *Christian Worker's Magazine* 19 (1919):534.

42. Yellow sheet, "Great Northwestern Series of Correlated Conferences"; *Christian Fundamentals in School and Church,* October-November-December 1922, 5, both in Riley Manuscripts.

43. *God Hath Spoken* (Philadelphia, 1919), 25. J. M. Gray noted the need for an "offensive and defensive alliance in the Church" (*Christian Worker's Magazine* 19 [1919]):328.

Chapter 8

1. Edward S. Ames, *The New Orthodoxy* (Chicago, 1918), 2.

2. Ralph Barton Perry, *The Present Conflict of Ideals: A Study of the Philosophical Background of the World War* (New York, 1918), 2.

3. J. Wilbur Chapman, "The New Era Movement of the Presbyterian Church, U.S.A.," *Union Seminary Review* 30 (1919):116.

4. For the social history of the 1920s, see Paula S. Fass, *The Damned and the Beautiful: American Youth in the 1920s* (New York, 1977); Frederick Lewis Allen, *Only Yesterday: An Informal History of the Nineteen-Twenties* (New York, 1931); Gilman M. Ostrander, "The Revolution in Morals," in John Braeman, ed., *Change and Continuity in Twentieth Century America: The 1920s* (Columbus, 1968); Samuel Drury, "What Are Our Young People Seeking in Their Apparent Revolt from the Moral Standards of an Earlier Day?" *The Influence of the Church on Modern Problems* (New York, 1922).

5. One contemporary counted at least twenty different sets of "fundamentals" which different Christian groups had supported at different periods of time. These ranged from predestination to foot washing, from premillennialism to hooks and eyes. He concluded that it was impossible to agree on a statement of *the* fundamentals for all Christians ("Fundamentals," *Scroll* 18 [December 1921]:50–56).

6. Charles G. Trumbull, "Fundamentalists Expose Modernism in the South," *Christian Fundamentals in School and Church,* April-May-June 1923, 15.

7. *Watchman-Examiner,* August 4, 1921, 973.

8. *Christian Fundamentals in School and Church,* July-August-September 1923, 7.

9. Ibid., 14; ibid., October-November-December 1922, 8–11, 18; ibid., July-August-September 1921, 14.

10. Ibid., July-September-October 1922, 25; William B. Riley, *The Challenge of*

Orthodoxy, pamphlet, originally a lecture delivered June 13, 1920, at the annual conference of the WCFA in Chicago, William Bell Riley Manuscripts, Northwestern College, Roseville, Minn.

11. Don B. Rood to author, June 9, 1971; Roland T. Nelson, "Fundamentalism and the Northern Baptist Convention" (Ph.D. dissertation, Divinity School of the University of Chicago, 1964), 131ff.

12. See Paul M. Harrison, *Authority and Power in the Free Church Tradition: A Social Case Study of the American Baptist Convention* (Princeton, 1959): "For years, the Baptists have been looking at an anarchy and seeing democracy" (p. 157).

13. *Christian Register* 101 (1922):218; *Christian Century* 39 (1922):326–27; *Baptist* 3 (1922):325.

14. *Christian Century* 39 (1922):327; Robert G. Delnay, "A History of the Baptist Bible Union" (Th.D. thesis, Dallas Theological Seminary, 1963), 32.

15. American Baptist Convention, *Annual* [1922] (Philadelphia, 1922), 38–40.

16. Quoted in *Christian Century* 39 (1922):886.

17. Ibid. 46 (1929):672.

18. Delnay, "History of the Baptist Bible Union," 52, 53.

19. T. T. Shields, "The Baptist Bible Union," *Christian Fundamentals in School and Church*, July-August-September, 1923, 59.

20. *Beacon* 1 (January 1924):5; William B. Riley, "Autocracy Intolerable to True Baptists," sermon given December 4, 1923, before the BBU, Sermons, Box 1, Riley Manuscripts.

21. William B. Riley, *Theological Liberty vs. the License of Infidelity*, pamphlet of address given before the BBU in 1924 in Milwaukee, Riley Manuscripts.

22. Delnay, "History of the Baptist Bible Union," 138; *Watchman-Examiner*, April 19, 1923, 488.

23. Bertha Henshaw to John R. Straton, December 21, 1922, John R. Straton Manuscripts, American Baptist Historical Society, Rochester, N.Y.

24. Chester E. Tulga, *The Foreign Missions Controversy in the Northern Baptist Convention, 1919–1949: 30 Years of Struggle* (Chicago, 1950), 27–28.

25. American Baptist Convention, *Annual* [1924], 51ff.; *Baptist* 4 (1924):1–2; *Watchman-Examiner*, November 15, 1923, 1466; John R. Straton, "The Menace of Modernism on Mission Fields," a sermon originally given at a BBU meeting May 26, 1924, and later printed as a pamphlet.

26. American Baptist Convention, *Annual* [1925], 93.

27. American Baptist Convention, *Annual* [1926], 81; Shailer Mathews, "Shall We Have a General Assembly?" *Baptist* 7 (1926):324.

28. *Watchman-Examiner*, June 10, 1926, 713; ibid., June 3, 1926, 683–84; American Baptist Convention, *Annual* [1926], 88; Delnay, "History of the Baptist Bible Union," 127; *Christian Century* 43 (1926):651.

29. Robert Hastings Nichols, "Fundamentalism in the Presbyterian Church," originally published in the *Journal of Religion*, January 1925, reprinted as a pamphlet (New York, 1925); Hay W. Smith, *Evolution and Presbyterianism* (Little Rock, 1923), offers a good contemporary account. Cf. James E. Clarke, *Points at Issue between 'Fundamentalists' and 'Modernists'* (Nashville, 1923), pamphlet, Presbyterian Historical Society, Philadelphia.

30. *Christian Century* 40 (1923):696.

31. *Presbyterian* 29 (1923):384.

32. Stewart G. Cole, *History of Fundamentalism* (Hamden, Conn., 1931; 1963), 121–30; *Christian Century* 40 (1923):696; *Presbyterian* 29 (1923):387; ibid. 30 (1924):342; cf. Edwin H. Rian, *The Presbyterian Conflict* (Grand Rapids, 1940).

33. John M. Wells, "What Is Modernism?" *Union Seminary Review* 34 (1923):90.

34. On Modernism or liberalism, see especially Sydney E. Ahlstrom, *A Religious History of the American People* (New Haven, 1972), 763–804; Kenneth Cauthen, *The Impact of American Religious Liberalism* (New York, 1962); William R. Hutchison, "Cultural Strain and Protestant Liberalism," *American Historical Review* 76 (1971):386–411; Henry Van Dusen, *The Vindication of Liberal Theology: A Tract for the Times* (New York, 1963).

35. "Modernism in Confusion," *New Republic* 48 (1926):33–34.

36. James T. Ely, *Glimpses of Bible Climaxes, from "The Beginning" to "The End"* (Garden City, Kan., 1927), 104; Joseph E. McAfee, "Who Wins—Fundamentalists or Fosdick?" *Christian Century* 41 (1924):1266; *Christian Century* 39 (1922):1381.

37. E. C. Cameron, "Fundamentalism and the Disciples of Christ," *Christian Standard* 66 (1929):532–33; Alonzo W. Fortune, "Fundamentalist or Modernist," *Christian Evangelist* 6 (1928):469–76; "The Big 'F' and the little 'f,' " *Christian Standard* 64 (1929):755.

38. *New York Times*, January 2, 1924.

39. Philip L. Frick, "Why the Methodist Church Is So Little Disturbed by the Fundamentalist Controversy," *Methodist Review* 107 (1924):421–26; Emory S. Burke et al., eds., *History of American Methodism*, 3 (New York, 1964), 270–73.

40. William W. Sweet, *Methodism in American History* (New York, 1933), 391–93.

41. "A Premillennial Methodist Church," *King's Business* 11 (1920):1018.

42. R. A. Torrey, "Is It *Pre*millenniarism or *Post*millenniarism That Is Divisive," *King's Business* 10 (1919):107–9.

43. O. E. Brown, "Modernism: A Calm Survey," *Methodist Quarterly Review* 74 (1925):390–92.

44. *Neither Fundamentalism Nor Modernism, but Belief in Jesus Christ, the Son of God* (New York, 1923), pamphlet, Historical Archives of the Protestant Episcopal Church, Austin, Texas.

45. The quotation is from Ernest R. Sandeen, "Fundamentalism and American Identity," *Annals of the American Academy of Political and Social Science* 387 (1970):59; see also his "Towards a Historical Interpretation of the Origins of Fundamentalism," *Church History* 36 (1967):66–83; and his "The Princeton Theology: One Source of Biblical Literalism in American Protestantism," *Church History* 31 (1962):307–21; Dwight Wilson, in *Armageddon Now! The Premillenniarian Response to Russia and Israel since 1917* (Grand Rapids, 1977), 12, estimates that premillennialists make up about three million of the forty million modern conservative evangelicals; Timothy P. Weber feels there may be sixteen million premillennialists, *Living in the Shadow of the Second Coming; American Premillennialism, 1875–1925* (New York, 1979), 209.

46. Jack Mills, "The Speaking of William Jennings Bryan in Florida, 1915–1925" (M.A. thesis, University of Florida, 1948), 34; Candler as quoted by Edwin Mims, *The Advancing South: Stories of Progress and Reaction* (New York, 1926), 284.

47. Charles Ferris, "The Place of E. Y. Mullins in the Evolution Controversy of the 1920s," *Quarterly Review* 35 (1975):53–57.

48. James J. Thompson, Jr., "Southern Baptists and the Anti-evolution Controversy of the 1920s," *Mississippi Quarterly* 29 (1975–76):65–81.

49. John M. Wells, "What Is Modernism?" *Union Seminary Review* 34 (1923):98.

50. *Presbyterian of the South* 99 (July 22, 1925).

51. Ray Dobyns, "The Second Coming," *Union Seminary Review* 35 (1923):334–45; James J. Vance, "Fundamentalism, Liberalism, Tolerance," sermon, June 17, 1923, Historical Foundation of the Presbyterian and Reformed Churches, Montreat, N.C.

52. As reported in *Presbyterian of the South* 93 (July 25, 1923).

53. John R. Straton to George F. Washburn, October 31, 1925, Straton Manuscripts. The name Bible Crusaders was selected over Evangelical Crusaders because of the desire to include Roman Catholics and Greek Catholics in the passing of antievolution legislation (Washburn to Straton, October 2, 1925, ibid.).

54. Washburn to Straton, August 21, 1925; *Crusader's Champion* 1 (December 25, 1925):6, ibid.

55. Bertha Henshaw to Straton, August 13, 1926; Washburn to Straton, May 13, 1929; Bertha Henshaw to Straton, May 22, 1929, ibid.

56. "Should Christians Play on Sunday?" *Literary Digest* 88 (January 30, 1926):57; Patsy Ledbetter, "Defense of the Faith: J. Frank Norris and Texas Fundamentalism, 1920–1929," *Arizona and the West* 15 (1973):45–62.

57. Norris to Riley, September 27, November 27, 1933, Box 36, J. Frank Norris Papers, Historical Commission of the Southern Baptist Convention, Nashville, Tenn.

58. Norris to Riley, July 30, 1931, ibid.

59. Nels Anderson, "The Shooting Parson of Texas," *New Republic* 48 (September 1, 1926):35–37; Marcet Haldeman-Julius, *A Report of the Rev. J. Frank Norris Trial* (Girard, Kan., 1927), 1–76.

60. See Donald George Tinder, "Fundamentalist Baptists in the Northern and Western United States, 1920–1950" (Ph.D. dissertation, Yale University, 1969).

Chapter 9

1. S. K. Ratcliffe, "America and Fundamentalism," *Contemporary Review* 128 (1925):288; S. K. Ratcliffe, "The Intellectual Reaction in America," *Contemporary Review* 122 (1922):14–22.

2. *Fundamentalist Magazine* 1 (September 1927):8.

3. "The Survival of the Fittest," *King's Business* 8 (1917):1065; Howard Kellogg, "Kultur—Applied Evolution," ibid. 10 (1919):110.

4. "The 'Taboo' on 'Made in Germany,'" *King's Business* 9 (1918):n.p.; cf. "The Collapse of German Authority," ibid. 6 (1915):943.

5. Glenn Gates Cole, "Evolution and Destructive Criticism," *Christian Standard* 54 (1919):551.

6. "The War and the Prophetic Word," given June 13, 1915, Sermons, Box 7; Sermon, June 16, 1918, Box 4; Scrapbook 20, William Bell Riley Manuscripts, Northwestern College, Roseville, Minn.

7. Charles M. Harger, "Bryan: Preacher and Politician," *Outlook* 89 (1908):64–65.

8. William Jennings Bryan Manuscripts, Box 30, Library of Congress.

9. Bryan to C. W. Bryan, December 25, 1915, William Jennings Bryan Manuscripts, Occidental College, Los Angeles, Calif.; Reverend George Zucker to Bryan, February 20, 1917, Bryan Manuscripts, Box 31, Library of Congress.

10. William Jennings Bryan, ed., *World Peace—A Written Debate between William Howard Taft and William Jennings Bryan* (New York, 1917).

11. Bryan to B. C. Hilliard, April 3, 1917, Bryan Manuscripts, Box 31, Library of Congress.

12. Bryan to C. W. Bryan, March 31, 1917, Bryan Manuscripts, Occidental College; Bryan Manuscripts, Box 31, Library of Congress.

13. William Jennings Bryan, *Heart to Heart Appeals* (New York, 1917), 102.

14. Bryan's speech is printed in *Moody Bible Institute Monthly* 23 (April 1923).

15. See William Grant Smith, "W. J. Bryan on Evolution," *Christian Standard* 52 (1917):1487.

16. G. McGinnis to Bryan, December 8, 1920; W. O. Garrett to Bryan, March 19, 1920; T. E. Stephens to Bryan, February 19, 1921, Bryan Manuscripts, Box 31, Library of Congress.

17. Walter W. Moore to Bryan, January 22, February 5, 1919, ibid.

18. " 'In His Image,'—A Review," *Union Seminary Review* 33 (1922):177–87; New York *Herald*, February 12, 1922; Kenneth K. Bailey, "The Anti-evolution Crusade of the Nineteen Twenties" (Ph.D. dissertation, Vanderbilt University, 1953).

19. Arthur W. Stalker to Bryan, November 15, December 1, 1920, January 31, 1921, Bryan Manuscripts, Box 31, Library of Congress.

20. Lloyd C. Douglas, "Mr. Bryan's New Crusade," *Christian Century* 37 (1920):11–12; "The Passing of Mr. Bryan," ibid. 38 (1921):6–7, 21.

21. *Capital Times*, February 7, 17, 1922, Box 61; Bryan to H. H. Hoard, December 17, 1921, Box 23; Bryan to Chester C. Platt, December 16, 1921, Box 34, Bryan Manuscripts, Library of Congress.

22. *Capital Times*, n.d., Box 61, ibid.

23. Quoted in Lawrence W. Levine, *Defender of the Faith: William Jennings Bryan, the Last Decade, 1915–1925* (New York, 1965), 287.

24. W. J. Bryan, "The Fundamentals," *Forum* 70 (1923):1665–80.

25. Glenn Frank, "William Jennings Bryan—A Mind Divided against Itself," *Century* 106 (1923):794.

26. *Moody Bible Institute Monthly* 23 (1923):334; cf. Alonzo W. Fortune, "The Kentucky Campaign against the Teaching of Evolution," *Journal of Religion* 2 (1922):225–35.

27. W. P. Merrill to Bryan, November 11, 1921, Box 34; J. D. Coon to Bryan, June 22, 1923, Box 37, Bryan Manuscripts, Library of Congress.

28. George Zucker to Bryan, December 15, 1922, Box 36, ibid.

29. Bryan to Reverend Stalker, dated December 9, 1923, but probably 1922, Box 38, ibid.

30. Bryan to Reverend John A. Marquis, May 4, 1923, ibid.

31. Republic Syndicate to Bryan, December 31, 1924; Guy T. Viskniskki to Bryan, June 9, 1923, ibid.; William Jennings Bryan, *Christ and His Companions: Famous Figures of the New Testament* (New York, 1925), 26, 27, 67, 166, 234.

32. *Commoner* 19 (May 1919).

33. Ibid.; miscellaneous letters in Folders 1919–1921; Bryan to Reverend Paul M. Strayer, December 19, 1921, Box 34; W. M. Covert to Bryan, January 5, 1922, Box 35, Bryan Manuscripts, Library of Congress.

34. A. C. Dixon to Bryan, January 5, 1923, Box 36; T. C. Horton to Bryan, September 15, 1923, Box 38; J. W. Porter to Bryan, April 14, 1923, Box 37, Bryan Manuscripts, Library of Congress.

35. *Christian Fundamentals in School and Church*, April-May-June, 1923; Bryan to Riley, March 27, 1925, Bryan Manuscripts, Box 40, Library of Congress.

36. Bryan to Riley, May 3, 1923, Box 40, Bryan Manuscripts, Library of Congress.

37. Frank T. Boyer, editor of the *Bible Champion*, to Bryan, Box 38, ibid.

38. James H. Larson to Bryan, January 28, 1922; Larson to Bryan, January 1922, Larson to Bryan, January 10, 1922, W. F. Riederwolf to Bryan, December 9, 1921, Bryan to Larson, January 28, 1922, Box 35, ibid.

39. Bryan to J. F. Norris, May 1, 1923, Box 37; Riley to Bryan, February 7, 1923, Box 36; W. J. Gray to Bryan, March 2, 1923, Box 37; J. F. Norris to Bryan, April 24, May 30, 1923, Box 37, ibid.

40. Bryan to W. J. Gray, March 8, 1923, Box 37; W. J. Gray to Bryan, March 2, 1923, Box 37, ibid.

41. *Moody Bible Institute Monthly* 26 (1925):3.

42. A. K. Foster, "Mr. Bryan's Responsibility," *Christian Century* 39 (1922):755; Clarence T. Wilson to Bryan, November 3, 1923, Bryan Manuscripts, Box 37, Library of Congress.

43. Malcolm Willey and Stuart A. Rice, "William Jennings Bryan as a Social Force," *Journal of Social Forces* (May 4, 1925):1–7; *New York Times*, January 13, 1924.

44. Harvard *Crimson*, April 7, 1925.

45. *Christian Fundamentals in School and Church*, April-May-June 1925, 6.

46. Bryan to Charles S. Thomas, July 1, 1925, Bryan Manuscripts, Box 37, Library of Congress. See my examination in "William Jennings Bryan, Evolution and the Fundamentalist-Modernist Controversy," *Nebraska History* 56 (1975):259–78.

Chapter 10

1. Butler said, "I never had any idea my bill would make a fuss. I just thought it would become a law, and that everybody would abide by it" (quoted in Leslie H. Allen, ed., *Bryan and Darrow at Dayton: The Record and Documents of the "Bible-evolution Trial"* [New York, 1925], 1). Willard B. Gatewood, Jr., ed., *Controversy in the Twenties: Fundamentalism, Modernism, and Evolution* (Nashville, 1969), contains an excellent collection of documents.

2. Tennessee General Assembly, *House Journal*, 1925, 741–45, quoted in Kenneth K. Bailey, "The Enactment of Tennessee's Antievolution Law," *Journal of Southern History* 16 (1950):484.

3. John Thomas Scopes and James Presley, *Center of the Storm: Memoirs of John T. Scopes* (New York, 1967), 49–51.

4. Ibid., 60; Roger Baldwin, "Dayton's First Issue," in Jerry R. Tompkins, ed., *D-Days at Dayton: Reflections on the Scopes Trial* (Baton Rouge, 1965), 55–57.

5. "The World's Christian Fundamentals Association and the Scopes Trial," article in Sermons, Box 7, William Bell Riley Manuscripts, Northwestern College, Roseville, Minn.

6. Scopes and Presley, *Center of the Storm*, 62; Baldwin, "Dayton's First Issue," 57. Irving Stone, *Clarence Darrow for the Defense: A Biography* (Garden City, 1941), is disappointing.

7. R. D. Owen, "The Significance of the Scopes Trial," *Current History* 22 (1925):881; John R. Straton, "Is Our Modern Educational System Developing a Race of Materialists, Sensualists and Unbelievers?" folder, "Evangelical," John R. Straton Manuscripts, American Baptist Historical Society, Rochester, N.Y.

8. Clarence Darrow, *The Story of My Life* (New York, 1932), 244; Scopes and Presley, *Center of the Storm*, 67ff.

9. Bryan to Ed Howe, June 30, 1925, Bryan Manuscripts, Library of Congress.

10. *New York Times*, July 10, 11, 1925, as quoted in Kenneth K. Bailey, "The Anti-Evolution Crusade of the Nineteen Twenties" (Ph.D. dissertation, Vanderbilt University, 1953), 156.

11. Scopes and Presley, *Center of the Storm*, 98.

12. George Gaylord Simpson, "Science by Jury," *Nation* 186 (1958):420–21; interview with George Gaylord Simpson, February 18, 1980, Tucson, Arizona.

13. Tompkins, *D-Days at Dayton*, 44.

14. William R. Manchester, *Disturber of the Peace: The Life of H.L. Mencken* (New York, 1951), 164.

15. Tompkins, *D-Days at Dayton*, 46.

16. H. L. Mencken, *Prejudices: Fifth Series* (New York, 1926), 64ff.

17. Manchester, *Disturber of the Peace*, 185.

18. Ferenc M. Szasz, "The Scopes Trial in Perspective," *Tennessee Historical Quarterly* 30 (1971):288–98, treats this question in fuller detail.

19. Scopes and Presley, *Center of the Storm*, 102.

20. Bryan to Straton, July 1, 13, 16, 1925, Straton Manuscripts; Bryan to Riley, June 7, 1925, Bryan Manuscripts, Box 37, Library of Congress.

21. Interview with Kirtley F. Mather, December 15, 1977, Albuquerque, N.M.; tape in the author's possession.

22. Kirtley F. Mather, "The Scopes Trial and Its Aftermath," typescript in the author's possession.

23. Bryan to S. K. Hicks, June 16, 1925; Alfred McCann to Bryan, June 30, 1925; S. K. Hicks to Bryan, June 13, 1925; Bryan to S. K. Hicks, June 10, 1925, Bryan Manuscripts, Box 37, Library of Congress; Bertnam Windle, "A Roman Catholic View of Evolution," *Current History* 23 (1925):337–38.

24. The story of those dramatic days in Dayton, Tennessee, in July of 1925 has often been told. Jerome Lawrence and Robert E. Lee have fictionalized the account in *Inherit the Wind* (New York, 1955), which was also made into a movie. Ray Ginger has written the most able account in *Six Days or Forever? Tennessee v. John Thomas Scopes* (Boston, 1958). The protagonists, Arthur Garfield Hays in *Let Freedom Ring* (New York, 1937) and Clarence Darrow in *The Story of My Life*, presented their

sides; Mary Bryan completed her husband's *Memoirs* (Chicago, 1925) from the other point of view. Lawrence W. Levine's account in *Defender of the Faith: William Jennings Bryan, the Last Decade, 1915–1925* (New York, 1965) and Paolo Coletta's three-volume *William Jennings Bryan* (Lincoln, 1964–69) treat Bryan's role. Two recent works are Jerry R. Tompkins's collection of essays, some by participants, *D-Days at Dayton,* and John T. Scopes's own account, *Center of the Storm.* The historian does not lack factual information regarding the Scopes trial. The problem lies in placing it in proper perspective.

25. Quoted in Tompkins, *D-Days at Dayton,* 22.

26. See Donald F. Brod, "The Scopes Trial: A Look at Press Coverage after Thirty Years," *Journalism Quarterly* 42 (1965):219–26.

27. Quoted in John Reddy, "The Most Unforgettable Character I've Met," *Reader's Digest* 49 (August 1956):86. *Commoner* 3 (May 1903), contains Bryan's address, "Religious Freedom," to the Thomas Jefferson Memorial Association.

28. Quoted in Scopes and Presley, *Center of the Storm,* 155.

29. Kirtley F. Mather, "The Scopes Trial and Its Aftermath," public lecture, November 3, 1976, University of New Mexico, tape in the author's possession.

30. Mather interview.

31. Allen, *Bryan and Darrow at Dayton,* 171.

32. Levine, *Defender of the Faith,* 357. The Bryan Manuscripts at the Library of Congress contain many clippings on his death, especially Scrapbook 57; see also *Washington Star,* July 27, 1925.

33. *Utica Press,* July 29, 1925.

34. G. O. Griffith, "William Jennings Bryan," *Watchman-Examiner,* August 20, 1925, 1037.

35. *Albany News,* July 27, 1925.

36. Quoted in *Literary Digest* 86 (August 8, 1925):5, 6; cf. Scrapbook 59, Bryan Manuscripts, Library of Congress.

37. *Memphis Commercial Appeal,* April 29, 1925.

38. *Pittsburgh Sun,* July 27, 1925.

39. *Little Rock Democrat,* July 27, 1925.

40. *Fundamentalist,* December 6, 1925; *Washington Post,* July 30, 1925; H. L. Mencken agreed, see Tompkins, ed., *D-Days at Dayton,* 46.

41. *Christian Register* 104 (1925):761; Stone, *Clarence Darrow,* 464.

42. J. F. Norris to Bryan, June 3, 1925, Bryan Manuscripts, Box 35, Library of Congress.

43. G. F. Washburn to Bryan, July 13, 1925; William Upshaw to Bryan, July 16, 1925, ibid.

44. Bryan to William J. Bryan, Jr., June 17, 1925, Bryan Manuscripts, Occidental College; Bryan, *Memoirs,* 486.

45. Frank Kent, "On the Dayton Firing Line," *New Republic* 43 (1925):259.

46. Paul Rood, "Bryan, the Modern Elijah," *Bryan Broadcaster* 1 (November 1925).

47. *Chicago Daily News,* August 18, 1925; see also *Manila Times,* September 8, 1928; *Waterloo Evening Courier,* August 31, 1925; *Grand Rapids Daily,* August 15, 1925; *Christian Register* 104 (October 1, 1925):962.

48. *Watchman-Examiner,* September 3, 1925, 1131.

49. *Christian Fundamentals in School and Church,* October-November-December, 1925, 56.

50. Callahan to Mark Sullivan, August 8, 1925, Josephus Daniels Papers, Library of Congress.

Chapter 11

1. Paula S. Fass, *The Damned and the Beautiful: American Youth in the 1920s* (New York, 1977), 44–46. Paul A. Carter, in *Another Part of the Twenties* (New York, 1977), feels that the "revolt of the youth" has been exaggerated.

2. Walter Lippmann, *A Preface to Morals* (Boston, 1929, rpt. 1960), is a model of pessimism; Joseph Wood Krutch, *The Modern Temper: A Story and a Confession* (New York, 1929, rpt. 1956.).

3. Edward A. Purcell, Jr., *The Crisis of Democratic Theory: Scientific Naturalism and the Problem of Value* (Lexington, 1973), 15–23, 31–46.

4. Maynard Shipley, "Growth of the Anti-evolution Movement," *Current History* 32 (1930):332; "Evolution and the Bible," *Science* 62 (July 31, 1925):3; Miriam Allen DeFord, *Up-Hill All the Way: The Life of Maynard Shipley* (Yellow Springs, 1956), esp. 47, 239, 244; *New York Times,* June 19, 1934.

5. *Sunset* 60 (May 1928):12–13.

6. William B. Riley, *Should Evolution Be Taught in Tax-supported Schools,* pamphlet of a Smith-Riley debate in Arkansas, Riley Manuscripts; "Resolved, that Evolution Is a Proven Fact and Should Be So Taught in the Public Schools," a reply to J. B. McCabe of London, as delivered in Chicago, December 22, 1925, sermons, Box 4, William Bell Riley Manuscripts, Northwestern College, Roseville, Minn. "Discussion and Correspondence," *Science* 62 (September 4, 1925):221.

7. *Should Evolution Be Taught in Tax-supported Schools?*

8. Joseph McCabe, *1825–1925: A Century of Stupendous Progress* (London, 1925), 10.

9. Willard B. Gatewood treats the North Carolina controversy in two works: "Politics and Piety in North Carolina: The Fundamentalist Crusade at High Tide, 1925–1927," *North Carolina Historical Review* 42 (1965):275–90, and *Preachers, Pedagogues, and Politicians: The Evolution Controversy in North Carolina, 1920–1927* (Chapel Hill, 1966).

10. Kirtley Mather, "The Scopes Trial and Its Aftermath," typescript in the author's possession, 210–11; Kirtley Mather, "The Scopes Trial and Its Aftermath," public lecture, November 3, 1976, University of New Mexico, tape in the author's posession.

11. *Alabama Baptist,* August 6, 1925, 13.

12. John R. Straton, lectures: "The Poison in the Pot of the American Magazines," "The New Infidelity in Our Baptist Theological Seminaries," "Resolved that Man Is a Product of Evolution instead of Divine Creation," all in John R. Straton Manuscripts, American Baptist Historical Society, Rochester, N.Y.

13. Quoted in *Christian Fundamentals in School and Church,* October-November-December 1925, 26; Willard H. Smith, "William Jennings Bryan and the Social Gospel," *Journal of American History* 53 (1966):41–61; Lawrence W. Levine,

Defender of the Faith: William Jennings Bryan, the Last Decade, 1915–1925 (New York, 1965), esp. 251–53, 358–65.

14. Sam Torgeson to Bryan, March 14, 1921; Bryan to Dr. Kelly, June 17, 1925; "Bryan on Tour," *Collier's*, May 20, 1916, William Jennings Bryan Manuscripts, Library of Congress, Boxes 33, 40, 37.

15. Glenn Gates Cole, "Evolution and Destructive Criticism," *Christian Standard* 54 (1919):551.

16. See Straton's article in the *International Biblical Encyclopedia*, 305.

17. Bryan to Graham Patterson, January 31, 1925, Bryan Manuscripts, Box 40, Library of Congress.

18. William G. Shepherd, "What Is Religious Liberalism?" *Christian Register* 103 (1924):125.

19. Quoted in *Christian Century* 39 (1922):1613.

20. William E. Ellis, "Edgar Young Mullins: Southern Baptist Theologian, Administrator, and Denominational Leader" (Ph.D. dissertation, University of Kentucky, 1974); William E. Ellis, "Edgar Young Mullins and the Crisis of Moderate Southern Baptist Leadership," *Foundations* 19 (April–June 1976):171–85.

21. J. J. Rice, "The Hypothesis of Evolution—Its Rise and Effect," *Union Seminary Review* 30 (1923):331; J. C. Calhoun Newton, "The Turning Tide of Evolution," *Methodist Quarterly Review* 75 (1926):443; G. F. Bell, *Religion and Science: A Protest against Dogmatism in Both* (ca. 1925), pamphlet, Historical Foundation of the Presbyterian and Reformed Churches, Montreat, N.C.; John W. Bucklaw, "Naturalism in Psychology and Ethics," *Methodist Review* 104 (1921):204–12.

22. *Baptist Courier*, August 21, 1924, 2; Frazer Hood, "The Challenge of Science," *Union Seminary Review* 36 (1925):326.

23. *Fundamentalist*, March 15, 1923; cf. Bryan Manuscripts, Box 35, Library of Congress; "The Evolution Trial," *Forum* 74 (1925):320.

24. See the comments by Hillyer H. Straton in Paul A. Carter, ed., *The Uncertain World of Normalcy: The 1920s* (New York, 1971), 142–45.

25. Alfred W. McCann, *God—or Gorilla* (New York, 1922); Alfred Fairhurst, *Atheism in Our Universities* (Cincinnati, 1923); George McCready Price, *The New Geology* (Mountain View, Calif., 1923); William M. Goldsmith, *Evolution or Christianity, God or Darwin?* (Winfield, Kan., 1924). The quotation is from George McCready Price, *Q.E.D.; or New Light on the Doctrine of Creation* (New York, 1917), 127.

26. George McCready Price to John R. Straton, March 25, 1924, Straton Manuscripts.

27. William B. Riley, "The World's Christian Fundamentals Association and the Scopes Trial," sermons, Box 7, Riley Manuscripts.

28. "The Troublesome Apostates," sermons, Box 7, Riley Manuscripts; *Bible Champion* 25 (March, April 1918):86.

29. Robert Frost to Sidney Cox, 1926, Frost Manuscripts, Dartmouth College Library, Hanover, N.H.

30. *Presbyterian of the South* 99 (August 5, 1925).

31. L. R. Scarborough, "A Four-Fold Answer to Modernism," *Alabama Baptist*, July 2, 1925, 5.

32. *Watchman-Examiner,* August 30, 1925, 1071.

33. *Bible Champion* 29 (October 1923):489.

34. John R. Straton, *The Salvation of Society and Other Addresses* (Baltimore, 1908), 21.

35. Brooks Adams, *The Degradation of the Democratic Dogma* (New York, 1920), 115.

36. George H. Daniels, "The Pure-Science Ideal and Democratic Culture," *Science* 156 (1967):1699–1705; George H. Daniels, "The Process of Professionalization in American Science: The Emergent Period, 1820–1866," *Isis* 58 (1967):151–66.

37. Nathan Reingold, ed., *Science in 19th Century America: A Documentary History* (New York, 1964), 324.

38. Richard C. Cabot, *Social Service and the Art of Healing* (New York, 1912), 471.

39. Quoted in Daniel Kevles, "Science in the Gilded Age," *California Institute of Technology Quarterly* 8 (Fall 1966):20.

40. Fisher as quoted in Carter, *Another Part of the Twenties,* 70; Edward L. Rice, "The Significance of the Scopes Trial, III: From the Standpoint of Science," *Current History* 22 (1928):893.

41. Carter, *Another Part of the Twenties,* 82.

42. Benjamin W. Bacon, "The Problem of Religious Education and the Divinity School," *American Journal of Theology* 8 (1904):682–98.

43. W. H. Griffith-Thomas, "Some Texts of Old Testament Criticism," *King's Business* 9 (1918):12–13.

44. "The Modern Man and His Bible," *Methodist Review* 105 (1922):285; Bryan, as quoted by *Truth-seeker* 26 (1929):402.

45. The court transcript, published under the title *The World's Most Famous Court Trial: Tennessee Evolution Case* (Cincinnati, 1925), contains many such statements.

46. Bryan as reported in *King's Business* 14 (1923):570.

47. David Swenson to John Dewey, no date but probably February 1927, David F. Swenson Papers, University of Minnesota, Minneapolis; cf. Herbert Croly, *The Promise of American Life* (Cambridge, 1965), 160; John L. Robinson, *Evolution and Religion* (Boston, 1923), foreword.

Conclusion

1. Each side has often predicted the demise of the other. During the 1920s, liberals considered the Fundamentalists as inevitably doomed. During the late 1970s and 1980s, however, the strength of Protestantism seems to have swung to the conservative side. See "Born Again!" *Newsweek,* October 25, 1976, 68–78; "Back to That Old Time Religion," *Time,* December 26, 1977, 52–54; cf. Dean M. Kelley, *Why Conservative Churches Are Growing: A Study in Sociology of Religion* (New York, 1972).

2. *Christian Century* 43 (1926), 799; Paul A. Carter, *The Twenties in America* (New York, 1968), 79.

3. Alfred North Whitehead, *Adventures of Ideas* (New York, 1933), 163.

4. Michael Grant's brilliant and provocative *Jesus: An Historian's Review of the*

Gospels (New York, 1977) would find little favor from the front pews. See "Gap Widens between Churchgoers and Scholars," *Arizona Republic*, September 17, 1977.

5. Henry Steele Commager, *The American Mind: An Interpretation of American Thought and Character since the 1880s* (New Haven, 1950), 165.

Bibliography

Abbott, Lyman. "The Message of the Nineteenth Century to the Men of the Twentieth." *Outlook* 102 (1912):351–54.

———. "The Progressive Movement." *Outlook* 102 (1912):57–59.

Abrams, Ray H. *Preachers Present Arms: A Study of the War-time Attitudes and Activities of the Churches and the Clergy in the United States, 1914–1918*. New York: Round Table Press, 1933.

Adams, Brooks. *The Degradation of the Democratic Dogma*. New York: Macmillan, 1920.

Adams, William. *Evolution Errors*. Augusta, Ga.: N.p., 1886.

Addresses of the International Prophetic Conference, Held December 10–15, 1901, in the Clarendon Street Baptist Church, Boston, Mass. Boston: Watchword and Truth, 1902.

Ahlstrom, Sydney E. *The American Protestant Encounter with World Religions*. Beloit: Beloit College, 1962.

———. *A Religious History of the American People*. New Haven: Yale University Press, 1972.

Allen, Frederick Lewis. *Only Yesterday: An Informal History of the Nineteen-Twenties*. 1931. Reprint. New York: Bantam Books, 1952.

Allen, Isabel D. "Negro Enterprise: An Institutional Church." *Outlook* 78 (1904):181–82.

Allen, Leslie H., ed. *Bryan and Darrow at Dayton: The Record and Documents of the "Bible-evolution Trial."* New York: A. Lee, 1925.

Allen, Stephen. *The Bible and National Prosperity*. Waterville, Maine: Maxham and Wing, 1851.

Ames, Edward S. *The New Orthodoxy*. Chicago: University of Chicago Press, 1918.

Anderson, Nels. "The Shooting Parson of Texas." *New Republic* 48 (September 1, 1926):35–37.

Armstrong, George D. *A Defense of the "Deliverance" on Evolution*. Norfolk, Va.: John D. Ghiselin, 1886.

Bacon, Benjamin W. "The Problem of Religious Education and the Divinity School." *American Journal of Theology* 8 (1904):682–98.

Bailey, Hugh C. *Edgar Gardner Murphy: Gentle Progressive*. Coral Gables: University of Miami Press, 1968.

————. *Liberalism in the New South: Southern Social Reformers and the Progressive Movement*. Coral Gables: University of Miami Press, 1969.

Bailey, Kenneth K. "The Anti-evolution Crusade of the Nineteen Twenties." Ph. D. dissertation, Vanderbilt University, 1953.

————. "The Enactment of Tennessee's Antievolution Law." *Journal of Southern History* 16 (1950):472–90.

————. "Southern White Protestantism at the Turn of the Century." *American Historical Review* 68 (1963):618–35.

————. *Southern White Protestantism in the Twentieth Century*. New York: Harper and Row, 1964.

Baker, Ray Stannard. *The Spiritual Unrest*. New York: Frederick A. Stokes, 1910.

————. "The Spiritual Unrest: A Vision of the New Christianity." *American Magazine* 69 (December 1909):176–83.

Baldwin, Roger. "Dayton's First Issue." In Jerry R. Tompkins, ed., *D-Days at Dayton: Reflections on the Scopes Trial*, 55–63. Baton Rouge: Louisiana State University Press, 1965.

Ball, Peter R., ed. *Darwin's Biological Work: Some Aspects Reconsidered*. Cambridge: Cambridge University Press, 1959.

Barnard, John. *From Evangelism to Progressivism at Oberlin College, 1866–1917*. Columbus: Ohio State University Press, 1969.

Baromé, Joseph A. "The Evolution Controversy." In Donald Sheehan, ed. *Essays in American Historiography*, 169–92. New York: Columbia University Press, 1960.

Bass, Clarence B. *Backgrounds to Dispensationalism: Its Historical Genesis and Ecclesiastical Implications*. Grand Rapids: Eerdmans, 1960.

Batten, Samuel Z. "The Church as the Maker of Conscience." *American Journal of Sociology* 7 (1902):611–28.

Beecher, Henry Ward. *Evolution and Religion*. 2 vols. New York: Fords, Howard and Hulbert, 1885.

Berman, Milton. *John Fiske: The Evolution of a Popularizer*. Cambridge, Mass.: Harvard University Press, 1961.

Binnie, William. *The Proposed Reconstruction of the Old Testament History*. 2d ed. Edinburgh: A. Elliott, 1880.

Blackstone, William E. *Jesus is Coming*. New York: Fleming H. Revell, 1908.

Boatright, Mody C., ed. *The Impact of Darwinian Thought on American Life and Culture*. Austin: University of Texas Press, 1959.

Bode, Frederick A. *Protestantism and the New South: North Carolina Baptists and Methodists in Political Crisis, 1894–1903*. Charlottesville: University Press of Virginia, 1975.

Bolce, Harold. "Christianity in the Crucible." *Cosmopolitan* 47 (1909):310–19.

Bowden, Henry W. *Church History in the Age of Science: Historiographical Patterns in the United States, 1876–1918*. Chapel Hill: University of North Carolina Press, 1971.

Bozeman, Theodore Dwight. *Protestants in an Age of Science: The Baconian Ideal and Antebellum American Religious Thought*. Chapel Hill: University of North Carolina Press, 1977.

Briggs, Charles A. "Sunday-School and Modern Biblical Criticism." *North American Review* 158, January (1894):64–76.

Brod, Donald F. "The Scopes Trial: A Look at Press Coverage after Thirty Years."
Journalism Quarterly 42 (1965):219–26.

Brooks, Phillips. *Lectures on Preaching*. New York: E. P. Dutton, 1873.

Brown, Herbert Ross. *The Sentimental Novel in America, 1789–1860*. Durham:
Duke University Press, 1940.

Brown, Ira V. "The Higher Criticism Comes to America, 1880–1900." *Journal of the
Presbyterian Historical Society* 38 (1960):193–212.

———. *Lyman Abbott, Christian Evolutionist: A Study in Religious Liberalism*.
Westport, Conn.: Greenwood Press, 1949.

Brown, Jerry Wayne. *The Rise of Biblical Criticism in America, 1800–1870: The New
England Scholars*. Middletown: Wesleyan University Press, 1964.

Brown, O. E. "Modernism: A Calm Survey." *Methodist Quarterly Review* 74
(1925):387–412.

Bruce, F. F. *History of the Bible in English*. 3d ed. New York: Oxford University
Press, 1978.

"Bryan on Tour." *Collier's* 57 (May 20, 1916):11–12.

Bryan, William Jennings. *Christ and His Companions: Famous Figures of the New
Testament*. New York: Fleming H. Revell, 1925.

———. "The Fundamentals." *Forum* 70 (1923):1665–80.

———. *Heart to Heart Appeals*. New York: Fleming H. Revell, 1917.

———, and Bryan, Mary. *The Memoirs of William Jennings Bryan*. Chicago: John C.
Winston, 1925.

———, ed. *World Peace—A Written Debate between William Howard Taft and
William Jennings Bryan*. New York: George H. Doran, 1917.

Bucke, Emory S., et al., eds. *The History of American Methodism*. 3 vols. New York:
Abingdon Press, 1964.

Burg, David F. *Chicago's White City of 1893*. Lexington: University Press of
Kentucky, 1976.

Burton, Ernest DeWitt. "The Present Problem of New Testament Study." *American
Journal of Theology* 9 (1905):201–37.

Cabot, Richard C. *Social Service and the Art of Healing*. New York: Moffatt, Yard,
1912.

Cameron, E. C. "Fundamentalism and the Disciples of Christ." *Christian Standard*
66 (1929):532–33.

Carter, Paul A. *Another Part of the Twenties*. New York: Columbia University Press,
1977.

———. *The Decline and Revival of the Social Gospel: Social and Political Liberalism
in American Protestant Churches, 1920–1940*. Ithaca: Cornell University Press,
1956.

———. *The Spiritual Crisis of the Gilded Age*. DeKalb: Northern Illinois University
Press, 1971.

———. *The Twenties in America*. New York: Crowell, 1968.

———, ed. *The Uncertain World of Normalcy: The 1920s*. New York: Pitman, 1971.

Case, Shirley Jackson. *The Millennial Hope: A Phase of War-Time Thinking*. Chicago: University of Chicago Press, 1918.

Cauthen, Kenneth. *The Impact of American Religious Liberalism*. New York: Harper
and Row, 1962.

Christie, Francis A. "Harnack's Chronology of the New Testament." *New World* 6 (1897):452–67.

Churchill, Winston. "The Modern Quest for a Religion." *Century* 87 (1913):169–74.

Clarke, Francis E. "Christianity as Seen by a Voyage around the World." In John Henry Barrows, ed., *The World's Parliament of Religions,* 2:1237–42. Chicago: Parliament, 1893.

Clarke, James E. *Points at Issue between 'Fundamentalists' and 'Modernists.'* Nashville: Advance, 1923.

Clarke, James F. "Affinities of Buddhism and Christianity." *North American Review* 136 (1883):467–77.

Clarke, William Newton. *Sixty Years with the Bible: A Record of Experience.* New York: Charles Scribner's Sons, 1909.

Coates, Willson H., White, Hayden V., and Schapiro, J. Salwyn. *The Emergence of Liberal Humanism.* Vol. 1. New York: McGraw-Hill, 1966.

Cockshut, A. O. J., ed. *Religious Controversies of the Nineteenth Century: Selected Documents.* Lincoln: University of Nebraska Press, 1966.

Cole, Stewart G. *History of Fundamentalism.* 1931. Reprint. Hamden, Conn.: Archon Books, 1963.

Coletta, Paulo E. *William Jennings Bryan.* 3 vols. Lincoln: University of Nebraska Press, 1964–69.

The Coming and Kingdom of Christ. Chicago: Bible Institute Colportage Association, 1914.

Commager, Henry Steele. *The American Mind: An Interpretation of American Thought and Character since the 1880s.* New Haven: Yale University Press, 1950.

Complaint of James Woodrow versus the Synod of Georgia. Columbia: Presbyterian Publishing House, 1888.

Cook, Joseph. *Boston Monday Lectures.* Boston and New York: Rand Avery, 1887.

Crapsey, Algernon S. *The Last of the Heretics.* New York: Knopf, 1924.

Cross, George. "Federation of the Christian Churches in America—An Interpretation." *American Journal of Theology* 23 (1919):129–45.

Cummins, Alexander G. "The Relationship of Social Service to Christianity." In Protestant Episcopal Church, *Papers and Speeches of the Church Congress,* 41–46. New York: T. Whittaker, Inc. (?), 1913.

Curtis, Edward L. "The Present State of Old Testament Criticism." *Century* 45 (1893):727–34.

Daniels, George H. "The Process of Professionalization in American Science: The Emergent Period, 1820–1866." *Isis* 58 (1967):151–66.

———. "The Pure-Science Ideal and Democratic Culture." *Science* 156 (1967):1699–1705.

———, ed. *Darwin Comes to America.* Waltham, Mass.: Blaisdell, 1968.

Darrow, Clarence. *The Story of My Life.* New York: Charles Scribner's Sons, 1932.

Darwin, Francis, ed. *The Life and Letters of Charles Darwin.* Vol. 1. New York: D. Appleton, 1891.

Dawley, Powel Mills. *The Story of the General Theological Seminary.* New York: Oxford University Press, 1969.

Day, William Horace, and Eddy, Sherwood. *The Modernist-Fundamentalist Controversy.* New York: George H. Doran, 1924.

A *Defense of True Presbyterianism against Two Deliverances of the Augusta Assembly*. Charleston: Presbyterian Publishing House (?), 1886.

DeFord, Miriam Allen. *Up-Hill All the Way: The Life of Maynard Shipley*. Yellow Springs: Antioch Press, 1956.

Deland, Margaret. *John Ward, Preacher*. New York: Houghton Mifflin, 1888.

Dobyns, Ray. "The Second Coming." *Union Seminary Review* 35 (1923):334–45.

Doherty, Herbert J., Jr. "Alexander J. McKelway: Preacher to Progressive." *Journal of Southern History* 24 (1958):177–90.

Dorn, Jacob H. *Washington Gladden: Prophet of the Social Gospel*. Columbus: Ohio State University Press, 1966.

"Dr. Shailer Mathews and the Premillenniarians," *King's Business* 9 (1918):3–5.

Dumbroski, James. *The Early Days of Christian Socialism in America*. New York: Columbia University Press, 1936.

Dupree, A. Hunter. *Asa Gray*. Cambridge, Mass.: Harvard University Press, 1959.

Dwight, Henry Otis. *The Bible among the Nations: A Brief Review of One Hundred Years of the American Bible Society*. New York: American Bible Society, 1916.

Eaton, Clement. "Professor James Woodrow and the Freedom of Teaching in the South." *Journal of Southern History* 28 (1962):1–11.

Eddy, Sherwood. *The Kingdom of God and the American Dream: The Religious and Secular Ideals of American History*. New York: Harper and Brothers, 1941.

Ehlert, Arnold D., ed. *A Bibliographic History of Dispensationalism*. Grand Rapids: Baker Book House, 1965.

Eighmy, John Lee. "Religious Liberalism in the South during the Progressive Era." *Church History* 38 (1969):359–72.

Eiseley, Loren. *Darwin's Century: Evolution and the Men Who Discovered It*. New York: Doubleday, Anchor Books, 1958, 1961.

Eliot, Charles W. "The Religion of the Future." *Harvard Theological Review* 2 (1909):389–407.

Ellis, William E. "Edgar Young Mullins and the Crisis of Moderate Southern Baptist Leadership." *Foundations* 19 (1976):171–85.

———. "Edgar Young Mullins: Southern Baptist Theologian, Administrator, and Denominational Leader." Ph.D. dissertation, University of Kentucky, 1974.

Ellis, William T. "A Union Preacher." *Outlook* 91 (1910): 838–42.

Ely, James T. *Glimpses of Bible Climaxes, from "The Beginning" to "The End."* Garden City, Kan.: Businessman's Gospel Association, 1927.

Ernst, Eldon G. *Moment of Truth for Protestant America: Interchurch Campaigns Following World War One*. Missoula: Scholars' Press, 1974.

Fairhurst, Alfred. *Atheism in Our Universities*. Cincinnati: Standard, 1923.

Fass, Paula S. *The Damned and the Beautiful: American Youth in the 1920s*. New York: Oxford University Press, 1977.

Faunce, William H. P. "Religious Advance of Fifty Years." *American Journal of Theology* 20 (1916):333–44.

Feinberg, Charles L., ed. *The Fundamentals for Today*. 2 vols. Grand Rapids: Kregel, 1958.

Feldman, Egal. "American Ecumenism: Chicago's World's Parliament of Religions of 1893." *Journal of Church and State* 9 (1967):180–91.

Ferris, Charles. "The Place of E. Y. Mullins in the Evolution Controversy of the 1920s." *Quarterly Review* 35 (1975):53–57.

Findlay, James F., Jr. *Dwight L. Moody: American Evangelist, 1837–1839*. Chicago: University of Chicago Press, 1969.

Flynt, Wayne. "Dissent in Zion: Alabama Baptists and Social Issues, 1900–1914." *Journal of Southern History* 25 (1969):523–42.

Fortune, Alonzo W. "Fundamentalist or Modernist." *Christian Evangelist* 6 (April 12, 1928):469–76.

———. "The Kentucky Campaign against the Teaching of Evolution." *Journal of Religion* 2 (1922):225–35.

Frank, Glenn. "William Jennings Bryan—A Mind Divided against Itself." *Century* 106 (1923):793–800.

Frick, Phillip L. "Why the Methodist Church Is So Little Disturbed by the Fundamentalist Controversy." *Methodist Review* 107 (1924):421–26.

"Fundamentals." *Scroll* 18 (1921):50–56.

Funk, Robert W. "The Watershed of the American Biblical Tradition: The Chicago School, First Phase, 1892–1924." Manuscript, Disciples of Christ Historical Society, Nashville, Tenn.

Furniss, Norman. *The Fundamentalist Controversy, 1918–1931*. New Haven: Yale University Press, 1954.

Gaebelein, Arno C., ed. *Christ and Glory: Addresses Delivered at the New York Prophetic Conference, Carnegie Hall, November 25–28, 1918*. New York: "Our Hope" Publication Office, 1919.

Gatewood, Willard B. "Politics and Piety in North Carolina: The Fundamentalist Crusade at High Tide, 1925–1927." *North Carolina Historical Review* 42 (1965):275–90.

———. *Preachers, Pedagogues, and Politicians: The Evolution Controversy in North Carolina, 1920–1927*. Chapel Hill: University of North Carolina Press, 1966.

———, ed. *Controversy in the Twenties: Fundamentalism, Modernism and Evolution*. Nashville: Vanderbilt University Press, 1969.

Giboney, Ezra P., and Potter, Agnes M. *The Life of Mark A. Matthews*. Grand Rapids: Eerdmans, 1948.

Gillett, Charles R. "The Briggs Heresy Trial." *New World* 2 (1893):141–69.

Ginger, Ray. *Six Days or Forever? Tennessee v. John Thomas Scopes*. Boston: Beacon Press, 1958.

Girardeau, John L. *The Substance of Two Speeches on the Teaching of Evolution in Columbia Theological Seminary Delivered in the Synod of South Carolina at Greenville, S.C., October 1884*. Columbia: William Sloane, 1885.

Gladden, Washington. *How Much Is Left of the Old Doctrines?* Boston: Houghton, Mifflin, 1899.

———. "The New Bible." *Arena* 9 (1894):296–97.

———. *Recollections*. Boston: Houghton, Mifflin, 1909.

———. *Who Wrote the Bible? A Book for the People*. Boston: Houghton, Mifflin, 1891.

God Hath Spoken (Philadelphia, 1919).

Goldman, Eric. "Books That Have Changed America." *Saturday Review* 36 (July 4, 1954):7–9ff.

Goldsmith, William M. *Evolution or Christianity, God or Darwin?* Winfield, Kan.: Anderson Press, 1924.

Gordon, A. J. "The Second Coming of Our Lord." *Watchman-Examiner*, February 5, 1920, 147.

Grant, Michael. *Jesus: An Historian's Review of the Gospels*. New York: Charles Scribner's Sons, 1977.

Grantham, Dewey W., Jr. "The Progressive Movement and the Negro." *South Atlantic Quarterly* 54 (1955):461–77.

Greene, John C. *The Death of Adam: Evolution and Its Impact on Western Thought*. Ames: Iowa State University Press, 1959.

Griffith, G. O. "William Jennings Bryan." *Watchman-Examiner*, August 20, 1925, 1037.

Griffith-Thomas, W. H. "Some Tests of Old Testament Criticism." *King's Business* 9 (1918):12–13.

Gusfield, Joseph R. *Symbolic Crusade: Status Politics and the American Temperance Movement*. Urbana: University of Illinois Press, 1963.

Haar, Charles M. "E. L. Youmans: A Chapter in the Diffusion of Science in America." *Journal of the History of Ideas* 9 (1948):193–213.

Haber, Samuel. *Efficiency and Uplift: Scientific Management in the Progressive Era, 1890–1920*. Chicago: University of Chicago Press, 1964.

Haldeman, Isaac M. *Professor Shailer Mathews' Burlesque on the Second Coming of Our Lord Jesus Christ*. New York: N.p., 1918.

Haldeman-Julius, Marcet. *A Report of the Rev. J. Frank Norris Trial*. Girard, Kan.: Haldeman-Julius, 1927.

Haller, John S., Jr. *Outcasts from Evolution: Scientific Attitudes of Racial Inferiority, 1859–1900*. Urbana: University of Illinois Press, 1971.

Handy, Robert T. *A Christian America: Protestant Hopes and Historical Realities*. New York: Oxford University Press, 1971.

———. "The Protestant Quest for a Christian America, 1830–1930." *Church History* 22 (1953):8–20.

———, ed. *The Social Gospel in America, 1870–1920: Gladden, Ely, Rauschenbusch*. New York: Oxford University Press, 1966.

Harger, Charles M. "Bryan: Preacher and Politician." *Outlook* 89 (1908):64–65.

Harrison, Paul M. *Authority and Power in the Free Church Tradition: A Social Case Study of the American Baptist Convention*. Princeton: Princeton University Press, 1959.

Hartt, Rollin Lynde. "The War in the Churches." *World's Work* 46 (September 1923):469–77.

Hartzler, Henry B. *Moody in Chicago*. New York: Fleming H. Revell, 1894.

Haskins, George L. *Law and Authority in Early Massachusetts: A Study in Tradition and Design*. New York: Macmillan, 1960.

Hatch, Carl E. "The First Heresy Trial of Charles Augustus Briggs: American Higher Criticism in the 1890s." Ph.D. dissertation, University of Buffalo, 1964.

Hays, Arthur Garfield. *Let Freedom Ring*. New York: Liveright, 1937.

Hays, Samuel P. *Conservation and the Gospel of Efficiency: The Progressive Conservation Movement, 1890–1920*. Cambridge, Mass.: Harvard University Press, 1959.

————. "The Politics of Reform in Municipal Government in the Progressive Era." *Pacific Northwest Quarterly* 55 (1964):159–69.

Henry, James O. "Black Oil and Souls to Win." *King's Business* 49 (1958):10–40.

Hillis, Newell Dwight. *The Influence of Christ in Modern Life: Being a Study of the New Problems of the Church in American Society.* New York: Macmillan, 1900.

Hodge, Charles. *Systematic Theology.* 3 vols. New York: Charles Scribner, 1873.

Holifield, E. Brooks. *The Gentlemen Theologians: American Theology in Southern Culture, 1795–1860.* Durham: Duke University Press, 1978.

Hopkins, Charles H. *The Rise of the Social Gospel in American Protestantism, 1865–1915.* New Haven: Yale University Press, 1940.

Horton, W. M. "The Development of Theological Thought." In Stephen C. Neill, ed., *Twentieth Century Christianity*, 253–83. Rev. ed. Garden City: Doubleday, 1963.

Hovey, Alvah. *An Epitome of Textual Criticism of the New Testament.* Boston: Youngjohn, 1905 (?).

Howe, Frederick. *The Confessions of a Reformer.* 1925. Reprint. Chicago: Public, 1967.

Hutchinson, John A. *We Are Not Divided: A Critical and Historical Study of the Federal Council of the Churches of Christ in America.* New York: Round Table Press, 1941.

Hutchison, William R. "The Americanness of the Social Gospel: An Inquiry in Comparative History." *Church History* 44 (1975):367–81.

————. "Cultural Strain and Protestant Liberalism." *American Historical Review* 76 (1971):386–411.

————. "Disapproval of Chicago: The Symbolic Trial of David Swing." *Journal of American History* 59 (1972):30–47.

————. *The Modernist Impulse in American Protestantism.* Cambridge, Mass.: Harvard University Press, 1976.

Huthmacher, J. Joseph. "Urban Liberalism and the Age of Reform." *Mississippi Valley Historical Review* 49 (1962):231–41.

Hyde, William DeWitt. "Reform in Theological Education." *Atlantic Monthly* 85 (1900):16–26.

The Influence of the Church on Modern Problems. Baltimore: Macmillan, 1922.

" 'In His Image,'—A Review." *Union Seminary Review* 33 (1922):177–87.

Iver, George. "How a Great Free Lecture System Works." *World's Work* 5 (1903):3327–34.

Janes, Lewis G. "The Comparative Study of Religion: Its Pitfalls and Its Promise." *Sewanee Review* 7 (1897):1–20.

Janick, Herbert. "The Mind of the Connecticut Progressive." *Mid-America* 52 (1970):83–101.

Jenks, Jeremiah W. *The Political and Social Significance of the Life and Teachings of Jesus.* New York: Association Press, 1912.

Jeschke, Channing R. "The Briggs Case: The Focus of a Study in Nineteenth Century Presbyterian History." Ph.D. dissertation, University of Chicago, 1967.

Jordan, David Starr. *The Call of the Twentieth Century: An Address to Young Men.* Boston: Beacon Press, 1903.

Jordan, Phillip D. "The Evangelical Alliance for the United States of America: An

Evangelical Search for Identity in Ecumenicity during the Nineteenth Century." Ph.D. dissertation, University of Iowa, 1971.

Kelley, Dean M. *Why Conservative Churches Are Growing: A Study in Sociology of Religion*. New York: Harper and Row, 1972.

Kent, Charles Foster. *The Social Teachings of the Prophets and Jesus*. New York: Charles Scribner's Sons, 1920.

Kent, Frank. "On the Dayton Firing Line." *New Republic* 43 (1925):259–60.

King, Henry C. *Reconstruction in Theology*. 1901. 2d ed. New York: Macmillan, 1907.

Knapp, Susan T. "The Relation of Social Service to Christianity." In Protestant Episcopal Church, *Papers and Speeches of the Church Congress*, 26–33. New York: T. Whittaker, Inc. (?), 1913.

Kolko, Gabriel. *The Triumph of Conservatism*. New York: Free Press of Glencoe, 1963.

Kraus, Clyde Norman. *Dispensationalism in America: Its Rise and Development*. Richmond: John Knox Press, 1958.

Krutch, Joseph Wood. *The Modern Temper: A Story and a Confession*. 1929. Reprint. New York: Harcourt, Brace, 1956.

Ladd, George. *The Blessed Hope*. Grand Rapids: Eerdmans, 1956.

Lawrence, Jerome, and Lee, Robert E. *Inherit the Wind*. New York: Random House, 1955.

Ledbetter, Patsy. "Defense of the Faith: J. Frank Norris and Texas Fundamentalism, 1920–1929." *Arizona and the West* 15 (1973):45–62.

Leverette, William E., Jr. "E. L. Youmans' Crusade for Scientific Autonomy and Respectability." *American Quarterly* 17 (1965):12–32.

Levine, Lawrence W. *Defender of the Faith: William Jennings Bryan, the Last Decade, 1915–1925*. New York: Oxford University Press, 1965.

Levy, Clifton Harby. "Professor Haupt and the 'Polychrome' Bible." *American Review of Reviews* 14 (1896):669–86.

Light on Prophecy. Philadelphia: Christian Herald, 1918.

Lingle, Walter L. "The Teachings of Jesus and Modern Social Problems." *Union Seminary Review* 27 (1916):191–205.

Link, Arthur S. "The Progressive Movement in the South, 1870–1914." *North Carolina Historical Review* 23 (1946):172–95.

Lippmann, Walter. *A Preface to Morals*. 1929. Reprint. Boston: Beacon Press, 1960.

Loetscher, Lefferts A. *The Broadening Church: A Study of Theological Issues in the Presbyterian Church since 1869*. Philadelphia: University of Pennsylvania Press, 1957.

Loewenberg, Bert James. "The Controversy over Evolution in New England, 1859–1873." *New England Quarterly* 8 (1935):232–57.

———. "Darwinism Comes to America, 1859–1900." *Mississippi Valley Historical Review* 28 (1941):339–68.

Long, Mason. *Save the Girls*. Fort Wayne, Ind.: Mason Long, 1888.

Love, John Smith. "The Task of Religion in the New Age." *Universalist Leader* 21 (December 28, 1918):1002–3.

Lovejoy, W. P. "Is a Christian Socialism Possible?" *Methodist Quarterly Review* 54 (1905):738–58.

Loveland, Frank L. "The Mutual Obligations of Church and State in Building Human Character." In Paul Little, ed., *The Pacific Northwest Pulpit,* 59–75. New York and Cincinnati: Methodist Book Concern, 1915.

Lubove, Roy. *The Professional Altruist: The Emergence of Social Work as a Career, 1880–1930.* Cambridge, Mass.: Harvard University Press, 1965.

———. "The Twentieth Century City: The Progressive as Municipal Reformer." *Mid-America* 41 (1959):195–209.

Lurie, Edward. *Louis Agassiz: A Life in Science.* Chicago: University of Chicago Press, 1960.

McAfee, Joseph E. "Who Wins—Fundamentalists or Fosdick?" *Christian Century* 41 (1924):1266–69.

McAllister, James Gray, and Guerrant, Grace Owings. *Edward O. Guerrant: Apostle to the Southern Highlanders.* Richmond: Richmond Press, 1950.

McCabe, Joseph. *1825–1925: A Century of Stupendous Progress.* London: Watts, 1925.

McCann, Alfred W. *God—or Gorilla: How the Monkey Theory of Evolution Exposes Its Own Methods, Relates Its Own Principles, Denies Its Own Inferences, Disproves Its Own Case.* New York: Devin-Adair, 1922.

McComb, Samuel. *Christianity and the Modern Mind.* New York: Dodd, Mead, 1910.

McCown, Chester C. *The Genesis of the Social Gospel: The Meaning of the Ideals of Jesus in the Light of their Antecedents.* New York: Knopf, 1929.

McCulloch, James E., ed. *Battling for Social Betterment.* Nashville: Southern Sociological Congress, 1914.

———. *The Call of the New South.* Nashville: Southern Sociological Congress, 1912.

———. *The South Mobilizing for Social Service.* Nashville: Southern Sociological Congress, 1913.

MacFarland, Charles. "The Progress of Federation among the Churches." *American Journal of Theology* 20 (1917):392–410.

MacLaurin, Richard E. "Science and Religion: The End of the Battle." *Outlook* 99 (1911):71–74.

McLoughlin, William G. *Billy Sunday Was His Real Name.* Chicago: University of Chicago Press, 1955.

———. *Modern Revivalism: Charles Grandison Finney to Billy Graham.* New York: Ronald Press, 1959.

McMath, Robert C., Jr. *Populist Vanguard: A History of the Southern Farmers' Alliance.* Chapel Hill: University of North Carolina Press, 1975.

Magnuson, Norris. *Salvation in the Slums: Evangelical Social Work, 1865–1920.* Metuchen, N.J.: Scarecrow, 1977.

Mallock, W. H. "Science and Religion at the Dawn of the Twentieth Century." *Fortnightly* 76 (1901):395–414.

"The Man with the Hoe in America." *Christian Standard* 35 (1899):1005.

Manchester, William R. *Disturber of the Peace: The Life of H. L. Mencken.* New York: Harper, 1951.

Mandelbaum, Maurice. "Darwin's Religious Views." *Journal of the History of Ideas* 19 (1958):363–78.

Mann, Arthur. "British Social Thought and American Reforms of the Progressive Era." *Mississippi Valley Historical Review* 42 (1956):672–92.

Manning, William Thomas. *Neither Fundamentalism nor Modernism, but Belief in Jesus Christ, the Son of God.* New York: Bishop's Office, Synod House, 1922.

Marcosson, Isaac F. "A Practical School of Democracy." *World's Work* 10 (July 1905):6414–17.

Maring, Norman H. "Baptists and Changing Views of the Bible, 1865–1918." *Foundations* 1 (July 1958):52–75; (October 1958):30–62.

Marsden, George M. *Fundamentalism and American Culture: The Shaping of Twentieth Century Evangelicalism, 1870–1925.* New York: Oxford University Press, 1980.

————. "Fundamentalism as an American Phenomenon: A Comparison with English Evangelicalism." *Church History* 46 (1977):215–32.

Martin, James L. *Anti-evolution, Girardeau vs. Woodrow.* Columbia: Presbyterian Publishing House, (?) ca. 1888.

————. *Dr. Girardeau's Anti-evolution.* Columbia: Presbyterian Publishing House, 1889.

May, Ernest. "Agassiz, Darwin, and Evolution." *Harvard Library Bulletin* 13 (1959):165–93.

May, Henry F. *The End of American Innocence: A Story of the First Years of Our Own Time, 1912–1917.* New York: Knopf, 1959.

————. *Protestant Churches and Industrial America.* New York: Harper and Brothers, 1949.

Mencken, H. L. *Prejudices: Fifth Series.* New York: Knopf, 1926.

Methodist Episcopal Church, South. General Conference. *Journal.* Nashville and Richmond: Methodist Episcopal Church, South, 1926.

Meyer, C. M. "An Apostle to Labor." *World's Work* 19 (1909):12217–21.

Meyer, D. H. "American Intellectuals and the Victorian Crisis of Faith." In Daniel Walker Howe, ed., *Victorian America,* 59–77. Philadelphia: University of Pennsylvania Press, 1976.

Meyer, Donald B. *The Protestant Search for Political Realism, 1919–1941.* Berkeley: University of California Press, 1960.

Miller, Perry. "The Garden of Eden and the Deacon's Meadow." *American Heritage* 7 (December 1955):54–61.

Miller, Robert Moats. *American Protestantism and Social Issues, 1919–1939.* Chapel Hill: University of North Carolina Press, 1958.

Mims, Edwin. *The Advancing South: Stories of Progress and Reaction.* Garden City: Doubleday, Page, 1926.

Mode, Peter G. "Aims and Methods of Contemporary Church-Union Movements in America." *American Journal of Theology* 24 (1920):224–51.

"Modernism in Confusion." *New Republic* 48 (September 1926):33–34.

Moore, James R. *The Post-Darwinism Controversies: A Study of the Protestant Struggle to Come to Terms with Darwin in Great Britain and America, 1870–1900.* Cambridge: Cambridge University Press, 1979.

Morris, George Perry. "Review of 1919." *Universalist Leader* 23 (1920):8.

Mott, John R. *History of the Student Volunteer Movement for Foreign Missions.* Chicago: N.p., 1892.

Mowry, George E. "The California Progressive and His Rationale: A Study in Middle Class Politics." *Mississippi Valley Historical Review* 36 (1949):241–50.

"Mr. Eliot's Religion of the Future." *World's Work* 18 (1909):11974–75.

"Mr. Herbert Spencer." *American Review of Reviews* 12 (1895):699–707.

Nash, Henry S. *The History of the Higher Criticism of the New Testament*. New York: Macmillan, 1901.

Niebuhr, H. Richard. *The Kingdom of God in America*. New York: Willett, Clark, 1937.

Neill, Stephen. *The Interpretation of the New Testament, 1861–1961*. New York: Oxford University Press, 1966.

Newton, R. Heber. *The Right and Wrong Uses of the Bible*. New York: John W. Lovell, 1883.

Osgood, Howard. *Christ and the Old Testament*. Rochester, N.Y.: Genesee Press, 1902.

Osofsky, Gilbert. "Progressivism and the Negro, 1900–1915." *American Quarterly* 16 (1964):153–68.

Ostrander, Gilman M. "The Revolution in Morals." In John Braeman, ed., *Change and Continuity in Twentieth Century America: The 1920s*, 323–49. Columbus: Ohio State University Press, 1968.

Owen, R. D. "The Significance of the Scopes Trial." *Current History* 22 (1925):875–83.

Paton, D. K. *The Higher Criticism: The Greatest Apostasy of the Age*. London: Marshall, 1898.

Perry, Alfred. *The Pre-eminence of the Bible as a Book*. Hartford, Conn.: Hartford Seminary Press, 1899.

Perry, Ralph Barton. *The Present Conflict of Ideals: A Study of the Philosophical Background of the World War*. New York: Longmans, Green, 1918.

Persons, Stow, ed. *Evolutionary Thought in America*. New Haven: Yale University Press, 1950.

Peterson, Walter F. "American Protestantism and the Higher Criticism, 1870–1910." *Transactions of the Wisconsin Academy of Sciences, Arts and Letters* 50 (1962):321–29.

Phelps, William Lyon. "Mrs. Humphrey Ward." *Essays on Modern Novelists*, 191–207. Chautauqua: Chautauqua Press, 1909.

Plantz, Samuel. *The Church and the Social Problem: A Study in Applied Christianity*. Cincinnati: Jennings and Graham, 1906.

Price, George McCready. *The New Geology: A Textbook for Colleges, Normal Schools, and Training Schools and for the General Reader*. Mountain View, Calif.: Pacific Press Publishing Association, 1923.

———. *Q.E.D.; or New Light on the Doctrine of Creation*. New York: Fleming H. Revell, 1917.

Professor Woodrow's Speech before the Synod of South Carolina, October 27 and 28, 1884. Columbia: Presbyterian Publishing House, 1885.

Prophetic Studies of the International Prophetic Conference. Chicago: Fleming H. Revell, 1886.

Protestant Episcopal Church in the U.S.A. *The Church Congress Journal: Papers and Addresses*. New York: T. Whittaker, Inc. (?), 1913.

Prussner, Frederick C. "The Covenant of David and the Problem of Unity in Old Testament Theology." In J. Coert Rylaarsdam, ed., *Transitions in Biblical Scholarship*, 17–41. Chicago: University of Chicago Press, 1968.

Purcell, Edward A., Jr. *The Crisis of Democratic Theory: Scientific Naturalism and the Problem of Value*. Lexington: University Press of Kentucky, 1973.

Rabinowitz, Howard N. *Race Relations in the Urban South, 1865–1890*. New York: Oxford University Press, 1978.

Rainsford, William Stephen. *The Story of a Varied Life: An Autobiography*. Garden City: Doubleday, Page, 1922.

Rall, Harris F. *Modern Premillennialism and the Christian Hope*. New York: Abingdon Press, 1920.

Ratcliffe, S. K. "America and Fundamentalism." *Contemporary Review* 128 (1925):288–95.

———. "The Intellectual Reaction in America." *Contemporary Review* 122 (1922):14–22.

Ratner, Sidney. "Evolution and the Rise of the Scientific Spirit in America." *Philosophy of Science* 3 (1936):104–22.

Rausch, David. *Zionism within Early American Fundamentalism, 1878–1918: A Convergence of Two Traditions*. New York: Edwin Mellon, 1979.

Rauschenbusch, Walter. *For God and the People: Prayers of the Social Awakening*. Boston: Pilgrim Press, 1910.

Reddy, John. "The Most Unforgettable Character I've Met." *Reader's Digest* 49 (August 1956):85–88.

Reingold, Nathan, ed. *Science in 19th Century America: A Documentary History*. New York: Hill and Wang, 1964.

Rian, Edwin H. *The Presbyterian Conflict*. Grand Rapids: Eerdmans, 1940.

Rice, Edward L. "The Significance of the Scopes Trial, III: From the Standpoint of Science." *Current History* 22 (1925):889–95.

Riley, William Bell. *The Menace of Modernism*. New York: Christian Alliance, 1917.

———. *Messages for the Metropolis*. Chicago: Winona, 1906.

Ripley, John W. "The Strange Story of Charles M. Sheldon's *In His Steps*." *Kansas Historical Quarterly* 34 (1978):241–65.

Roberts, Robert R. "The Social Gospel and the Trust Busters." *Church History* 25 (1956):239–57.

Robinson, John L. *Evolution and Religion*. Boston: Stratford, 1923.

Roosevelt, Theodore. "The Church and the People." *Outlook* 100 (1912):161–63.

Ross, Edward Alsworth. *Sin and Society: An Analysis of Latter-Day Iniquity*. 1907. Reprint. New York. Harper and Row, 1973.

Rudolph, L. C. "Fundamentalism." In Arnold B. Rhodes, ed., *The Church Faces the Isms*, 45–67. New York: Abingdon Press, 1958.

Runyan, William M., ed. *Dr. Gray at Moody Bible Institute*. New York: Oxford University Press, 1935.

Russell, C. Allyn. "Mark Allison Matthews: Seattle Fundamentalist and Civic Reformer." *Journal of Presbyterian History* 57 (1979):446–66.

———. *Voices of American Fundamentalism: Seven Biographical Studies*. Philadelphia: Westminster Press, 1976.

Russett, Cynthia Eagle. *Darwin in America: The Intellectual Response, 1865–1912*. San Francisco: W. H. Freeman, 1976.

Sandeen, Ernest R. "Fundamentalism and American Identity." *Annals of the American Academy of Political and Social Science* 387 (1970):56–65.

———. "The Princeton Theology: One Source of Biblical Literalism in American Protestantism." *Church History* 31 (1962):307–21.

———. *The Roots of Fundamentalism: British and American Millennarianism, 1800–1930.* Chicago: University of Chicago Press, 1970.

———. "Towards a Historical Interpretation of the Origins of Fundamentalism." *Church History* 36 (1967):66–83.

Savage, Minot J. *The Irrepressible Conflict between Two World-Theories.* Boston: Arena, 1892.

Scarborough, L. R. "A Four-Fold Answer to Modernism." *Alabama Baptist,* July 2, 1925, 5.

Schaff, Philip. "The Old Version and the New Testament." *North American Review* 132 (1881):427–36.

Schneider, Herbert W. "The Influence of Darwin and Spencer on American Philosophical Theology." *Journal of the History of Ideas* 6 (1945):3–18.

Schneider, Robert W. *Novelist to a Generation: The Life and Thought of Winston Churchill.* Bowling Green: Bowling Green University Popular Press, 1976.

Scopes, John Thomas, and Presley, James. *Center of the Storm: Memoirs of John T. Scopes.* New York: Holt, Rinehart and Winston, 1967.

Scott, Anne F. "A Progressive Wind from the South." *Journal of Southern History* 29 (1963):53–70.

Selleck, Willard Chamberlain. *The New Appreciation of the Bible: A Study of the Spiritual Outcome of Biblical Criticism.* Chicago: University of Chicago Press, 1907.

Sharpe, Charles M. "Professor Orr and Higher Criticism." *Scroll* 4 (1907):85–89.

Sharpe, Dores R. *Walter Rauschenbusch.* New York: Macmillan, 1942.

Shepherd, William G. "What Is Religious Liberalism?" *Christian Register* 103 (February 7, 1924):125.

Sherwood, Andrew. "Lincoln and Darwin." *World's Work* 17 (1909):11128–32.

Shipley, Maynard. "Growth of the Anti-evolution Movement." *Current History* 32 (1930):330–32.

Shriver, George H., ed. *American Religious Heretics: Formal and Informal Trials.* Nashville: Abingdon Press, 1966.

"A Sign of the Times: 'Lux Mundi' as the Book for May." *Review of Reviews* 1 (1890):434–45.

Simpson, George Gaylord. "Science by Jury." *Nation* 186 (May 10, 1958):420–21.

Small, Albion W. "The Bonds of Nationality." *American Journal of Sociology* 20 (1915):629–83.

Smalley, Beryl. *The Study of the Bible in the Middle Ages.* Oxford: Clarendon Press, 1941.

Smith, Benjamin E. "The Darwin Centenary." *Century* 78 (June 1909):299–300.

Smith, Charles Sprague. "Ethical Work of the People's Institute." *Outlook* 79 (1905):1001–3.

Smith, Gerald Birney. "Christianity and the Spirit of Democracy." *American Journal of Theology* 21 (1917):339–57.

Smith, Hay W. *Evolution and Presbyterianism.* Little Rock: Allsopp and Chapple, 1923.

Smith, Willard H. "William Jennings Bryan and the Social Gospel." *Journal of American History* 53 (1966):41–61.

Smith, William Grant. "W. J. Bryan on Evolution." *Christian Standard* 52 (1917):1487.

Smith, William Henry. *Modernism, Fundamentalism, and Catholicism*. Milwaukee: Morehouse, 1926.

Spain, Rufus B. *At Ease in Zion: Social History of the Southern Baptists, 1865–1900*. Nashville: Vanderbilt University Press, 1967.

Speer, Robert E. "The Achievements of Yesterday." In Jesse R. Wilson, ed., *Students and the Christian World Mission*, 173–86. New York: Student Volunteer Movement for Foreign Missions, 1936.

Stead, Francis Herbert. "The Story of the World's Parliament of Religions." *American Review of Reviews* 9 (1894):299–310.

Stelzle, Charles. *American Social and Religious Conditions*. New York: Fleming H. Revell, 1912.

———. *Christianity's Storm Centre: A Study of the Modern City*. New York: Fleming H. Revell, 1907.

———. *The Church and Labor*. Boston: Houghton, Mifflin, 1910.

———. "Jebusites versus Chicagoites." *Outlook* 92 (1909):76–77.

———. *Messages to Working Men*. New York: Fleming H. Revell, 1906.

———. "Proposals with Regard to the Labor Temple." Typescript dated February 21, 1911, Presbyterian Historical Society, Philadelphia, Pa.

———. *A Son of the Bowery: The Life Story of an East Side American*. New York: George H. Doran, 1926.

———. *Why Prohibition!* New York: George H. Doran, 1918.

———. "The Workingman and the Church: A Composite Letter." *Outlook* 68 (1901):717–21.

———. *The Workingman and Social Problems*. New York: Fleming H. Revell, 1903.

Stewart, John T. *The Deacon Wore Spats: Profiles from America's Changing Religious Scene*. New York: Holt, Rinehart and Winston, 1965.

Stone, Irving. *Clarence Darrow for the Defense: A Biography*. Garden City: Doubleday, Doran, 1941.

Stone, William A. *The Tale of a Plain Man*. N.p., 1917.

Straton, Hillyer H. "John Roach Straton: Prophet of Social Righteousness." *Foundations* 5 (1962):17–38.

Straton, John R. *The Gardens of Life: Messages of Cheer and Comfort*. New York: George H. Doran, 1921.

———. *The Menace of Immorality in Church and State: Messages of Wrath and Judgment*. New York: George H. Doran, 1920.

———. *The Salvation of Society and Other Addresses*. Baltimore: Fleet-McGinley, 1908.

———. *The Scarlet Stain on the City*. Norfolk: N.p., ca. 1916.

Stuart, George R. *Sermons*. Philadelphia: Pepper, 1904.

Sweet, William W. *Methodism in American History*. New York: Methodist Book Concern, 1933.

Szasz, Ferenc M. "The Progressive Clergy and the Kingdom of God." *Mid-America* 55 (1973):3–20.

————. "The Scopes Trial in Perspective." *Tennessee Historical Quarterly* 30 (1971):288–98.

————. "Three Fundamentalist Leaders: The Roles of William Bell Riley, John Roach Straton, and William Jennings Bryan in the Fundamentalist-Modernist Controversy." Ph.D. dissertation, University of Rochester, 1969.

————. "William Jennings Bryan, Evolution and the Fundamentalist-Modernist Controversy." *Nebraska History* 56 (1975):259–78.

Talmage, T. DeWitt. *The Earth Girdled: The World as Seen To-day*. Philadelphia: Historical Publishing Co., 1896.

————. *500 Selected Sermons*. 20 vols. Grand Rapids: Baker Book House, 1956.

————. *Live Coals*. Chicago: Fairbanks, 1886.

Taylor, Graham. "The Social Function of the Church." *American Journal of Sociology* 5 (1899):305–21.

Teilhard de Chardin, Pierre. *The Phenomenon of Man*. New York: Harper, 1964.

Thayer, Joseph Henry. *The Change of Attitude towards the Bible*. Boston: Houghton, Mifflin, 1891.

Thompson, Ernest T. *Presbyterians in the South*. 3 vols. Richmond: John Knox Press, 1973.

Thompson, James J., Jr. "Southern Baptists and the Anti-evolution Controversy of the 1920s." *Mississippi Quarterly* 29 (1975–76):65–81.

Timberlake, James H. *Prohibition and the Progressive Movement, 1900–1920*. Cambridge, Mass.: Harvard University Press, 1963.

Torrey, Reuben A. "Is It Premillenniarism or *Post*milleniarism That Is Divisive?" *King's Business* 10 (1919):107–9.

Toy, Crawford H. *Modern Biblical Criticism*. Boston: American Unitarian Association, n.d.

Tulga, Chester E. *The Foreign Missions Controversy in the Northern Baptist Convention, 1919–1949: 30 Years of Struggle*. Chicago: Conservative Baptist Fellowship, 1950.

Turner, William S. *Story of My Life*. Cincinnati: Western Methodist Book Concern, 1904.

Van Dusen, Henry. *The Vindication of Liberal Theology: A Tract for the Times*. New York: Charles Scribner's, 1963.

Van Dyke, Henry. "The Influence of the Bible in Literature." *Century* 80 (1910):893.

Vedder, Henry C. *Our New Testament: How Did We Get It?* New York: Griffin and Roland Press, 1908.

Ward, Mrs. Humphrey. *Robert Elsmere*. 1888. Reprint. Lincoln: University of Nebraska Press, 1969.

Warren, William F. "Comparative Religion, So-called." *Methodist Review* 96 (1914):9–13.

Weber, Timothy P. *Living in the Shadow of the Second Coming: American Premillennialism, 1875–1925*. New York: Oxford University Press, 1979.

Weinstein, James "Big Business and the Origins of Workmen's Compensation." *Labor History* 7 (1967):156–74.

Weiss, Nancy J. "The Negro and the New Freedom: Fighting Wilsonian Segregation." *Political Science Quarterly* 84 (1969):61–79.

Wells, John M. "What Is Modernism?" *Union Seminary Review* 34 (1923):89–109.

West, Nathaniel, ed. *Premillennial Essays of The Prophetic Conference Held in the Church of the Holy Trinity, New York City, 1878*. Chicago: Fleming H. Revell, 1878.

Wheeler, Everett P. "The Church of Today as a Factor in Human Progress." *The Church Congress Journal; Papers and Addresses*. New York: T. Whittaker, Inc. (?), 1910.

White, Lynn, Jr. *Dynamo and Virgin Reconsidered*. Cambridge, Mass.: MIT Press, 1968.

White, Ronald C., Jr., and Hopkins, C. Howard, eds. *The Social Gospel: Religion and Reform in Changing America*. Philadelphia: Temple University Press, 1976.

Whitehead, Alfred North. *Adventures of Ideas*. 1933. Reprint. New York: Macmillan, 1958.

Wilbur, Earl M. *The First Century of the Liberal Movement in American Religion*. Boston: American Unitarian Association, 1916.

Willett, Herbert L. "The Corridor of Years." Manuscript, Disciples of Christ Historical Society, Nashville, Tenn.

———. "The Deeper Issues of Present Religious Thinking." *Campbell Institute Bulletin* 10 (1914):4–8.

Willey, Malcolm, and Rice, Stuart A. "William Jennings Bryan as a Social Force." *Journal of Social Forces*, May 4, 1925, 1–7.

Wilson, Dwight. *Armageddon Now! The Premilleniarian Response to Russia and Israel since 1917*. Grand Rapids: Baker Book House, 1977.

Wilson, R. J., ed. *Darwinism and the American Intellectual*. Homewood, Ill.: Dorsey Press, 1967.

Wilson, Samuel Paynter. *Chicago by Gaslight*. Chicago: Wilson, 1909.

Windle, Bertnam. "A Roman Catholic View of Evolution." *Current History* 23 (1925):335–39.

Witmer, Safara Austin. *The Bible College Story: Education with Dimension*. Manhasset, N.Y.: Channel Press, 1962.

Woodrow, James. *Evolution*. Columbia: Presbyterian Publishing House, 1884.

———. *A Further Examination of Certain Recent Assaults of Physical Science*. Columbia: Presbyterian Publishing House, 1884.

The World's Most Famous Court Trial: Tennessee Evolution Case. Cincinnati: National Book Company, 1925.

Wright, Alfred A. *Anticipated Improvements in the New New Testament*. Lynn, Mass.: N.p., 1881.

Wyllie, Irvin G. "Social Darwinism and the Businessman." *Proceedings of the American Philosophical Society* 103 (1959):629–35.

Zimmerman, Jane. "The Penal Reform Movement in the South during the Progressive Era, 1890–1917." *Journal of Southern History* 17 (1951):462–92.

Major Manuscript Depositories

Austin, Texas
 Historical Archives of the Protestant Episcopal Church
  Journals of the various dioceses and of the general convention, *Papers and Speeches* of the various church congresses, *Catholic Champion, Church Defence;* pamphlets
Boston, Massachusetts
 Congregational Library
  Congregationalist; pamphlets
Chicago, Illinois
 Moody Bible Institute
  Manuscripts: James M. Gray
  Christian Worker's Magazine (Moody Bible Institute Monthly)
Columbus, Ohio
 Ohio Historical Society
  Manuscripts: Washington Gladden
Denver, Colorado
 Colorado Heritage Center
  Dawson Scrapbooks
 Western Room, Denver Public Library
  Vertical Files
Lake Junaluska, North Carolina
 Association of Methodist Historical Societies
  Methodist Review, Methodist Quarterly Review, Social Service Bulletin, Journals of the general conferences; pamphlets
Los Angeles, California
 Bible Institute of Los Angeles
  Manuscripts: Lyman and Milton Stewart
  King's Business; pamphlets
 Occidental College
  Manuscripts: William Jennings Bryan, available on microfilm
Minneapolis, Minnesota
 University of Minnesota
  Manuscripts: Lotus D. Coffman, David F. Swenson
  Minnesota *Daily*

Montreat, North Carolina
  Historical Foundation of the Presbyterian and Reformed Churches
    Union Seminary Magazine, Presbyterian of the South, Minutes of the General
    Assembly; pamphlets
Nashville, Tennessee
  Disciples of Christ Historical Society
    Manuscripts: Herbert L. Willett
    Campbell Institute Bulletin (Scroll), Christian Standard, Christian Evangelist
  Historical Commission of the Southern Baptist Convention
    Manuscripts: Amzi C. Dixon, Carver Family, Albert W. Newman, J. Frank
    Norris
    *Alabama Baptist, Baptist Courier, Bible Champion, Baptist Standard, Proceed-
    ings* of the Southern Baptist Convention; pamphlets
Newton Centre, Massachusetts
  Andover-Newton Theological Seminary
    Pamphlets
Philadelphia, Pennsylvania
  Presbyterian Historical Society
    Manuscripts: Labor Temple
    Presbyterian, Proceedings of the General Assembly; pamphlets
Rochester, New York
  American Baptist Historical Society
    Manuscripts: John R. Straton
    *Baptist, Watchman-Examiner, Baptist Beacon, Religious Searchlight, Crusad-
    ers Champion*
Roseville, Minnesota
  Manuscripts: William Bell Riley
  Christian Fundamentals in School and Church
Seattle, Washington
  University of Washington Library
    Manuscripts: Mark A. Matthews, Sidney Strong
Tucson, Arizona
  Arizona Historical Society
    Vertical Files
Washington, D.C.
  Library of Congress
    Manuscripts: William Jennings Bryan, T. DeWitt Talmage, Josephus Daniels,
    Clarence Darrow, Alexander J. McKelway
    *New World, American Journal of Theology, Christian Register, Christian Cen-
    tury, Truth-seeker, Universalist Leader, Commoner, Lutheran Quarterly*

Index